MADCAP

best wishes ——————>

Donald Spoto.

MADCAP

The Life of Preston Sturges

by DONALD SPOTO

LITTLE, BROWN AND COMPANY

Boston Toronto London

FIRST EDITION

Unless otherwise identified, photographs are courtesy of Sandy Sturges.

LIBRARY OF CONGRESS CATALOGING-IN-PUBLICATION DATA
Spoto, Donald, 1941–
    Madcap : the life of Preston Sturges / by Donald Spoto.
        p.   cm.
    Includes bibliographical references.
    ISBN 0-316-80726-5
        1. Sturges, Preston.   2. Motion picture producers and directors—
United States—Biography.   3. Screenwriters—United States—
Biography.   I. Title.
PN1998.3.S78S66   1990
812'.52—dc20
    [B]   89-13510
                                                              CIP

10   9   8   7   6   5   4   3   2   1

MV-PA

Designed by Barbara Werden

Published simultaneously in Canada
by Little, Brown & Company (Canada) Limited
PRINTED IN THE UNITED STATES OF AMERICA

FOR JOHN

with gratitude for thirty years of devoted friendship

"Mercy falls like summer rain . . . light comes down in living beams." — CARYLL HOUSELANDER

Contents

CONTENTS

Sabrina fair,
Listen where thou art sitting
Under the glassy, cool, translucent wave . . .
Listen for dear honor's sake,
Goddess of the silver lake,
    Listen and save.

— MILTON, *Comus* (1634).

Acknowledgments

SANDY STURGES, Preston Sturges's widow, provided invaluable, uninterrupted assistance in the preparation of this book; without her constant generosity, *Madcap* could never have been written. Almost daily during my research and through the time of writing, she granted interviews, answered questions, suggested sources and topics to consider, made crucial materials and photographs available to me, provided unrestricted access to the Preston Sturges archives and gave permission to quote her husband's memoir, letters and papers.

Her sons Preston Sturges and Thomas Sturges were also invariably courteous and helpful, smoothing the way toward access to important interviews and in every way giving me their encouragement and their confidence.

My subject's third wife, Louise Sturges, cordially agreed to a crucial interview, answering frankly and fully some particularly important and delicate questions. I am grateful for her trust and her generosity of spirit. She, too, provided some of the best photographs here published for the first time.

And her son Mon Sturges, Preston's firstborn, could not have been more kind and cooperative, and I am grateful for his assistance.

The Preston Sturges papers are on deposit in the Special Collections Department of the University of California at Los Angeles. I was warmly greeted and aided each day by the entire staff — especially by the department head, David Zeidberg, and the manuscripts librarian, Anne Caiger.

ACKNOWLEDGMENTS

Howard Green and Marvin Eisenman very kindly enabled me to view and study the early Sturges films that are especially difficult to locate, and I am grateful for their generosity.

For giving their time to be interviewed, I am greatly indebted to the following people, each of whom knew Sturges, spoke enthusiastically and made unique contributions to an emerging portrait of him: Jody Carter, Marvin Chesebro, Phyllis Feldkamp, Edwin Gillette, Richard J. Goggin, Jr., Dolores Gray, Katharine Hepburn, Bernard Hiatt, Lilith James, Muriel Angelus Lavalle, Sidonie Lederer, Robert Lescher, Maxine Merlino, Jean La Vell Nugent, Robert Pirosh, Frances Ramsden, Cesar Romero, Peter Turgeon, Vivian Werner, Billy Wilder, Marie Windsor, Priscilla Bonnar Woolfan and Lillian Sturges Woolford.

For ten years, I have been fortunate to have Elaine Markson for my literary representative; she is a wise and highly respected agent, a good and generous lady and a true friend. Her associates — Geri Thoma, Lisa Callamaro, Sally Wofford and C. J. Hall — also deserve my thanks for their daily attentiveness.

My attorney, Kirtley Thiesmeyer, is not only a prudent counselor but a dear friend, and I cherish his unerringly acute suggestions as much as his devoted, daily support.

I am also grateful to Donna Haynes for her warmly personal and astute attention to the details of my business life, and to Sally Altabet for her kind professionalism.

At Little, Brown and Company, I have been fortunate to enjoy the guidance of William Phillips, editor-in-chief, who always inspires me to dig deeper. Nothing escapes his quick eye, thank goodness. Also in my publisher's offices, Karen Dane has been a constant support, cheerfully facilitating an endless skein of tasks small and great; and Mike Mattil — with his usual grace and good humor — polished the last draft as copyeditor *non pareil*.

I am especially grateful on many counts to my research and editorial assistant, Douglas Alexander — first of all, for his alacrity and for the constant application of his considerable talents. Douglas is a first-rate researcher and a sharp reader, and he is ever the most cheerful colleague and loyal companion. The final draft of this book, in fact, owes much to his keen editorial skills. I acknowledge very deeply these assistances and contributions, his endorsement of me and my work, and most of all his abiding friendship.

*　　*　　*

ACKNOWLEDGMENTS

John Darretta and I first met as undergraduates, and our friendship has never had a dark day or an interrupting season — thus the dedication page of this book. A continent's distance separates us the last several years, but I record this with astonishment, since we are always in contact. John's humor ever refreshes my life, his patience — always remarkable! — is a sustaining force, and his intelligence, kindness and compassion are unfailingly inspiring. I am, in other words, the beneficiary of his prodigious gifts of mind and heart. My life would be incalculably poorer without his fraternity on the journey.

D.S.
28 June 1989
Los Angeles

MADCAP

ONE

Weaned on Champagne

O N AUGUST 29, 1898, in Chicago, a Canadian immigrant named Mary Estelle Dempsey, the wife of Edmund C. Biden, gave birth to their only child and named him Edmund Preston. Before adolescence, Edmund Preston Biden was known as Preston Sturges.

Mary's father had been Dominick Dempsey, a Dublin-born merchant seaman. Over six feet tall, handsome and flirtatious, he came from Ireland to Michigan before moving to an Irish neighborhood in the city of Quebec. There he met and married Mary Smythe, a thin, brown-haired beauty with alabaster skin, who bore him six children. The last, born October 11, 1871, was Mary Estelle.

At thirty-six, Dominick succumbed to tuberculosis, leaving his wife with enormous responsibility but no money. In 1876, when little Mary was five, her mother decided to relocate to Chicago, her sister having emigrated there earlier and married a saloonkeeper. "Working-man's clubs," as saloons were called there, routinely offered patrons a complimentary lunch, and there was always enough food and even some work for a barmaid's family.

Mary was a pretty, vibrant, outgoing child with dark hair, a strong personality and a vivid imagination. At the age of ten, she gladly went to work in a candy factory, where with a team of other children she wrapped taffy six days a week, for a total of five dollars' pay. By thirteen, she had blossomed into a bright-eyed, attractive girl with a radiant smile, intelligent eyes and a cheerfully aggressive manner.

Meanwhile, Mary's mother (a devout Catholic whose family included several nuns) took a job in a Chicago convent. One day little Mary found her mother scrubbing floors there, and seeing her "in a loathsome, servile position [thus her son, many years later], she developed an instantaneous allergy toward religion."

Very little else is known of Mary's early years, or of her erratic education, which apparently went no further than a year of high school. She was, however, an avid reader, she loved music and she fancied ladies and gentlemen of style, whom she knew more from the pages of books and journals than from personal acquaintance. Preston later believed that Mary had eloped with a singer when she was fifteen, but that the marriage was declared invalid, and there were rumors of a second annulled marriage and the birth of a stillborn child. Hard evidence for these is lacking (Cook County records, alas, are woefully incomplete for Chicago before 1900), but in his adult life Preston was convinced that his mother was a prodigal collector of husbands.

Perhaps most intriguing about Mary Dempsey was her vivid fantasy life, as her son later wrote in a rambling, unpublished memoir on which he was working at the time of his death.

> My mother was in no sense a liar. She was, however, endowed with such a rich and powerful imagination that anything she had said three times she believed fervently. Often twice was enough. This gave rise to some tall stories . . . [and] the one that gave her the most satisfaction, and lasted the longest, was undoubtedly the figment concerning her maiden name and her illustrious Italian origin.

Perhaps because she knew so little of her father and his ancestry, and because her mother claimed there was no one eminent on either side of the family, Mary Dempsey invented a scintillatingly glamorous lineage. From the wish to be better connected came the "conclusion," as her son noted,

> that the name [Dempsey] was a misnomer, bestowed upon us in error by the vulgar Irish varlets of her ancestor, a distinguished Italian prince, unfortunately on the lam in Ireland because of a romantic duel. What these flunkies were trying to say was "d'Este," the gentleman being a member of that celebrated Italian family — only they couldn't pronounce it.

Thus Mary Dempsey had the idea (while still in her teenage years) that she was an Italian princess. Presently she resumed what she now proclaimed was her true name, Mary d'Este Dempsey — the designation that appears on most of her marriage certificates (of which there were at least four and perhaps as many more).

In time, Mary developed a passion for a cultural life befitting her noble ancestry. She had studied piano with Italian neighbors from the age of nine, and by eighteen she yearned for European travel, the better to deepen her association with her Continental roots. She got only as far as New York, however, and then — for reason or reasons that may never be known — she made her way to Baltimore, New Orleans and San Francisco. By the summer of 1897 she had returned to Chicago, where she met Edmund C. Biden, and before year's end they were wed in Milwaukee.

Biden's parents — Edmund S. Biden and Isabelle Missouri Parry — had been married in 1864. The older Biden was remembered by his grandson Preston as "a drinking man who had fought for the North during the Civil War." His wife (whose mother had been a Miss Preston) was from a Virginia family that had settled in St. Louis, where Parry became a building contractor. Isabelle "was a confirmed grouser on practically every subject," according to her grandson, but she was also famous for her cooking, which assured her a respectable income as proprietor of a boardinghouse.

The Bidens had two sons. The older, Sydney, had a successful career as a concert singer in Europe and America, but the younger son, Edmund, seems not to have had a stable career at all; at various times he was a traveling salesman, a bill collector or unemployed.

Even before the birth of their son in August 1898, the marriage of Mary Dempsey and Edmund Biden was in deep crisis, for despite her quest for intellectual, social and artistic stimulation, Mary Dempsey had somehow married a shiftless alcoholic. While Preston was still an infant, Mary was welcoming the attentions of one of Chicago's wealthiest men — a stockbroker named Solomon Sturges. She had perhaps first met him through a connection between her mother-in-law and his family, although Mary's son later had the distinct feeling that she had known Sturges even before she had known Biden ("but how they all met is lost in the swirling mists of time").

Solomon Sturges was born October 18, 1865, in Chicago. One of three surviving children (of fifteen) of the successful banker and broker Albert Sturges and his wife, Eliza Graham, the child was raised in considerable comfort and with a strong sense of family tradition. His ancestor Edward

Sturges had come from England to America in 1634 with a coat of arms and a motto — *Esse Quam Videri* (To Be Rather Than to Seem).

By 1865, the Sturgeses had acquired substantial wealth and had settled mostly in Illinois, and the men of the family were invariably bankers, brokers or land barons. Solomon was sent to study business at Yale in the autumn of 1883, but an epidemic of measles in the university dormitory prevented his enrollment. He matriculated instead at the Massachusetts Institute of Technology. After his graduation in 1887, he returned to Chicago, and the following year, with Charles A. Wilson, he formed Wilson and Sturges, stock and bond brokers.

In 1897, Sturges joined Alfred L. Baker and Company and his fortunes accumulated magnificently: by this time he was (along with Cyrus McCormick and Potter Palmer) one of Chicago's millionaires. Later, with the firm of Noyes and Jackson, he did so well in financial management and investment that even the Great Depression beginning in October 1929 did not entirely ruin him.

Gentle and pleasant-looking rather than strikingly handsome, and modest, ambitious and sincere, Solomon Sturges had remained single, earnestly pursuing the life of a financier and a privileged roué. Then he met Mary Biden. Extroverted and willful, always eager for diversion and stimulation, and as passionate about the arts as she was about romance, she impressed Solomon and he began to think of marriage.

She was certainly not a great beauty, but she had skin like porcelain, sparkling hazel eyes and luxuriant hair she twisted into a variety of daring designs. Inclined to plumpness, she was nonetheless enormously appealing, with a vibrant humor and relentless energy. She also seemed to cultivate an iconoclastic, almost aggressively sexual manner. When the very marriageable and very suitable Solomon Sturges entered her life, she saw an attractive potential mate who might be a good provider.

By Christmas 1898, Mary and Solomon were certainly on warm terms, for she mentioned in a notebook years later that he offered gifts to her and baby Preston. (The child was always known as Preston, the better to differentiate him from his uncongenial father.)

The Bidens were still nominally a family unit, however, and Mary was living and occasionally traveling with her husband. During a family trip to New Orleans the baby required surgery for an ear affliction, the cost of which Biden would exploit later as an excuse to attempt extortion money from his adult son.

But by 1900 Mary was firm in her desire for separation, and soon she was living with her baby apart from Biden, while encouraging the wealthy and well-known financier who lavished attention and gifts on them both. Later that year, she obtained a divorce from Biden.

Mary's greatest passion was for a European journey, and (on the advice, she later claimed, of a Chicago music teacher) Mary accepted a monthly allowance from Solomon Sturges, assuring him she would consider his marriage proposal. She packed several steamer trunks, and she and her baby embarked for Paris, where, she hoped, a musical or theatrical career awaited. They arrived in January 1901.

Major portions of the next several years drift uneasily in a sea of chronological obscurity whose tides and eddies are impossible to chart exactly. There are two reasons for the confusion, and they are the accounts left by the two participants in the events.

Following the death in 1927 of her friend Isadora Duncan, Mary (as Mary Desti, her settled variation on d'Este) wrote a memoir of the last years of that dancer's life, published as *The Untold Story*. The text is seriously flawed by grammatically obtuse and hyperbolic diction ("This goddess [Isadora] in a poor frail human body, what glimpses of heaven she gave us through her pure inspiration and marvellous interpretations of art. . . . No religious ceremony has ever moved its believers to a higher ecstasy than did Isadora's dance").

The Untold Story is also marred by Mary's invention of lengthy dialogues, recounted as if they were recorded conversations. There is also a cavalier disregard for accuracy of time and place, dates and facts. "In January 1901 . . . I was scarcely more than a child myself," she wrote of the year she turned thirty, and then states her son's age as a year and a half — one year younger than he was.

Equally unfortunately, Preston Sturges's own incomplete and unedited memoir is the second reason for the confusion. He often endorses Mary's dubious ordering of events while admitting their highly problematic structure, and his narrative is as maddeningly nomadic as it is frequently entertaining. Mary and son were strong on dramatic color but not always on the kind of accurate, authorial care that facilitates a biographer's task. As a result of their dual accounts, their adventures during the decade 1899–1909 can often be verified, but the exact sequence may forever remain uncertain.

It is easy to understand why a restless, eager woman of thirty would head for Paris. Mary was a passionate creature, hungry for culture and determined to leave behind the memories of a poor childhood and a disastrous marriage, and Paris was at the height of *la Belle Époque*, a time of social luxuriance and cultural experimentation. The city was also far more tolerant and morally freewheeling than fin-de-siècle Chicago.

Within days of her arrival at the Hotel Terminus in Paris, Mary had reconnected with some of her shipmates, who insisted she join them at the Paris Opera Ball, where "one Frenchman after another swept me off my feet, crying, 'Oh, la belle Américaine, la belle Américaine.' " But the day after the ball, little Preston was ill with a severe cold, and Mary knew they required better lodging than their poorly heated, drafty room at the hotel.

On the rue Scribe was an American named Donald Downey, who offered, for a steep fee, to find lodging for Americans in Paris. "This really meant taking everything you had if he could," according to Mary, who was forthwith whisked off to a dark, overpriced apartment on the rue de Douie, in Montmartre. She was accompanied by a tall, majestic woman she had met in Downey's office who called her "a darling" and announced that Mary must meet her daughter later that same day. The daughter was Isadora Duncan, and she and Mary quickly formed a friendship that lasted until Duncan's death.

Born in San Francisco in 1877, Isadora Duncan became one of the most significant developers of modern dance. After studies in America, she departed for England and Europe at the age of twenty-one. Duncan spurned the traditional forms of classical ballet, insisting on natural, free rhythms and gestures in interpreting music, and her rejection of rigid formulas and mere technical virtuosity were among the contributions that paved the way for, among others, Martha Graham.

In addition to her iconoclastic approach to dance, Isadora led a life she herself called "more interesting than any novel and more adventurous than any cinema," which is not too great an exaggeration. Dedicated both to the art of dance and to the defiance of social conventions, she traveled round the world, took a number of lovers and refused to marry the fathers of her children. She laughed at national taboos and social prejudices, inspired thousands of young artists and influenced the next generation of dancers.

Months after her bizarre death in 1927, Isadora Duncan's autobiography was published, in which she hoped "to write the truth of all that happened to me and I greatly fear that it will turn out to be an awful mess." This, too, is no exaggeration, for Duncan had hardly any interest in dates, chronological accuracy or the careful arrangement of facts. The memoir does, nevertheless, offer a curious combination of humor and high-toned artiness. Of her prenatal life, for example:

> Before I was born my mother was in great agony of spirit and in a tragic situation. She could take no food except iced oysters and iced champagne. If people ask me when I began to dance I reply, "In my mother's womb, probably as a result of the oysters and champagne — the food of Aphrodite."

The humor, however, is not always easy to identify as deliberate. After the birth of her daughter Deirdre, Duncan left for a dance tour in Russia. But she was still lactating, and "often when I danced the milk overflowed, running down my tunic, and causing me much embarrassment." Her deduction from this occurrence may not be intentionally facetious: "How difficult it is for a woman to have a career!"

Isadora had arrived in Paris late in 1900, after some professional success in London. From the time of her meeting Isadora in early 1901, Mary claimed a constant companionship with her except for Mary's sporadic returns to America. There is good reason to believe this — for the most part — since Mary was the first to recount events later verified by more scrupulous Duncan biographers. Her closeness to Duncan is not a reality to be gathered from Duncan's own book, however; Mary Sturges is mentioned only six times, as "my friend Mary," without surname. But the lack of identifying detail is not surprising: Duncan rarely wrote extensively about anyone but herself. In *The Untold Story* — her account of the last years of Duncan's life — Mary redressed the situation.

Very soon after their first meeting, Mary was spending long hours with Isadora, her mother and Isadora's brother Raymond. But Preston's cold and fever worsened into pneumonia, a condition only alleviated, as his mother later wrote, when

> Mrs. Duncan came with a bottle of champagne of which she gave the baby a spoonful and every few hours thereafter she repeated this. The next morning the baby opened his eyes and looked up at us both with the sweetest smile in the world.

Mary and her son then moved in to Isadora's studio at 45 avenue de Villers, where there was ample space for them, the dancer, her family and assorted visitors. Almost immediately, however, Preston was sent off with Isadora's mother to an inn at Giverny, a tiny village about fifty miles northwest of Paris whose fame derives from Claude Monet's residence and achievements there. They were accompanied by Raymond Duncan, a cheerful eccentric who had just then begun to dispense with a traditional wardrobe and to dress in a loose, flowing Graeco-Roman tunic, his hair long, his feet covered only in leather sandals. Mary and Isadora occasionally visited Giverny, but only for a weekend. Isadora was busy in her Paris studio and Mary attended her there as a faithful companion. (Mary also took an occasional music lesson, courtesy of Solomon's one hundred fifty–dollar monthly support.)

The friendship between the two women flourished and deepened. Mary — capricious, often impetuous, but warm and empathetic — was a devoted admirer and a constant support to Isadora, who appreciated Mary's practical assistance, her tough feminine independence and her disregard for convention. With Mary, wrote one of Duncan's biographers, Isadora for the first time "became the carefree girl she had never been able to be during her childhood in America" — carefree, perhaps, because that adjective so aptly described Mary.

For her part, Mary found in Isadora the glamour she coveted and perhaps also the famous artist she longed to be. "You [were] an antique goddess reborn that man might again catch a glimpse of pure beauty," Mary wrote of Isadora in a typical passage of *The Untold Story*. "I should have thrown myself on my knees before [Isadora], believing I was worshipping a celestial being. . . . My heart went out to Isadora, and she still has it with her in eternity," she added, and this is in fact the theme of her book. But more than merely praising Isadora as a devoted admirer, Mary seems in fact to have had a fanciful identification with her.

Victor Seroff, also a Duncan biographer, recalled Mary as

> a robust woman with a liberal amount of unspent energy, bringing with her wherever she went more noise and disorder than harmony and peace. In her approach to life, she thought everything "terribly funny," except, perhaps, for one thing — she seriously believed that she was Isadora. . . . While her intentions were sincere, their being carried out usually meant trouble and confusion. Nevertheless . . . they always remained good friends.

Mary's identification with Isadora is indeed a motif announced from the first page of *The Untold Story*. After Isadora's death, Mary traveled to the Duncan dancing school in Moscow, where, she wrote, she was welcomed by the young students: " 'But Mary,' the children cried, 'you look out of the eyes like Isadora. You are like our Isadora.' " Richard Wagner's widow, Cosima, according to Mary, had greeted the two friends by stating flatly, "Isadora, I thought you were one, but you are two." And Mary further insisted that the similarities between them became so marked that when Cosima Wagner saw Mary dance and remarked to Isadora "how she [Mary] resembles you," Isadora's reaction was a furious remonstrance to Mary. Her friend must never dance again, Isadora insisted, must never imitate her, must never *threaten* her that way.

It is difficult to judge if these latter incidents occurred as Mary recounted them or if they represent several of her more fervent fantasies. In any case, the accounts reveal what Mary *felt* about her relationship with Isadora, and how closely she wished to identify with her. And regardless of the accuracy of Mary's scenes, Duncan's biographers do confirm the extremes to which Mary went in her identification with Isadora. From the earliest days of their friendship, Mary imitated her friend's style, and eventually she began to dress like Isadora, in loose, flowing Greek garments, with cape and sandals.

Ilya Ilyich Schneider, who knew both women, recalled that

> Desti [as everyone knew her later] told me that she worshipped Duncan, and there is no reason why one should not believe her. . . . Desti tried to imitate Isadora in everything. She wore the same kind of cloaks and hats, she had the same kind of hair style as Isadora, she even tried to imitate Isadora's way of walking.

And writer and socialite Mercedes de Acosta, who knew both women, wrote in her provocative autobiography that Mary

> worshipped [Isadora] to such an extent that in a curious way she had taken on some essence of Isadora. . . . Isadora completely dominated Mary.

By the time he was five, Preston was dressed by Mary the way Isadora dressed herself and Mary — in a Greek tunic with cape and open sandals. What suited the Duncans would be suitable for Mary and son.

Preston's time in Giverny — and his subsequent separations from his mother — at least partially explain his virtual absence in Mary's book. Briefly mentioned on the early pages, he then vanishes, and as the narrative limps along he is only an occasional presence in the life of Mary and Isadora.

This separation from his mother while still a baby began a pattern that continued throughout his childhood and adolescence, for he was routinely left in the care of others while his mother followed her cultural and personal whims. It would be easy, in this regard — but perhaps unfair — to judge Mary as a negligent mother, attentive only when it was convenient and rather coolly detached from a child who already lacked a father's presence.

Mary seems to have had no feeling for motherhood precisely because she had no model for it. Her background, after all, had ill prepared her for parental responsibilities. Catherine Dempsey had worked outside the home throughout Mary's childhood, and a kind of minimum care — until Mary herself began working quite young — was provided by an aunt or siblings or neighbors. Denied mothering, Mary knew nothing of it.

Later, Mary's only child was the product of a miserable marriage she tried her best to forget. She felt a basic responsibility for Preston — to see that he was fed and clothed and sheltered — but otherwise she felt no special emotional duty, and there seems to have been no affective conviction behind her obligation. Mary Desti seems, quite simply, not to have developed much in the sense of a warmly maternal feeling at all. Her intentions were good, but she had no idea that most mothers might be more attentive to their children.

Mary's background, then, and her ambition to be a cultured and artistic woman effectively short-circuited what might have been more nurturing sentiments. There seems no doubt, however, that a dimension was missing in her life — and, therefore, in the life of her small son.

TWO

Noblesse Oblige

F OR WHATEVER monetary reasons may have prevailed, Mary decided to return to her apartment on Superior Street, Chicago, in early autumn 1901. That October, she and Solomon Sturges were married in Memphis, and on their return to Chicago, Mary and her son moved into Solomon's spacious, elegant apartment on Goethe Street. In January 1902, Solomon formally adopted Edmund Preston Biden, who was thenceforth known as Preston Sturges.

Preston's tender devotion to Solomon Sturges — whom he always regarded as his only true father — was reiterated constantly in letters over the years, both to his stepfather and to many others. "I revere his memory," he wrote in his unpublished memoir many years after Solomon's death. "We never stopped loving each other [and] he never ceased being my father." To anyone who would listen, he routinely praised him as a man "whose love and protection and generosity and constant patience made him much more my father than a simple circumstance of birth."

The declarations of love were mutual. Solomon was unfailingly supportive, emotionally and materially, from Preston's childhood through the financial vagaries and irresponsibilities of his adult years. He was proud of Preston's accomplishments, lavish in praise, lenient with his faults and benevolent when advising. On his side, Preston appreciated the time he spent with his stepfather in his childhood — however brief and irregular — and he was certainly grateful for everything offered. And in Solomon's old age, Preston was as attentive and provident as any son could be.

Occasional visits to Chicago meant not only financial and emotional security for Preston but also connection to one of the city's most venerable and sometimes most flamboyant families.

In his childhood, for example, Preston was regularly taken to the home of Solomon's cousin Kate Buckingham, a charmingly eccentric maiden lady who was the daughter of his stepfather's sister Lucy Sturges and her husband, Ebenezer Buckingham. After the death of her brother Clarence, who every Sunday escorted her and her sister Lucy Maud to church, Kate expressed her gratitude for his weekly constancy by erecting on Lake Shore Drive an elaborate and expensive fountain. She personally supervised its design and operation, with the vertical sprays illuminated at night by changing patterns of electric light and accompanied by cheerful calliope music. (A century later, the Buckingham Memorial Fountain remained a major tourist attraction in Grant Park.)

After the death of her father, sister and uncles, Kate Buckingham inherited enormous wealth, and she generously endowed museums and symphonies. She then had the odd idea of financing a grand memorial to Alexander Hamilton. Preston (then a schoolboy) suggested a monument to Christ instead, adding that if placed in a poor neighborhood and surrounded with a reflecting pool it would dignify the area and, in the summer heat, provide a wading pond for children. "But you haven't understood, Preston dear," Kate replied, "it is *Alexander Hamilton* I want to do something for — Christ has so much already!"

Mary, however, was soon bored by what she called the "conventional life in Chicago," and she longed for her "old simple way of living" in Europe: Grecian tunics, oysters and champagne, weekends with the painter Eugène Carrière and the Prince de Polignac (occasional visitors, among others, to the inn at Giverny) and the glamorously unpredictable life with Isadora and her family, her lovers, her students and her audiences. To such a "simple way of living" many others might eagerly aspire.

After some serious discussions, Mary and Solomon agreed in the spring of 1904 that thenceforth she would travel for half a year in Europe and spend the other half in Chicago, and so — eager to return to Isadora — Mary sailed for Europe with Preston. Years later, Preston remembered being carried one day on the ship's deck by the great tenor Enrico Caruso, who drew a caricature of Mary that apparently displeased her.

In Berlin, Preston and little Temple Duncan (Isadora's niece, a few months older than Preston) were at first left at Isadora's apartment with Mrs. Duncan, and Preston endured several weeks in a local schoolroom, where he understood nothing but learned a few German melodies he never forgot. Mary — ever zealous for her son's cultural development — had supplied him with portfolios of classical artwork and had arranged for violin and piano lessons. She also insisted that when she booked seats at an evening opera later that summer, he had to take an afternoon nap "instead of playing in the municipal gardens with the other children, and this poisoned my existence." Her child had to submit to the doctrines of serious culture, and at times his cultural education seemed to have been rather forcefully imposed.

Mary and Isadora had proceeded at once to the Bavarian town of Bayreuth, where Isadora was scheduled to dance in the "Bacchanale" sequence of *Tannhäuser* at the Wagner festival. When the children finally arrived in late June, they were lodged not with Mary and Isadora at Phillip's Rest (the former hunting lodge of King Ludwig of Bavaria) but nearby, at the Hermitage Gardens — a lovely residence on a hillside, landscaped with gently splashing fountains and manicured parks. The entire region was magnificently tended, in fact, with wide, shaded streets and eighteenth-century gardens designed like those at Versailles. The center of Bayreuth was the Festspielhaus, where for three decades Wagner's operas had been performed in summer festivals; by 1904, the events were under the supervision of his widow and son.

When not at rehearsals for her dance sequence, Isadora and Mary leaped gaily into the social circle around Richard Wagner's widow, Cosima, where they met a number of colorful celebrities that included the composer Engelbert Humperdinck (best known for his opera *Hänsel und Gretel*); the conductors Hans Richter and Karl Muck; the king and queen of Württemberg and the Ab-Princess of Meiningen, sister of the Kaiser; and the actors and musicians in rehearsal. Preparing dinner for Ferdinand of Bulgaria, brewing coffee for Siegfried Wagner, listening to music and poetry in the summer evenings — that time was remarkable for what Mary, with perhaps unconscious irony, called "the joy and sheer beauty of its unreality." Preston, who marked his sixth birthday that summer, was present for it all.

Although his youth prevented full recognition of the romantic intrigues swirling around Isadora, he was never far away while the women orchestrated the tricky medleys of her admirers.

There were, for example, Isadora's recently assumed, torrid affair with Hungarian actor Oskar Beregi; her equally feverish but noncarnal relationship with art historian Heinrich Thode, son-in-law of their hostess, Cosima Wagner; and the warm but innocent attentions of the seventy-year-old Darwinian evolutionist Ernst Haeckel.

At the same time, Mary had an affair with the Maltese tenor Alfred Erwin von Bary. ("In my boyhood," her son allowed later, "I found that wherever Mother went, there was a man.") Von Bary, who had a medical degree, had given up his practice when he was told he had a fine dramatic singing voice. From 1902 he was at the Dresden court opera, and then, after some success in Munich, he was engaged to sing Parsifal and Tristan at Bayreuth. A romance with Mary blazed in 1904.

Some diversions, however, were more hazardous. When the two women and Beregi took the children to the German island of Helgoland in the North Sea, there was very nearly a disaster. After a day's swimming on a tiny cay a short distance from the island, Mary and Isadora left Preston and Temple on the cay with an innkeeper and returned to spend the evening on the island with Beregi. A fierce storm arose, and the women just barely rescued Preston and Temple in a rowboat before a torrent swept over the cay. "The children were put to bed," Mary noted in her book, "after being given hot tea and whiskey" — a toddy, Preston added years later, that repeated the boozy medication he had received in infancy ("I never seemed to stop drinking!").

Beregi and Isadora separated forever after that holiday, and the women and children returned briefly to Bayreuth, where von Bary eagerly awaited Mary. After toying with the man's feelings and discussing a possible elopement, she rather callously abandoned him — "and drove gleefully home," Mary admitted without a trace of remorse, "looking for some new adventure."

The new adventure was a journey to Italy. Preston, Mary and Isadora went first to Florence where, according to Mary, they "danced gaily through the deserted streets . . . singing at the top of our voices." In Venice, they were joined by Solomon, who had come to take his wife and son back to Chicago at the end of the prearranged six months.

Back in Chicago that autumn, Preston was enrolled in first grade at the Coulter School. Extracurricular culture proceeded, of course, and Mary saw to it that her son attended performances of Shakespeare and Molière at Ravinia Park. But he remembered as much more interesting a screening of Edwin S. Porter's recent twelve-minute film *The Great Train Robbery* — one of the first American silents that economically and effectively told a simple dramatic story and anticipated future developments in film narrative, in creative editing and in both the western and thriller genres.

At the same time, Mary herself seemed to have developed her first pretensions toward playwriting. Over the next twenty years, usually with a collaborator, she wrote several plays and drafted ideas for others. Preserved among the Preston Sturges papers, these exercises (they can hardly be called more) lack any verbal facility, wit or dramatic structure and are gravid with worn melodramatic devices and limp stories of beleaguered heroines and hypocritical lawmen, of ignoble greed denounced and angelic virtue rewarded. A sampling of her titles, like the dialogues, suggests nothing so much as melodrama and soap opera: *Getting a Passport* or *The Woman without a Country, Jobless Jerry, The Little Mother of the Neighborhood, Nicholas Nobody, Oh, My!, Paddy Patch of the Daily Dispatch, The Scented Hat* and *Two Young Fools*. Scenes are occasionally written in verse:

> Lost in the wilds of heart's despair
> Seeking the path to find
> That led us together through gardens fair
> Before you left me behind.

Solomon, ever long-suffering and indulgent, funded a modest staging of one of Mary's efforts, *The Law*. The Chicago press took no notice.

But again after the contracted six months — like the mythic Persephone pining for her half year back on Earth after a half year in the underworld — Mary swept off to Europe in early 1905 with Preston in tow. By this time Isadora's lover was Edward Gordon Craig, the English director and designer who would father her daughter Deirdre (born September 24, 1906), and Mary at once reimmersed herself in Isadora's personal life as well as in the details of the dance school in Paris.

Preston was deposited in the care of a family named Rousseau, who had a school in Joinville, east of Paris. There he felt welcome and loved, and with the Rousseaus' son Preston attended classes, quickly learning an excellent French he retained for the rest of his life.

The actual time he spent with the Rousseaus was apparently less than ten months, but for a child who had not known a warm and constant family, that was sufficient time to impart his first sense of domestic security. Occasionally, "a beautiful lady in furs and a shining automobile would arrive with expensive presents for everyone" — the lady being his mother, living handsomely on Solomon's allowance and benefiting materially, perhaps, from both the Duncan-Craig liaison and from a new one of her own.

Preston's sense of security was not to endure, however, and later that year he was brought to his mother's Paris apartment on the rue Villarette de Joyeuse, where there also resided a parrot that soiled the carpet, chewed the furniture and screeched sometimes obscene insults. Not long after, he accompanied Isadora's pupils and Temple on a dance tour of more than a dozen German cities and towns.

After another American interval with Solomon in 1906, Mary and Preston were about to depart New York by steamship for Europe when they received news from home that Solomon had been seriously injured in an auto accident, sustaining several broken bones and a fractured skull. They returned at once to Chicago, where after some time in a coma Sturges began a long and slow recuperation. For several years, however, he showed signs of frequent mental dysfunction, erratic behavior and inappropriate responses. Once, walking through Lincoln Park with Preston, he began to laugh hysterically for no apparent reason, and then, just as suddenly, he threw his walking stick at the boy. "I was terribly frightened because I loved him so and was so sure of his love for me, and I am sure he didn't mean me any harm."

Mary nursed her husband for several months, and then the three Sturgeses went west for a California vacation near San Diego, where Preston learned to swim. Among their neighbors were L. Frank Baum (author of *The Wizard of Oz*) and a woman whose Christian Science faith renewed Mary's dormant interest in religion — a topic she tossed into her cultural grab bag along with Wagner, dancing, the art of table-setting and poems by Shelley. She might have been "allergic" to spiritual matters, as her son stated, but she knew it had at least cultural significance.

In early 1907, Solomon accompanied Mary and Preston to Paris — not a pleasant time, the boy remembered, because by now it was clear that the Sturges marriage was crumbling. After a brief stay at a Paris hotel, where he climbed onto a window ledge and threatened suicide, Solomon was shipped back to Chicago and Mary and son went on to the Duncans in Dresden. One of Isadora's students — a dancer later known as Maria Theresa Bourgeois — remembered the young Preston Sturges years later and wrote to him:

> You wore the Grecian tunic and looked exactly as in the photograph with your mother. Ah, what a cherub you were — but how deliciously devilish at the same time. Then, we were fellow acolytes in the cause of art and Hellenic culture, and more often the rogue in you schemed how you could evade becoming a Grecian and fulfill the role of a Frenchman or an English squire. . . .

In Dresden, Mary took a new lover, a Mexican composer named José Velasquez with whom she tried to compose lyrics for an operetta called *The Vendor of Dreams.* "I suspect," Preston wrote later, "he had some idea of marrying Mother, as most of the gentlemen who came around seemed to have." While awaiting her decision (negative, as it turned out), Velasquez taught the boy to play some piano tunes. In the now typical style of her whirlwind life, Mary then dismissed Velasquez and told Preston and their maid to pack for departure.

The trio boarded the train in Dresden, burdened with much luggage, a cageful of singing canaries, the furniture-chewing and hot-tempered parrot and three yelping dogs. An hour after departure, Mary absentmindedly left her purse with the train tickets and her cash at their seats, and she, her son and their maid went to the dining car.

On their return from dinner, they discovered that the compartment they had occupied in the rear of the train had been disconnected at Cologne as scheduled and was proceeding to Paris without them. Her purse, their luggage and the animals had gone along, while they were now on the express route back into Germany.

Arriving in Berlin without tickets or cash, Mary was told that since she had no ticket stubs (as is customary in Europe, to allow exit from the station) she must pay again for the journey just completed — as well as buy new tickets for the next segment of the trip next morning. The price would be refunded when she found and presented the other set of tickets. She protested that her cash was on the disconnected train, too.

"But you will get the money back," said the stationmaster.

"Get *what* back?" asked Mary. "I haven't anything to *give* you until I get my bag."

"But you can't leave the platform without tickets — it's against the rules!"

"Well, you are certainly not going to keep us standing here all night! You let us off this platform immediately or I will telephone my friend, the Ab-Princess of Meiningen, immediately — and your name will be mud!"

"You mean His Imperial Majesty's sister?" asked the poor man nervously.

"I most certainly do — take me to the telephone!"

The threat was enough, and soon the three were waved on. With a few pennies from the maid they spent the night at the dreary station hotel, and next day managed to sneak aboard the Paris express. Eventually they found their bags and animals at the Cologne train station, where a soldier with a bayonet was guarding everything while the parrot barked insults in French.

Like many episodes in Preston Sturges's life, this adventure was vividly recalled by him many years later — in the incomplete, witty, fragmented and frequently embellished memoir he was compiling at the time of his death. His account of this particular journey very likely reflects his creative reconstruction of it, especially in the snappy dialogue he had by then mastered as a writer and director of enormously popular motion picture comedies.

A chaotic sudden trip to New York followed, where Mary unsuccessfully tried to interest producers in her operetta, and then they visited Solomon in Chicago. Preston was, as usual, delighted: "It was heaven to sit upon his lap," he wrote of this time, years later. "I loved to kiss the top of his bald head, and the perfume of my father, a mixture of maleness and the best Havana cigars — was the breath of Araby to me."

But Mary and Solomon then began fighting: she protested her hatred of Chicago and he berated her for allowing their marriage to evaporate.

"Mother is going to live in Paris, darling," Mary then announced to Preston, "and Father is going to stay here in Chicago. What do you want to do?" When the boy said he preferred to stay with his father, Solomon replied flatly: "I am not your father."

Until that moment, Preston had assumed — since no one had informed him to the contrary — that he was the natural son of Solomon Sturges. The news was shattering. "I looked at him in stupefaction for a moment, then at my mother to see if he was joking, then back at Father. Then I started to cry. . . . I think that night he thought I was going to die of grief."

Despite the boy's wish to remain with Sturges, however, he was taken back to Paris with Mary. The Atlantic crossing was memorable only for marking Preston's first theatrical performance, before a group of fellow passengers in the ship's salon. While Mary read the nursery tale of Little Miss Muffet, Preston and a girl playmate acted it out. He later remembered wearing a green veil over his head, and he "leapt upon the little girl violently, knocked her off the tuffet, stepped in the curds and whey, then chased her, screaming. I need hardly add that the play was an immense success, being full of sex, suspense and surprise."

Back in Paris that autumn of 1907, Mary took up with a handsome French actor named Jacques Grétillat, fourteen years younger than herself. When the subject of Preston's education arose, it was decided that he should attend Grétillat's former school, and so Preston was outfitted in a new wardrobe and forthwith enrolled as a *pensionnaire* in the junior boys' division of the Lycée Janson-de-Sailly. Of twenty-one hundred students enrolled that year, Preston was one of two hundred who boarded.

Occupying eight acres on the avenue Henri Martin (later, rue de la Pompe) between the Trocadéro and the Bois de Boulogne, the school, completed in 1886 and named for a nineteenth-century French jurist, was considered one of the best in Paris.

A central sports gymnasium dominated the property. The instructional buildings occupied only a third of the land, the rest being given over to carefully maintained open courts, a covered playground and yards with attractive trees and plantings. The brick and stone buildings housed classrooms on the first floor, laboratories and several dormitories were on the second and the remaining dormitories (and those for servants) were on the top floor.

As a younger boarder, Preston occupied one of the spacious top-floor dormitories, where thirty-two could be accommodated without crowding. The only furniture for each boy was a metal-frame bed, a small floor rug beside it and a clothes hook, for nighttime use only, on the wall; clothing was kept in lockers in a separate room. In the vast lavatory, each boy had his own washbasin, but toilets were few. According to Preston years later, the boys washed only their hands and faces at the school and were marched only once weekly to hot showers at a public bath, a half mile distant. In 1915, an English scholar wrote of French schools:

> The bath does not play the same part in continental life that it does in our own, partly, perhaps, because the children are less given to those violent forms of athletic exercise that make such conveniences essential. In France the shower never forms an accessory to the equipment of the school gymnasium.

Breakfast in the long, echo-filled refectory was invariably coffee or chocolate with bread; luncheon and dinner meant white or red beans, occasionally with some meat. Each boy was given a quarter bottle of red wine with both meals (pure for the older boys, diluted for the younger).

Within the school, black cravats were required but day students could choose the color of their light wool trousers and waistcoats. Preston and the other boarders, however, were required to wear a dark blue uniform with long trousers, a buttoned vest and a blue jacket. The shirt had a starched, detachable collar and gilt studs; there was a hooded cape for inclement weather, and the boys wore berets year round.

*   *   *

21

Cold, dimly lit, cramped and uncomfortable, the classrooms (with forty to fifty boys in each) were certainly malodorous, but they were also places of earnest instruction and serious learning. Latin, French, mathematics and history were taught daily. There were also recitations several times each week in history, geography, nature study, writing and singing, and for excellence in drawing Preston won first prize at the end of his second year. The teachers, he recalled, were all cheerful, kind and competent, except for the Frenchman who taught English and resented Preston's superior accent in both languages.

After classes, there were games and sports, and the exercise equipment in the gymnasium was surprisingly elaborate, with wooden and iron dumbbells, Indian clubs, wall pulleys, parallel bars, rowing machines, wrestling mats, ropes, trapezes and hanging rings. Following supper, there was a study hour until bedtime.

Several afternoons weekly Preston was compelled to continue the violin lessons he had taken for almost two years. For this he never showed any talent. "My mother did everything [she] could to make me an artist, but I didn't want to be an artist," he told *Time* magazine decades later. "I wanted to be a good businessman like my father [Sturges]."

His French classmates called Preston a "chic type" who had, according to one of them, André Moldavan,

> a kind of far west flavor polished by Fifth Avenue. . . . He was tall for his age. He held his back straight à la West Point in contrast with the easy relaxed muscles of the French boys. He kept his head high with a somewhat far-away look. He had the unhurried gait of the Yankee or the Texan and which is so unlike the leg motion of the French. He wore at the time an American navy blue suit . . . black stockings and New York–made low boots. . . . That alone would have left its mark on our sensitive youthful memories.

Occasionally, Preston went to his mother's apartment on the rue Octave Feuillet. Dashing young Jacques Grétillat frequently took them to dine at the Hôtel Meurice or at the Majestic. Jacques knew the best restaurants in and outside Paris, and even before adolescence Preston knew the gastronomic delights of La Rue, Marguery, Foyot, and Prunier. He soon learned house specialties, too — lobster bisque at the Café de Paris, the famous lamb at Volney, wild duck at Tour d'Argent, Italian cuisine at Frascati, caviar and blinis at Caneton, pastries at Rumplemaier's and virtually anything at La Coupole, Le Dôme, Le Panthéon, La Reine Pédauque and La Pavillon de Dauphine. They enjoyed the shadow plays at Le Clou restaurant and the singers and brandied cherries at Le Lapin Agile. "Sometimes," Preston recalled later, "we went as far as Rouen to eat a duck with turnips and I remember going all the way up to a restaurant on the English Channel to eat lobster."

One of their gastronomic journeys took them to the village of Fleurines, north of Paris, where Grétillat recommended the dining room and wine cellar of the centuries-old Hôtel du Grand Cerf, operated by a couple named Bruneau. Mary was impressed not only with the meal but also with the lovely surroundings, and she immediately decided to build a house on a nearby hill overlooking the village. Avoiding the expense of an architect, she presumed that a local builder could provide something as charming as the antique tile and stucco cottages of the neighborhood.

In this she could not have been more mistaken, however, for the builder saw an affluent American lady and stretched his imagination — but in the wrong directions. The place was, it turned out, badly designed, the rooms were ill proportioned, the terrace collapsed, the plumbing and drainage were virtually nonexistent and there was no insulation.

During construction of the house, Preston was lodged with the Bruneaus while Mary and Jacques capered in Paris, visiting occasionally to groan over the builder's progress. Some time later, the place caught fire, but Preston and a friend managed to douse the flames and save the house. Soon his mother returned, and when he proudly told her what he had done she asked, "Why didn't you let it burn, for heaven's sake? It's heavily insured and we'll never get another chance like this in our whole lives."

Preston continued to thrive on the fresh experiences life offered him, and his time in Fleurines (which extended for periods in 1908 and 1909) provided happy memories. Mary was there part of the time — at least on his birthday, for she celebrated the event by inviting the neighbors to a lawn party, where there were races and games, prizes and delicacies. On that occasion and after, she cultivated an elegant and almost formal manner, and Preston was soon called "Monsieur Preston" even by adults: "I very rapidly became the small lord of the manor."

Fancying herself mistress of an estate, Mary soon added an elaborate series of chicken coops and runs, intending to breed exotic species of game for diners near and far. She then further augmented her domain by purchasing two cottages. One she loaned to the Duncan dancing students; the second she rented, reserving the stable for a horse she bought Preston. He loved to ride in the early mornings, in the slanting rays of sunlight in the forest of Hallate, and I have never seen anything lovelier. . . . Looking down the fern-lined and leaf-covered paths was like looking into a green cathedral, except that a deer would stick its head out and look at you, rather than a priest.

Maria Theresa Bourgeois, one of the Duncan dancers who visited Fleurines, wrote years later to Preston that she cherished

a vision of you riding a horse through the fields at Saint-Christophe, Fleurines. . . . I adored it when you came along on our promenades through the forest and you taught us all the lovely French folk songs. How sweet and innocent we all were, yet even then you had that sauciness and delightful mischievousness. . . .

Mary, like some early prototype of Auntie Mame, believed that exposure to life and culture was the best education for her son and that formal schooling was very much subordinate. Perhaps because his attendance at the Lycée Janson was so erratic during his second year, his grades suffered and many of his subjects had to be repeated. For Preston's remedial lessons, Mary engaged a tutor, but she insisted that the work be done at Fleurines, perhaps so that her private life in Paris would not be affected.

After a second summer in the country, Preston compensated for his earlier grades and was readmitted to classes with his peers in the autumn of 1909. He returned to the Lycée Janson as a day student, however, and lived with his mother — and with Jacques Grétillat, who was then living with her in yet another new apartment she had taken at 13 avenue Elysée Reclus. The tenant above was the playwright René Fauchois, whose *Beethoven* Preston saw that season, and whose best-known work was adapted into English by Sidney Howard as *The Late Christopher Bean* in 1932.

Each day Preston rode his bicycle to school, passing the Eiffel Tower, crossing the Seine and climbing past the Trocadéro to the avenue Henri Martin. His boxing skills, begun the previous year in gymnasium classes, were tested at school when he got into "a whole series of fights with some Portuguese boys when I decided to stamp out homosexuality that was rampant in the bushes" at school. When he arrived home one day with a black eye, Jacques wisely advised him, "Why don't you mind your own business?"

Preston's education in 1910 included meeting the twenty-year-old daughter of a Cincinnati tailor. Later, for a decade beginning in 1914, she was renowned as Theda Bara, the original femme fatale, an exotic vamp whose pallor and exaggerated eyeliner immortalized her in roles such as Salome, Cleopatra, Madame Du Barry and Carmen.

Born Theodosia Goodman, she met Preston through the Duncans and was then calling herself Theodosia De Coppet. She stayed briefly at Mary's apartment while awaiting travel fare back to America, and young Preston was deeply struck by her assertion of mystic powers:

> She used to receive messages from the spirits which she would write down with her right hand while holding her left over her eyes, and [she was] absolutely astonished when she looked and saw what the spirits had written to her . . . she explained to me that she was not like other women, but much more primitive.

At the time, Preston was twelve, curious, a schoolboy in *Belle Époque* Paris. Preston's visitor Theodosia struck him as "dark and snakey," embodying a mysterious and slightly perverse carnality. For the present, however, his virginity remained intact.

He was, of course, maturing amid an ethic of sexual freedom: the two women he knew best thought little of fidelity and less of marriage. His mother and Isadora seemed to vie with one another in the shifting objects of their passional lives, and so their men may have seemed to Preston objects of pleasant, more or less serious involvement — like Beregi and Craig, von Bary and Grétillat.

By this time, Isadora Duncan had taken a new lover — an enormously wealthy American named Paris Singer, heir to the sewing machine fortune and eventually the father of Isadora's son Patrick (born May 1, 1910). Singer also became a kind of paternal figure to Preston in the years the boy rarely saw Solomon Sturges. He was always as generous and attentive to Mary and her son as he was to Isadora and her children, and they frequently all traveled together — in the spring of 1910, for example, to Beaulieu on the French Riviera, all of them subsidized by Singer's benevolence.

That summer, Mary, Preston and Jacques spent at Houlgate, a resort on the English Channel. By September, Jacques was out of Mary's life and she was on the move again — this time to a large apartment at 19 avenue Charles Floquet, where Mary acquired a gray automobile and a chauffeur named Marcel Bouhiron, remembered by Preston as "a stinking driver, although so fond of automobiles and curious about them that he had usually taken ours completely apart to see what made it work just when Mother needed it."

Prior to taking the spacious new apartment, however, Mary had leased a smaller one in the same building. When the landlord refused to cancel the lease on it, Mary decided to loan it to Isadora's brother Raymond — he of the shoulder-length hair and floor-length tunics — who by this time traveled with a retinue of lady admirers, most of them pregnant or nursing his progeny, and with goats to provide milk for those being weaned. This unlikely band of nomads moved at once into Mary's smaller apartment, where the goats fouled everything and, when tethered on the terrace, also rather nastily surprised pedestrians below. Presently the landlord agreed to cancel the lease.

In the autumn of 1910, Mary (for unstated reasons of her own) transferred Preston from the Lycée Janson to the École des Roches, near Verneuil-sur-Avre in Normandy. "We propose to create in France," wrote the École's founder, "a new type of school, better adapted to the exigencies of actual life." With the motto "Well equipped for life" as the standard, and with a firm commitment to belief in the superiority of English education and English manners, the place was fiercely Anglophilic. Patterned after the Abbotsholme Priory, where primary emphasis was accorded physical activity and a close relationship between pupils and teachers, the founder's goals did not endear the school to Frenchmen.

Languages and history were Preston's major studies at the École, and one of the literature selections he always recalled was the tenderly elegiac ode to Sabrina from John Milton's *Comus,* with its gentle request that she "listen and save." By this as by other poetry, the romantic within the child was aroused. Also memorable that year were the school's performances of *Le Bourgeois Gentilhomme,* accompanied by student musicians; in it, Preston wore a flamboyant period French costume. "The audience enjoyed me more than Molière," he later wrote.

On January 25, 1911, the *Chicago Examiner* reported that Solomon Sturges had filed for divorce on grounds of desertion, and a major story ran under a flamboyant drawing of Mary dressed in Grecian tunic and the headline "Sturges Suit Blamed to Art — Wife to Acquiesce in Decree."

> The love of Mrs. Mary d'Estes [*sic*] Sturges, wife of Solomon Sturges, wealthy Chicagoan and head of the brokerage firm of Solomon Sturges and Company, for all forms of art, and especially for that form of which Isadora Duncan is the country's greatest exponent, is blamed by friends of both Mr. and Mrs. Sturges for the marital differences that led to the filing of a

suit for divorce by Mr. Sturges in Chicago on Monday. As one friend expressed it yesterday: "Mrs. Sturges was wedded to her art and Mr. Sturges was wedded to the ticker-tape in his office. How could there have been compatibility?" . . . Mrs. Sturges, it is said, will be represented by counsel and will make a formal denial of the charge of desertion. She will not contest the suit. . . . Mrs. Sturges is in Paris, where she has spent the greater part of her time in the last two years.

Mary took the news of her divorce with an insouciant relief; for Solomon, however, the matter was not so simple. For years he felt that Mary's absence reflected badly on him as a good husband:

I do not know exactly what the matter with me was [he wrote to Preston two decades later], but I always concluded she had some good reason. . . . I cannot tell you how badly I felt for years about your mother leaving me, because I was foolish enough to feel I had done nothing to deserve it. After a time I became wholly reconciled to the psychology of it and knew we were both better off.

While the divorce was in the Chicago courts, Mary arrived at Preston's school one day with a dark-haired Turk, six feet four inches tall and radiating exotic charm; he was, she said, soon to be her new husband. Like most of her partners, he was several years younger. His name was Vely Bey, and his father, Ilias Pasha, had been personal physician to the recently deposed Turkish sultan Abdülhamid II. Vivid and intense, courtly and unpredictable, Vely Bey was the bearer of kismet.

THREE

Turkish Delights

BUT THERE was a bizarre interruption in Mary d'Este's romance with Vely Bey.

In October 1911, she decided to celebrate her birthday with Isadora Duncan, who was then in London. During a boisterous party at the Savoy Hotel on that occasion (October 11), Mary was introduced to the English occultist Aleister Crowley, a strange and unsavory character sporting one tufted square of hair on his shaved head.

Four years younger than Mary (who was then forty), he had developed a pathological overreaction against his fundamentalist Christian upbringing, and by 1911 — proudly claiming to be the Antichrist — he had begun to develop a complex occultism characterized by numerology, drug-induced sex rituals and a fervent, perverse commitment to personified powers of darkness.

According to Crowley's own account, he found Mary "a most powerful personality [with] terrific magnetism which instantly attracted my own. We forgot everything. I sat on the floor like a Chinese god, exchanging electricity with her."

Oriental deity or no, their electrical exchanges generated sensational blue sparks for the next few months. Crowley enjoyed Mary as an ardent mistress — "a voluptuous and passionate woman of the world," he wrote later, "an amorous . . . lioness . . . quick-tempered and impulsive, always eager to act with reckless enthusiasm." Ever impressionable, attracted to bohemians and sexually venturesome, Mary became a fresh, willing victim of Crowley's exploitive charm, his outlandish magical claims, his seductive romantic gloom and his unquenchable sexual appetite. Preston recalled him as

> a sinister buffoon . . . depraved, vicious and revolting . . . [and he had] the unappetizing habit of taking out a penknife and adding a small fresh slice to . . . his forearm . . . each time my poor mother had so far forgotten his teachings as to begin a sentence with "I."

First the lovers proceeded to Paris, thence for a winter holiday in Switzerland, where he also discovered that she could be useful to him (as he had, earlier, found other mistresses useful). Crowley was inspired to use Mary as a collaborator in his writing after she had a wild, prophetic vision one night at the National Hotel in Zurich. A spirit named Abuldiz, Mary raved, was — through her as medium — ordering Crowley to write about his system of magic and mysticism, and to go to southern Italy to do so. The instructions from beyond continued at the Palace Hotel in St. Moritz, and on to Milan and Rome where, Mary's voice insisted, a villa for their literary task awaited them. (Abuldiz, remarkably like Mary, seemed to have appreciated the Italian coast.)

Immediately after they had found a place to work at Posilippo, near Naples, her son joined them for Christmas. Familiar though he was with Mary's habitually offbeat, idiosyncratic life, Preston still found the holiday bizarre. He found his mother calling herself "Soror Virakam" (a name coined from Latin and Sanskrit: Sister I-will-perform) and taking dictation from Crowley (Frater Perdurabo: Brother I-will-triumph) for his book on the occult arts. Mary's own signed testimony is found in Crowley's work, *Book Four* (there are no first three): "I wrote this book down from [Crowley's] dictation at the Villa Caldarazzo, Posilippo, Naples, where I was studying under him, a villa actually prophesied to us long before we reached Naples. . . ." There is, however, no mention of Crowley in her own book.

Early in the new year 1912, Preston returned to school and Mary — after a surfeit of Crowley's cruelty and his weird sexual habits (which included an avid sadomasochism) — fled back to Paris, and Aleister Crowley returned to a former mistress. Preston later wrote he felt fortunate to have escaped with his life.

Back on the avenue Charles Floquet, Mary found Vely Bey waiting; Preston she installed in the family quarters of a nearby tutor, his attendance at the École des Roches now terminated.

In due course Mary and her Turk were married. Vely Bey's parents arrived from Istanbul with carloads of Turkish furniture for the newly-weds, and artifacts which they quickly moved into Mary's apartment as a wedding surprise.

> When [Mother] found her lovely Louis XVI apartment . . . covered with piles of priceless Turkish carpets, inlaid sandalwood tabourets and screens, pierced brass braziers, precious metal narghiles with tubes and mouth-pieces that looked like enema attachments, bonbonnieres [and] silk rugs . . . she got hysterical and couldn't stop laughing for an hour. At each new piece they tried to get her to admire, she'd go off again and laugh till the tears rolled down her cheeks.

Preston liked Vely Bey and his parents, all three of them in Paris exile after the deposition of the Turkish tyrant. Vely's father, Ilias Pasha, was a distinguished physician, having graduated from a German university and worked with the doctor who advanced the success of cataract surgery. He treated Preston kindly and generously and, wearing narrow, pointed, upturned yellow shoes, offered him guided walking tours of Paris. Ilias Pasha's wife was a cheerfully obese woman who wore huge diamonds and applied wide circles of black kohl eye powder — to prevent infections, she insisted.

The old man also became Preston's mentor in adult sex life: "You have no idea, my dear little grandson," he said one day, "what the taking on of a new little wife every ten years or so, preferably one about fifteen or sixteen, can do for a man." This was counsel Preston recalled in word — and later (albeit with somewhat older partners) in deed.

The family had an abundance of exotic perfumes, powders and pomades. When Mary developed a rash on her face, Ilias Pasha treated her with a lotion used by all the major harems in Turkey; the lotion also, he insisted, removed wrinkles. When the rash quickly vanished, she hit on the idea of marketing the remedy as "Le Secret du Harem." And with that the course of Mary d'Este's life — and her son's — was changed.

Within days, Mary decided to become a cosmetician and perfumer. She engaged a decorator to renovate a small mezzanine space she found at 4 rue de la Paix, and then she brought in a German manicurist, a French hairdresser, a Chinese chiropodist and an old provincial chemist. A French *parfumeur* assisted her with various alcohols and new scents, and soon she had a beauty institute ready for customers — to be called the Maison d'Este, after herself and her fancied Italian ancestor, the illustrious Marie Beatrice d'Este (Mary of Modena [1658–1718], second wife of England's

King James II). But the Paris branch of the d'Este family objected to the announcement of a Maison d'Este and threatened a lawsuit.

Mary was forced to comply, but she succeeded in opening the Maison Desti, and from that time to her death she called herself Madame Desti. Glass bottles from Venice held her new scents, the Paris box manufacturer Tolmer designed containers for Desti products, and Baccarat and Lalique sold her crystal bottles and alabaster jars. Rouges and face powders completed her line of products, and soon the Maison Desti was doing brisk business — so brisk, in fact, that in October Mary hustled Preston off to New York for a selling trip, where B. Altman and Company bought ten thousand dollars' worth of her products. Soon after, a manufacturer offered Mary a deal to distribute her cosmetics with his perfumes. She distrusted him, however, and rejected his offer — to her perpetual regret, for the man's name was Coty.

Then fourteen, Preston preferred New York entertainment to selling cosmetics, although the latter endeavor was facilitated by his polish, sophistication and mature appearance. For him the highlight of the journey was an evening at the Moulin Rouge theater on Broadway at Forty-fifth Street, where he first saw the *Ziegfeld Follies*.

Two players he especially remembered. Bert Williams, the gifted comic, had perfected a routine as a railroad porter trying to work at Pennsylvania Station, then under construction. He walked along girders, his arms laden with baggage and a mountain climber's rope round his waist, until another popular comedian named Leon Errol entered, tied to the other end of the rope. Verbal and physical gags abounded, and for Preston the evening had a great impression; almost a half century later he recalled the show as "terribly funny . . . a hell of an act." Over the next several years, he saw Williams often in the *Follies*. He loved the alchemy of swift verbal wit, slapstick, outrageous puns and dashes of risqué humor. This was his introduction to theatrical comedy.

Back in Paris late that October, Preston's memorable evening in the theater was followed by another, when Vely Bey took him and his mother to see Sacha Guitry and his wife Charlotte Lysès in a performance of Guitry's successful comedy *La Prise de Berg-op-Zoom*, Guitry's twenty-fifth play (and his third in 1912). The performance cultivated even further Preston's love of comic theater: "I howled along with everybody else," he noted in his memoir.

Based on the legend of Bergen, the Dutch town that resisted many sieges throughout history, Guitry's play was set in contemporary Paris and shifted the focus from military to romantic conquest.

31

But Preston saw only a portion of the comedy. Vely Bey, after several futile warnings to the boy to muffle his loud laughs, slapped his face. Shocked and humiliated, Preston responded automatically, as he would to a nasty schoolmate, by punching his stepfather in the nose. A melee ensued, the play was interrupted, the spectators roared their disapproval and the offenders were evicted from the theater. The brawl between them continued in a taxi and became even more violent, with blows and kicking and bloody noses — until finally their driver hailed policemen, who were given Vely Bey's assurance that this was only a minor family dispute.

"That is a dirty lie!" Mary rejoined, and then pointed at her husband: "I have never seen this man before in my life!" Vely Bey was detained by police while Mary and Preston fled into a gathering crowd.

Not long after, the marriage was understandably in its final declension. After scuffles and threats, raised voices and fists, Vely Bey withdrew from their lives, but not forever.

In early 1913, Preston Sturges was a strikingly handsome teen-ager, almost six feet tall and slim, with a full crop of thick, brown-black hair and alert hazel eyes. Like most men of that time, he also smoked — increasingly heavily as years passed — and by his fifties he finished five packages of cigarettes daily.

Preston also had an easy poise and an engaging charm, for his innate intelligence and quickness of wit had been naturally augmented by an exposure to the widest variety of cosmopolitan influences. His life had, after all, included dancers, artists, writers and singers, Europeans and Americans of every background, Chicago businessmen and wealthy international travelers on ocean liners — all of them various kinds of teachers and tutors in the school of his experience.

He had become, in fact, a young Continental, with a keen appreciation of good food and wine, of wit, sensuality and sociability — a *flâneur*, a connoisseur of city life who observed news and manners and deposited images and anecdotes in a memory bank. He could see a millionaire pursue a sweet young clerk or a sophisticate longing for a peasant girl, and he found amusement and beauty in both the ordinary and the unexpected. He was familiar, by this time, with journalists and essayists like Aurélien Scholl, Georges Courteline and Maurice Donnay — each of them a *flâneur* mentioned in Sturges's notes fifty years later.

Although he claimed to resent the enforcement of high culture his mother provided, he could not indeed ignore the effects of his upbringing, of the diversity absorbed from so much travel from continent to continent, from one European city to another, from the salons of the wealthy and famous to the chilly classrooms and dormitories of French schools. The whimsical locomotion that disallowed stability also introduced him to an extraordinary range of colorful human characters.

That year, Preston often assisted at the Maison Desti, putting to good use his talent for drawing, poster-making and designing windows, boxes and placards for new Desti products. Not long after Vely Bey's departure, there was, predictably, a new man in Mary's life: "there was always *some kind* of a male around to nail up things or carry heavy parcels," Preston commented later. "I cannot remember any time when there wasn't."

Mary's favor that year fell upon a gentle-spirited Mexican named Gabriel Elizaga — the second, after José Velasquez, of that nationality. (Mary's lovers may have been chosen at least partly for their exoticism — there were, among others, two Latins, at least two Frenchmen, a German and a Turk.) Elizaga was a professional gambler she did not marry because he lost a vast amount playing baccarat and was soon reduced to dealing cards at hotels and casinos on the Right Bank.

A friend of Elizaga took Preston to Trouville in Normandy — a northwestern resort town on the Channel — when his bronchitis during the winter of 1913 was particularly severe. But his cough worsened, and it was soon determined that there was the first sign of a small tubercular lesion. Mary decided to ship him off to La Villa, a school in Lausanne, on the north shore of Lake Geneva in western Switzerland.

The exact dates of Preston's attendance at his new school are not clear, for as usual Mary — with not much regard for traditional academic schedules — felt free to pluck him back and forth for whatever business or cultural reason seemed warranted.

La Villa was "a very high-toned school," Preston wrote later, "stinking with Barons and Counts and Marquis, like the École des Roches," and he later mostly remembered the school's emphasis on sports — rowing, soccer and hockey especially. His classmates included the Duke of Alba's nephew and a young German baron who, with Preston, took piano lessons.

The good result of these lessons was almost immediate. Within weeks, Preston had whistled a tune for which the young German transcribed notes. To their astonishment they had composed a little ragtime melody called "Winky," which they sold to a music publisher in Latvia, where the baron's family had great wealth and influence. (The tune, which Preston called "really pathetic," has vanished with time and war —

like the French arts journal that, about 1913, published Preston's drawing of the eccentric Raymond Duncan.)

For at least part of the spring term of 1913, however, Preston was
back in Paris, a fact confirmed by his presence at a singularly tragic
funeral.

On April 19, Preston was to join Isadora Duncan's two children on
an afternoon's excursion from her studio in the Paris suburb of Neuilly to
the house at Bellevue which Paris Singer had provided for her. Temporarily without her driver, Isadora had accepted Mary's offer of her own
chauffeur, Marcel Bouhiron. Just before the outing, however, Preston did
something to annoy his mother, and she forbade him to go to Bellevue.

Marcel arrived at Neuilly. Isadora kissed her children, bundled
them into her Renault with their nurse, and waved them off. A few
hundred yards distant, the car momentarily stalled, and Marcel jumped
out to crank the engine, absentmindedly leaving the gear engaged. The
auto suddenly lurched forward, crashed through a guardrail and plunged
into the Seine. Hours later, far down-current, it was recovered with the
bodies of the wide-eyed children and of their nurse embracing them
tightly against the hideous death they all had time to see approaching.

Mary Desti, revealing the stronger and more serious side of her
complex personality, rushed to Isadora and assumed all the painful responsibilities. She went to the hospital to identify the bodies, attended
Isadora night and day, ran interference with the press and arranged the
funeral details. Preston was among those who attended the heartbreaking
services and then accompanied the remains to a Montmartre crematory.

In spite of occasional trips from Lausanne, however, Preston seems to
have spent several uninterrupted months there from 1912 to 1914 (at
least two full terms were completed). By spring of 1914, his health had
greatly improved, and as he was about to turn sixteen in August Mary felt
he would be of good use to her in a new venture: she planned to open a
branch of Maison Desti in Deauville, a new resort town opposite Trouville on the English Channel.

The Desti shop was rented in a portion of the building owned by the
restaurant Ciro's (which had branches in Paris and London, and eventually gave its name to a famous nightclub in Los Angeles); Mary's lease
included three meals daily and lodgings for Preston. The elegant culinary
experiences of that summer further supplemented what he had learned
during the restaurant tours with Jacques Grétillat, and by summer's end
Preston knew the right temperature for truffles in champagne, the names

of the best French vineyards and the details of an extraordinary variety of precious cuisine.

That summer was one of the pleasantest of his youth, although a brief flirtation with a nineteen-year-old girl had a rude finale. By pretending to be the same age — which his appearance easily attested — Preston was getting on very well until Mary arrived one weekend. "Isn't he *big* for fifteen?" Mary asked the girl as Preston approached their café table. The girl's exit was swift and permanent.

There were morning duties in the shop — dusting and restocking the shelves — and then a few hours selling, for which Preston outfitted himself in white flannel trousers, saddle shoes and a tan jacket. The famous and fashionable social set had just discovered Deauville, and he saw one glamorous entourage after another on the streets and shores of the town that summer — Rothschilds and maharajahs, gigolos and opera stars, actors, gamblers, jewelers and the merely wealthy.

The pleasures of Deauville ended suddenly after the assassination of Archduke Ferdinand in Sarajevo on June 28 and the gathering war that was to have ended all wars. Because of its strategic position on the Channel, Deauville was thought especially unsafe, and in August Preston rejoined Mary in Paris. Very soon thereafter, his mother booked passage for him to return to America, while with sheer tenacity and admirable pluck, she returned to Deauville and helped the staff at a receiving station for French soldiers in the Great War. Later, she rode in a Red Cross truck as far as the Loire Valley to obtain necessary medical supplies. Mary Desti never turned down a chance for adventure, no matter the circumstances.

Capricious fantasist Mary could be, but she also had a compassionate nature. That quality was summoned on Isadora Duncan's behalf again that summer of 1914, when, hours after Isadora gave birth to a baby, he died in her arms. Mary, ever faithfully attentive, stayed with her grieving friend day and night for a week. From the tragic losses of her three children, according to her biographers, the dancer never recovered. In spite of her art and her travels, Isadora — compulsive, insecure, emotionally precarious — spent her last years in a coda of decline that was only occasionally relieved by the most gallant effort.

With a trunkful of perfumes, bottles and cosmetics, Preston arrived at 347 Fifth Avenue, New York City, where his mother had arranged for the American branch of Maison Desti. Her representative and manager there was a stout, gin-tippling lesbian named Daisy Andrews, who relieved him of his luggage and promptly sent him on to Solomon Sturges in Chicago. This was their first reunion in over seven years, and Preston never forgot the details of their meeting at Union Station:

> Suddenly, out of the stream of strangers, [I] appeared, a young man about six feet tall who seized him fondly in his arms and then making joyful sounds, kissed him, European style, on both cheeks. This amused my father very much, and the next time I came to Chicago having learned the American style of *not* kissing your father, he grabbed me in *his* arms, kissed *me* on both cheeks and said: "I've been saving that for you."

Lavishly and lovingly, Solomon bought Preston a new wardrobe, took him to restaurants, introduced him to friends and quietly pressed money into his wallet.

By October, it was decided that Preston should attend high-school classes in New York, where he could also work at the Desti store. On the Upper West Side of Manhattan was the Irving Preparatory School, and Preston rented a room on Madison Avenue near Thirty-second Street, very near Desti's. Business was disappointing, however, and soon Preston moved to a cheaper apartment at Fifth Avenue and 129th Street.

Also disappointing was a second paternal reunion, this one with Edmund Biden, who had not seen his son since infancy and had located him while he, too, was in New York. They dined together, and during the evening, Biden said something rude about Mary. Preston rose from his place, quit the restaurant and never saw the man again.

The months at the Irving Preparatory School would be, as it happened, his final formal education — not only because he was drafted into full-time service for his mother, but also because, quite simply, he found classes boring and unrewarding, and so they must have seemed after the episodes of his earlier life with Mary and Isadora and their motley crews.

When Mary arrived in New York in December 1914, the affairs of her business were a shambles. Daisy Andrews was dismissed, and mother and son together began to salvage their finances. This was no simple task, since neither of them had either talent for or interest in bookkeeping details.

Mary first relocated her shop from 347 Fifth Avenue to less expensive quarters at 23 East Ninth Street, near University Place. Then at her most impecunious, she could afford only a small apartment on East Twelfth Street for herself and her son (who moved down from Harlem) — a "rotten little apartment, the only banal one I have ever known her to take," according to Preston. But at least the Hotel Brevoort and the Café

Lafayette were a few steps away, both of them maintained with a Continental style by their French owner, who welcomed Mary and Preston as unusually sophisticated New Yorkers. After the employment of a new chemist, a new line of powders and rouges was soon on the shelves at Desti's — Aurore Rouge, Youth Lotion and ochre and lavender powders being the best sellers.

Early in 1915, Isadora Duncan arrived in New York, and Mary was invited to move in with her friend at the Hotel Ritz — a typically sudden change of circumstances for Mary, who moved Preston into the Hotel Irving in Gramercy Park. Isadora's lover underwrote the maintenance of a nearby dance studio, and a residence for the students a few blocks away. When not busy at the shop, Preston was expected to assist with various chores at both places.

Another benefactor late that winter was the banker Otto Kahn, who offered Isadora the use of his Century Theater, on Central Park West at Sixty-second Street. In addition to several dance recitals, Isadora had the idea of staging a production of *Oedipus Rex,* and into her production she put everyone she knew except Mary, who claimed she was too busy at the shop. Preston, however, could not escape and was pressed into service as assistant stage manager, general errand boy and backstage elevator operator. He was also orchestra librarian — Isadora having inserted musical interludes into the production — and this provided him with a crash course in the names of orchestra instruments and where their various players sat.

At the premiere on April 23, Isadora's brother Augustin Duncan played the title role and Margaret Wycherly was Jocasta. There were eighty musicians and a choir of one hundred voices. At least one duty misfired on opening night, however. Positioned backstage, given red and green flashlights and instructed to signal to a technician high above for the stage effects of lightning and thunder, Preston confused the red (for thunder) and green (for lightning); the result was a farcical mix-up in which the stage actors' speeches were repeatedly drowned out by iron thundersheets when they should have been illuminated by an electrical arc.

Also in April, Mary and Preston were surprised by the appearance in New York of Vely Bey, who apparently tried to rehabilitate his marriage by suggesting that he and Mary manufacture a new kind of paperless Turkish cigarette. For a brief time, Desti's Ambre Cigarettes were New York's latest affectation. Business and personal considerations were soon ignored, however, when Isadora announced in May that she had had enough of New York and was returning with her students to Europe.

Mary, Preston, Vely Bey and everyone else in Duncan's retinue went to the New York harbor for the farewell, and Preston vividly remembered the scene. From the deck of the *Dante Alighieri,* Isadora cried to her friend, "Mary! If you don't come with me, I don't know what I'll do!" and promptly collapsed into sobs. Vely Bey, seeing what might happen, turned to Mary:

"You aren't going to fall for anything *that* stupid, are you?" he asked. "You have no passport! You have no clothes! You have no baggage and you have no money!"

"You don't understand!" Mary replied. She kissed Preston, saying, "Do the best you can, darling! Keep things going! I'll send you some money as soon as I can!" And with that she leaped onto the moving gangplank and joined Isadora. (The dancer's account — which typically diminishes her own manipulative pleading — is probably less accurate than Preston's eyewitness: "My friend Mary, who had come to see me off, could not, at the last moment, bear to part from me, and without luggage or a passport, she leapt on to the deck and joined us in singing, and said, 'I am coming with you.' ")

As the ship departed, Vely Bey announced the immediate closing of Desti's, but Preston was adamant, insisting that even at sixteen he was capable of managing the business and fulfilling his mother's expectations. After an exchange of harsh words about loyalties, Vely Bey departed and Preston moved to a rooming house across from the store, where for the next several years he constantly tried to improve the fortunes of a declining business.

This time of Sturges's life only perpetuated the residential instability he had as a child. Moving often from hotel to boardinghouse to tiny apartment and then repeating the cycle, he seems not to have remained at any single address longer than a few months. He was suddenly thrust into adulthood, self-reliant, psychologically independent and for his livelihood counting only on what receipts he could bring in to Desti's. Preston was also without any constant adult emotional support, guidance or encouragement. Solomon sent an occasional check and wrote regular letters, but Chicago was far distant in those days without jet travel or easy long-distance telephone access.

Still resourceful, cheerful and optimistic, however, Preston managed to enjoy New York life in those days before America joined the Great War. At the Domino Club, Columbus Circle, he saw the financier and bon vivant "Diamond Jim" Brady with Jenny and Rosie Deutsch, the glamorous singing actresses known as the Dolly Sisters. For several weeks he went almost every night to that club while he had a teenage crush on the Spanish dancer Isabelle Rodriguez. ("She never even kissed me, but her mother used to invite me once a month for [dinner].")

At seventeen, Preston Sturges was not lured by easy money any more than he was impressed by notoriety. Thus he quickly and easily turned down an offer from Vely Bey, who reappeared on Ninth Street one day with no less exotic a companion than Daisy Andrews, Mary's former gin-tippling manager. This odd couple had decided to open a restaurant-cabaret, and they offered Preston one hundred dollars a week (an extraordinary sum in 1915, especially for one who ordinarily survived on one-tenth that). All he had to do was dance with women customers of their new establishment. This offer he rejected, no doubt because a kind of sentimental *noblesse oblige* took hold of him, for he later wrote that he felt

> the name of "Sturges" was not actually mine by rights, but had been *given* to me. . . . I tried always to behave as I imagined I would have done had I been a *real* Sturges . . . not to bring dishonor upon this name, nor tarnish it in any way. . . . I couldn't see a Sturges as a gigolo . . . [and] my exaggerated care of this name that had been lent to me kept me reasonably straight and out of trouble for years.

Out of trouble he certainly was, but not out of the normal range of romantic experience. In July 1916, he spent a night (what he called his "first and rather important night in my life") with a girl he remembered only as Doris, a chorine from London. But toward morning, suffering a chronic illness, the girl had a pulmonary hemorrhage, thus giving the memorable occasion a faintly Dumas *fils* tone. Gallantly, Preston offered to pay the rent for her little apartment on Washington Square South, where he presumed their rendezvous would continue. When he called on her without warning several days later, however, she was with another young man and Preston walked out forever.

Almost immediately thereafter, Mary summoned Preston to London, where she was busily trying to succeed with yet another branch of Maison Desti, this one at 6-8 Old Bond Street. She had taken a small but charming flat at 7 St. Martin's Lane, near Trafalgar Square, and she was also enjoying the companionship of one Captain Kelly of the Royal Flying Corps. Preston was soon having an affair, too — with a shopgirl at Desti's, "and my progress toward manhood proceeded at the full gallop." The galloping continued later that year in New York, when he had a brief affair with a divorcée several years older than himself.

*   *   *

The swift currents of events and the premature adult responsibilities of Preston Sturges's adolescent years effected a certain rootlessness and instability. He had been denied reliable parental attention, and apart from his haphazard attendance at a variety of European schools, he had also been deprived of strong relationships with peers. Most of his life, on the contrary, had been spent with wildly unconventional grownups in unpredictable, ever-shifting settings. Then, even before he completed a high-school education, the burdens of business responsibility had been imposed on him, precipitously and heavily. He had, in other words, no youthful experience that encouraged him to deep personal relations. This set a somewhat poignant pattern for his later life.

The whirlwind childhood, free of familial, emotional and cultural moorings, led finally to a certain shallowness of expectation, as he seemed to develop the unarticulated attitude that no relationships were enduring, that no one could really be relied upon, that everything was of the moment. The early years were too unusual to be forgotten, and they gave him a fund of stories he later used to entertain millions. But those same years did not give him a basis for forming an adult life. There were dramatic, zany scenes and a colorful supporting cast in his life, but that life did not often have as much coherence as his later screenplays.

Mary, in 1916, had managed to ingratiate herself with people of fashion with whom she, Preston and Captain Kelly dined regularly at Simpson's on the Strand. She also outfitted her son with a stylish new wardrobe. There were, however, more disturbing interludes, for England was at war with Germany. On several evenings that summer, the sky was illuminated with great searchlights, with a zeppelin suddenly hanging in the sky and fighter planes taking aim from below. For safety and for business, Mary shipped her son back to America.

Back in New York, Preston was less interested than ever in cosmetics, and he persuaded Solomon to contact a New York colleague in the brokerage business. He wanted, he said, nothing so much as to be a stockbroker like his adored stepfather. Leaving the daily tasks at Desti's to a hired girl, Preston took a minor office job at seven dollars a week, at F. B. Keech and Company, 2 Wall Street. This was, however, an exercise in futility, for he discovered that whereas he had little penchant for retail business he had less for the complexities of high finance.

He was distracted from his job, however, by the sudden arrival of Isabelle Parry Biden, his paternal grandmother, who had just visited her son Sydney in Germany and, stopping in New York, announced to her grandson that she was old, sad, penniless and homeless.

> She was, of course [Preston wrote years later], as strong as a horse, looked like a woman of fifty with plenty of curves, played the piano wonderfully and sang extremely well [and] . . . was such a superb cook . . . that she was really in no trouble at all and could have laid her head anyplace she pleased.

Notwithstanding her melodramatics, Preston rented some furniture and an upright piano and installed the lady in an upper Manhattan apartment, which he shared with her. This turned out to be an amiable arrangement — thanks to his grandmother, he even refined his knowledge of basic musical chords — until April 6, 1917, when the United States declared war on Germany.

Preferring the Aviation Section of the Signal Corps to the trenches abroad, Preston volunteered later that month. He was, however, rejected for service when told the physical examination revealed an overlarge blind spot in one eye — a surprise to him, since he enjoyed excellent vision. He was, on the contrary, convinced that the rejection was caused by his low income. Cadets were to be paid one hundred dollars monthly, a sum that attracted very many volunteers that spring. But those who were earning less than that sum as civilians were routinely rejected, on the presumption that they were only volunteering for the salary.

Preston then attempted to enter the British or Canadian flying corps (which had a certain cachet for sophisticated Americans), but when he told this to Solomon, his stepfather immediately cabled Mary in London. She returned in July and set to the task of getting her son into the military service of his own country, if duty was what he demanded. An old friend, she said, was one Major General Barry. With that they departed for Washington, and days later Preston was told to await his call.

Back in New York, Mary insisted that Preston stay with her in an apartment she leased at 1 East Fifty-sixth Street, above the Élysée Restaurant. (Isabelle Biden was so infuriated at Preston's departure from her that she quit New York, and they never met again.) The new place was a spacious, elegant home, and it was paid for by Solomon Sturges, who frequently covered Mary's debts and contributed to her living expenses. His generosity sprang not only from his compassion, but also because by supporting the mother he was in a sense guaranteeing a continuing relationship with her son, whom he loved dearly. In addition, that year, Solomon increased Preston's allowance to three hundred dollars a month.

No sooner had mother and son settled in than Mary attracted what Preston called "the usual collection of mild eccentrics . . . forming a little society of which she was the nucleus." Among the visitors were the "anti-artist" Marcel Duchamp, whose *Nude Descending a Staircase* had just caused a sensation and who later sent a toilet seat as contribution to an art exhibit; writer John Colton, with whom Mary was planning another futile writing collaboration (and who later had much better success with a play titled *Rain,* based on a tale by Somerset Maugham); Patrick Leary, a millionaire lawyer who had to keep drinking alcohol in order to prevent delirium tremens; and Bob Chanler, an artist and cocaine addict.

After several months of part-time preparatory training and marching practice in New York (while still holding his Wall Street clerkship), Preston was at last summoned to report as a cadet in the Aviation Section, United States Signal Corps at Camp Dick, in Dallas, on March 4, 1918. That summer was brutally hot — the temperature reached one hundred twenty degrees on several days — and the forced marches and parade routines of basic training were constantly decimated by fainting cadets. Further casualties followed in the great influenza epidemic that year, and a great number of cadets at Camp Dick were buried there on government property.

> Why some of us had high resistance and some had none, I don't know [Preston wrote later]. Nothing happened to my close friends or myself, although we were down at the hospital most of the time on the pallbearers detail, because we were six feet [tall].

From Dallas, Preston was transferred for a twelve-week course at the School of Military Aeronautics at Austin. In addition to seven hours of daily classroom instruction and weekly written examinations in aeronautics, there were hikes, trapshooting and machine-gun practice. Among his companions were Ralph Damon (later president of American Airlines) and a plump Greek-American named Spyros Skouras, who later became president of Twentieth Century–Fox Film Corporation. With them and the others, Preston — "a rather versatile fellow even at that date," according to fellow cadet Marion Denton — became quite popular singing French love songs and café ballads.

The three-month course complete, Preston and his fellow cadets were then dispatched for advanced flight training and warplane maneuvers at Park Field, in Millington, about twenty miles outside Memphis, Tennessee. During the autumn of 1918, the tedium was interrupted only by weekend outings to Memphis and by a request the camp newspaper made of Preston (called "Frenchy" by his friends) to contribute a weekly comic strip. "I obliged with the gruesome adventures of a flying cadet and his instructor, called *Toot and His Loot* . . . [which] was supposed to be funny," but was not. Not long after — on November 11 — the war ended. The cadets were, however, to finish their flight training and receive a reserve commission.

A furlough preceded that final stage of their government-sponsored training; Preston divided the interval between his stepfather in Chicago and his mother in New York, at her new business quarters on West Fifty-seventh Street. Then he was sent to Carlstrom Field, in Arcadia, Florida:

> We were fed for nothing, housed for nothing, clothed for nothing, insured for nothing, and given, of course, free medical and dental care. We had absolutely nothing to do except fly through the air and do stunts, which was great fun, and for this we received a high base pay, plus flying pay.

On May 9, 1919 — after fourteen months of service and training — he received his commission as second lieutenant and was honorably discharged from the United States military. He was twenty years old, a skilled pilot and a tinker with gadgets and mechanical contraptions. A return to Desti's looked very unrewarding indeed, but he had not the remotest notion of how to embark on any other career.

FOUR

Landed Gentry

"I DIDN'T care much for it," Preston Sturges wrote of his return to civilian life in 1919, and the reason for his disaffection was "the Desti business . . . the perfumed warm atmosphere of the place did not suit me." Without alternatives, however, he rejoined Mary's company as New York manager and sole salesman.

Mary had devised a motto for the company — "Youth and Beauty 'til 90" — and to fulfill the promise she had developed the line of products to include perfumes and toilet waters (with names like Moi-Même, Invitation à la Danse, Saphir and Jasmin), powders, antiwrinkle creams, whitening lotions, and bath salts (advertised as a reducing aid) and perfumed cigarettes. To the list, in 1920, Preston added a product of his own development — a lipstick that would last all day, "Red-Red Rouge."

Supervising the chemist and the store clerk (a pretty Dutch girl named Biddy Kleitz), ordering containers and managing the books quickly became a full-time occupation again, but not a lucrative one. Preston learned to work in the chemist's laboratory, and by 1920 he was assisting in the manufacture of Desti's red rouge. This and the other products he then personally marketed to Bonwit-Teller, Franklin Simon, Lord & Taylor, R. H. Macy, Arnold Constable, John Wanamaker, Bloomingdale Brothers and other New York department stores, as well as to drugstores and beauty parlors as far as eastern Long Island. "I was so innocent of any selling technique whatsoever that the customers used to help me . . . 'You shouldn't put it that way, Preston! You should say something like *this!*' After which they sold themselves a bill of goods."

44

Soon after Preston's discharge from military service, Mary had departed for England and France — this time to begin a new business venture, a supper club. Preston was left to manage the store on Fifty-seventh Street and to live in the apartment she had taken at Fifth-sixth and Fifth. Several romances occupied him in rapid succession in 1919 and 1920. The first, with a model named Laura Grove, ended when Preston introduced her to Paris Singer's son Cecil, whom she married soon after. The second was with a young Englishwoman "of unpredictable temper" named Lady Eve Waddington-Greeley (whose title and first name Preston memorialized in a film years later).

The third was more problematic than Laura or Eve. She was a hard-drinking woman named Dixie Bliss, a young woman of some mystery with no visible means of support who was somehow forever staying in large hotel suites. During the time of their romance, Dixie frequently went to northern New York by train — to visit her parents, she said.

One day, when Preston complained of a headache, Dixie offered as remedy a powder she said should be inhaled. Reaching for it, he accidentally knocked it from her hand. "You goddamn fool!" she shouted. "That cost sixteen dollars!" As Preston later learned, Dixie was a Canadian heroin runner (thus the trips to northern New York, thus the hotel suites), and after she had got drunk and talked too much, poor Dixie was found in an abandoned New York taxicab, murdered.

In early 1920, Preston closed the retail branch of the Desti business on Fifty-seventh Street and moved to a thirty-dollar-a-month shop at 84 Boerum Street, Brooklyn, to produce the Desti products. He hired as packager a young sign painter named John Wenzel, a genial employee who, like the unfortunate Dixie, turned out to be a hardcore drug addict. With regrets, Preston had to dismiss him.

In the tightest financial predicament thus far (the business consumed all his allowance but was barely surviving) Preston also moved from the fashionable apartment on Fifty-sixth Street. Several years earlier, he had met the French actor Georges Renavent, with whom he had established a great friendship, and now Georges invited him to his house in Douglaston, Long Island — a modest cottage already crowded with Georges and his wife, her mother, a Belgian war orphan they had adopted and a menagerie of canaries, dogs, cats and a monkey. Here Preston lived several months, in a cold paddock that had been the chicken coop.

The train fare to New York was an added expense, however, and finally Preston returned to New York, where he took a one-room apartment on East Fifty-ninth Street. Then a message arrived from Mary in

Paris: there was a steamship ticket at a local agent, for him to come to France, where she said there was much news. The Desti shop could be left in the care of Biddy Kleitz and the trusted chemist.

Before his departure, however, Cecil and Laura Singer invited Preston to join them in Fairfield, Connecticut, at the home of friends — a wealthy couple they had met in Palm Beach, Florida, named Mr. and Mrs. Jonathan Godfrey.

Godfrey, a white-haired gentleman over sixty, met them at the railway station. He struck Preston as "new-rich, uneasy and pretentious" — like the man's elaborate house with its Greek porticoes, butlers and museum art. Moments after they arrived, however, a beautiful young woman introduced herself. She was five feet three inches tall and slim, with bright eyes and an easy, gay manner. She wore her brown hair parted in the middle and coiled flat over her ears with bangs in front, in the style of the twenties. She was the host's wife, Estelle Godfrey, and she was nineteen years old.

The weekend passed pleasantly, but not without tension. The five dined at the Godfreys' country club and danced late Friday evening. Next morning, Preston sketched a pastel drawing of Estelle.

Saturday afternoon, Estelle took Preston to see her horses, and he learned more about her background. Estelle de Wolfe Mudge had come from a wealthy family in Bristol, Rhode Island, but her mother (following a crippling accident) had become a drug addict, and her father was an emotionally distant businessman she hardly ever saw. At eighteen Estelle had left home and married the first wealthy man who might not only sustain her comfortable style but who could also provide the parental security she had never known, and this happened to be wealthy Jonathan Godfrey, more like a father than a husband. The marriage, however, was a passionless travesty, and she was miserable: Godfrey, as it happened, was more the stern, vigilant guardian than the loving spouse or comforting parent.

Saturday night the Godfreys, the Singers and Preston went dancing again, and Preston partnered Estelle. But there were no surreptitious embraces by Preston, no trysts with her in the moonlight.

Sunday morning, Preston took an earlier train than the Singers back to New York, to pack for his trip to Europe. While Godfrey and the Singers breakfasted, Estelle drove Preston to the depot. From an open window onboard, he said to her as the train departed, "I love you." It was the first time, he later recalled, that he said these words to anyone. They could not have had a more eager audience.

*　　*　　*

Arriving in Paris, Preston learned that there was indeed much news in Mary's life.

In London, she had relocated the Desti branch to 47 Albemarle Street, where she had spotlighted the manufacture of Turkish and Virginia perfumed cigarettes. That was not all. She had also established Desti's Club at 70 New Bond Street — a supper club open to members only for an annual fee of £7.7s. Not only would meals be served, however. The culture maven Mary intended it to be a place where creativity would flourish. She also decided to offer complimentary memberships to a number of notables. H. G. Wells accepted with a cryptic reply, calling the privilege "the sort of thing I have been living for."

In her handbook of members' regulations, Mary stipulated that Desti's Club was an establishment

> for dancing, tea and supper. It will exhale the spirit of today — the renewed homage to Art . . . the cultivation of good humour . . . the revolt from snobbery and stodginess . . . where the music will be rhythmetic [sic] rather than rowdy, where the talk will be sane rather than noisy, where the drink will be good rather than dear, where the food will be well cooked rather than wasteful, and where the decorations will be right rather than modern.

The *Tatler* for February 1920 called the club "one of the most amusing places in London," and so it was. The *Daily Sketch* commented that "while it is smart and comfortable enough to attract [residents of the elegant neighborhood] Mayfair, Madame Desti will make it the kind of place in which painting, writing and acting people will feel at home." And the *Weekly Despatch* added that the place had "a good band, jolly music, and savouries so varied and appetising — including caviare."

A fancy dress ball that Mary had hosted on Saint Valentine's Day 1920 had been called a huge success by the press, and soon after she was welcoming writers (James M. Barrie, St. John Ervine, John Galsworthy, and H. Rider Haggard), actors (Cathleen Nesbitt, Phyllis Monkman, Ivor Novello, Godfrey Tearle and Ellen Terry) and — most welcome of all — those with titles (Prince Youssoupoff, Lady Norah Spencer Churchill, Lord Dunsany and the Princess of Monaco).

But there was another important event, and it had an odd angle. In the spring of 1921, at the Buckingham Palace Road Registry Office, Mary d'Este Vely (as she wrote her name) was married to Howard Griffith Perch, an ex-army officer. She was almost fifty, he was thirty. ("Oh,

Preston," she lamented later, "I really wanted to be a playwright, or a great director or a famous producer. At least I would have liked to own a fine restaurant. And look what I am — a perpetual wife!")

In response to the registrar's query about marital status, Mary's fantasy life flourished: she listed herself as a widow, which may have been wishful thinking but was certainly not the truth. Vely Bey had happily returned to Paris and was working there. She had no cause to think he had died, and by marrying Perch she had effectively contracted an invalid marriage and made herself a bigamist. ("I am not even sure that Mr. Perch was Mother's husband," Preston wrote the year after Mary's death, "as she married him in the belief that Vely Bey was dead, and the latter showed up after the war. It is all very complicated.")

Also in London, Mary had begun writing a column for the *Daily Sketch* — hints for ladies, such as how restful it was to put cold slices of lemon between the toes after a hard day at the office, and how refreshing to wash the face with a cucumber.

Mary and Howard (who was always known as "Punch") had the idea of repeating the minor success of the Desti Club in Paris, and he agreed to subsidize operating expenses when they opened on the rue de Colisée. All these developments were told to Preston when he met them at the Hotel Meurice.

On avenue de la Muette, the Perches had taken an apartment for Preston — a fantastic place with Chinese yellow walls and vermilion striping over black woodwork. From there he went out to the department stores and perfumeries of Paris, marketing Aurore Rouge and the other products with little more success than he had in New York, perhaps because the competition in Paris was more severe than ever and because the welcome extended to a young American cosmetics vendor was something less than enthusiastic.

Mary went forth, too. One afternoon, in fact, she was quite surprised during a walk along the Champs-Élysées with her new husband.

> My mother saw her old one [Vely Bey] walking up. She hoped for a moment he might prove to be a ghost and considered ignoring him entirely, but at this instant, emitting a happy cry of recognition, the spectre hurried over, took her in his arms and bussed her on both cheeks. There being nothing else to do, she introduced everybody all around, after which they retired to the terrace of the nearest café for some refreshments and a little talk.

The results of the little talk have not been documented — nor have the legal tangles surrounding Mary's simultaneous marriages. It seems, however, that Vely Bey agreed to an annulment.

Whatever the depth of Preston's feelings for Estelle, he was certainly not immune to feminine charms in Paris. A slender beauty he met at a Paris nightclub — "a Russian wildcat" singer — responded to him, and soon they were having an intense affair at an hotel on the rue Bergère. All the doors on the hotel rooms were outfitted with reverse peepholes, so that all the guests could be voyeurs at will. For Preston, "[All] these eccentricities seemed merely to add piquancy to my little girlfriend, and I couldn't see enough of her." But he had apparently had a sufficiency by early 1922, for after that he never saw her again; she seems to have developed dining and traveling preferences beyond his monetary means.

Mary, too, had financial concerns, but one day she lit upon a strange idea with an equally strange logic. In his unpublished memoir Preston artfully reconstructed the event, rather in the style of a scene from a Sturges movie.

"I never paid it back, did I?" Mary asked suddenly one morning.

"Probably not," Preston and Howard replied. "Paid *what* back?"

"Then it must still be good!" Mary added, triumphantly. "Since I didn't pay it back, it must still be *there!*"

"*What* must still be there?" the two men begged.

"Don't upset my train of thought!" she replied.

As it turned out, Mary was thinking of a cash loan tendered to her in 1915 through the Morgan bank, guaranteed by the wealthy industrialist Harold McCormick, a former Chicago acquaintance. Later that same day, the three were in the offices of Morgan, Harjes and Company, on the Place Vendôme.

"I was trying to remember," Mary began innocently, "whether I ever paid back that loan I got from you in 1915."

"We will soon find out," replied the banker, excusing himself. Moments later he returned with a file, and after examining it he was able to answer, "No, you never paid it back. No doubt you would like to do so now?"

"Well, not exactly," Mary continued, calmly. "What I really wanted to find out was whether Mr. Harold McCormick's guarantee was still good."

"Well, of course it's still good! Did you think he had gone bankrupt? With the McCormick Harvester Company and the Rockefeller fortune behind him, that would be difficult to do, wouldn't it?" The banker laughed at the question.

"Yes, wouldn't it?" said Mary, joining in the laughter. "Then the guarantee is still good!"

"Well, of course it's still good!"

And then, rather like Gracie Allen, Mary persisted in her oddly logical illogic.

"I would like the rest of my money," she said matter-of-factly.

"What money was that?"

"The loan guaranteed by Mr. McCormick. His signed guarantee is right in there."

"But you've already *had* that money, you see? Mr. McCormick guaranteed your account in the amount of ten thousand dollars on the twenty-ninth of August, 1915, and you withdrew the amount on the same day, cabling two thousand dollars to Mr. Preston Sturges in New York [for the Desti business debts] and taking the balance in French francs — forty thousand of them!"

"That's exactly what I'm talking about," Mary continued. "I would like the balance of my money — three hundred and sixty thousand francs!"

"But you already *had* all the money Mr. McCormick guaranteed your account *for* — the two thousand to your son and the forty thousand francs which was at that time eight thousand dollars! Two and eight is ten!"

"All I had," Mary continued doggedly, "was two thousand dollars and forty thousand francs. Since I never paid off the loan, the account is still *open* — and the guarantee is still *good*. The franc is now fifty to the dollar instead of five to the dollar as it was. Mr. McCormick's guarantee is therefore good for five hundred thousand francs, less what I already had. I have had two thousand dollars and forty thousand francs, that is to say one hundred forty thousand francs. I would like the other three hundred sixty thousand francs that my guarantee calls for!"

"But —"

"I am quite sure," Mary persisted, "that when you think this over, you will see that I am completely right. You must admit that I could go out and buy forty thousand francs for eight hundred dollars, which, with two thousand dollars added, would pay off my loan. Isn't that a fact?"

"Well, I suppose it is, in a way, but —"

"Not 'in a way' — in the only *honest* and *fair* way. I am quite certain that if Mr. McCormick were here himself, he would tell you the same thing. He *wanted* to loan me ten thousand dollars. I am sure he would be very much upset if he found he had loaned me only two thousand eight hundred."

Bizarre though it seems, Mary was given the money. She, Howard and Preston forthwith enjoyed a holiday in Deauville. There, Preston continued a series of brief romances with girls whose names he never mentioned in his memoir.

In New York by March 1922, Preston received a letter from Estelle Godfrey, inviting him to tea at the Ritz Hotel, and that afternoon was immediately followed by several others. Estelle was twenty, whimsical, energetic and fun-loving, she could hold her liquor (and large doses of it), and she was full of plans and suggestions for New York nightlife. She loved to dance, to walk through Central Park, to daydream about foreign travel. She had few plans beyond next week, and she seemed always fresh, always alert for amusement.

By the end of March, Estelle had told Preston she was leaving her husband and moving to Boston, where she would live temporarily with her aunt. Loving sentiments were by then regularly exchanged between her and Preston, but they had not yet spent a night together.

And so began an earnest and intense courtship, and a regular exchange of passionate, unselfconscious and remarkably frank letters. Hungry for affection and afraid of her husband's anger, Estelle seems to have touched something previously dormant in Preston Sturges. She was vulnerable, but she was also daring; she obviously needed him, his strength, his confidence — in a way that no woman had ever relied on him before — and in her dependence she made him feel important, critical to her happiness.

Estelle found irresistible Preston's imposing figure, his open charm, his urbanity, his witty optimism and his calm, unpretentious sophistication. Even before they made love, Preston wrote to her (in an undated note from late March 1922):

> I am going to say something frightfully indecent and shock you to death. I feel terribly lonely in bed at night. In other words I don't want only your intellectual companionship. Oh, darling! I want to take you in my arms and forget the world. Don't scold me for being so naughty . . . I love you.

Preston's affirmation seems to have sprung as much from her need to be reassured as from his own ardor, for throughout their courtship,

Estelle was terrified he would weary of her. On April 3, 1922, she wrote, typically: "Please tell me you love me — I can't understand why you do — and I'm so afraid it won't last." At least two other letters from the same month had an identical conclusion: "Do you still love me? I love you more than ever."

By May 1922, Preston had leased a small apartment on Lexington Avenue. He feared it would disappoint her after her opulent life in Rhode Island and with Godfrey, and that — if she would one day be free to marry him — she would find his modest circumstances intolerable. But she banished his fears, saying that they could both survive very nicely on the income from her trust fund, which amounted to something over eleven thousand dollars a year. Although Preston hesitated at the idea of marrying a woman with financial means he lacked, his caution was only momentary. He was certainly no fortune-hunter, but if the accident of her birth ensured she would never want necessities (even with him), that was acceptable.

That autumn, after the visit with her aunt in Boston, Estelle rented a house in New Jersey and bought a roadster. Because the relationship was by then more passionate, she told Preston that a friend had asked her

> if I had never known the pleasure of it [sex] — and I realized I never have. I am glad of this — because I am going to have it all with you and I know it will be wonderful — I love you so.

Finally, they spent several nights together, after which Preston was rhapsodic:

> You shall be my religion, darling. It is to you I shall address my prayers, to you I shall confess my sins, and when you put your arms around me and absolve me, I shall have reached my Heaven, an earthly paradise of whose reality I may harbor no doubt.

He, too, feared disappointing the beloved: "I know that you would be a darling little wife, but I wonder what kind of husband I'll be. Awful probably."

Estelle's reply ignored his protest and reiterated her need:

> I want to be with you always, darling, and when I am with you I am perfectly happy and contented, no matter what we are doing or where we are. . . . It is when I have to leave you that I realize how much you mean to me. Absolutely, you are my life — everything to me, darling. My one

hope is that I shall be Mrs. Sturges *very* soon and that I will always make you happy. . . . *Please* love me.

Meantime, Jonathan Godfrey's patience with his wife's absence was ending with a melodramatic threat. Through a friend he let it be known, in dark earnest, that he would have no hesitation in turning his hunting rifles on his young competitor. Perhaps thinking of legendary doomed lovers, Estelle wrote to Preston: "Even if he killed you (which I don't think he will), I will kill myself at once and be with you. I have the courage to do it and you can depend on me."

This notion was, however, not acceptable to the more pragmatic Preston, who chose to avoid confrontation by taking Estelle to meet his stepfather in Chicago. She and Solomon formed a fast friendship.

By the time the lovers returned to New York, Godfrey had agreed to a separation. There would be, however, the customary interval before the divorce was effective — the perfect time, Preston reasoned, for Estelle to meet Mary in Paris.

He had hoped his mother's reaction to Estelle would be as enthusiastic as Solomon's, but in this he was disappointed. Not long after they arrived in Paris in the spring of 1923, Mary ominously confided to Preston that there were things she did not like about Estelle. These were not enumerated — indeed, Mary may not have been able to list specifics — but there was obvious tension.

Mary may have regarded Estelle as a threat. Although she always acted on her slightest caprice and presumed others would cater to her needs as to her whims, Mary seems to have been deeply insecure — which may at least partly explain her endless search for the ultimately satisfying mate. In addition, apart from Isadora and Preston she had no strong emotional ties in her life to anyone. She relied on Preston's presence, support and assistance; his marriage, she may have felt, could alter that perpetual accessibility.

But Estelle was even more insecure than Mary and so apprehensive about gaining her approval — a surrogate mother's approval — that she may have sent out precisely the wrong social cues. Attractive and articulate, she could also appear nervous and high-strung.

For the moment, however, Preston chose to ignore his mother's disaffection. He and Estelle moved to a residential hotel on the rue Pergolese, a handsome house with a large garden. After a week, they realized they were living in a bordello, but since the proprietress was an amiable woman and managed a quietly discreet establishment, they remained. Preston led Estelle on a bicycle tour of Paris, Fleurines and the other scenes of his boyhood — a mode of travel not to her liking, but which she gallantly endured for his sake. In August, they received word that her divorce had been officially recorded on July 1, and they departed for New York after a farewell luncheon with Mary, Isadora Duncan and her husband, the Russian Sergei Essenin (a sad and confused man who shortly thereafter committed suicide).

With financial help from his fiancée, Preston moved the Desti factory from 84 Boerum Street to a ground floor at 33 Throop Street, Brooklyn. Here the cosmetics were not only manufactured but also labeled, boxed and shipped, and when a few rooms on the upper floor also became available after they were married, they moved there together.

Not long after, Preston contracted to have the cosmetics represented and distributed exclusively by the Lionel Trading Company, whose management agreed to purchase no less than a thousand dollars of Desti products monthly. Delighted with this decision and with the sudden increase in revenue, Preston was just as suddenly shocked. Mary, returning from Paris shortly after Preston married Estelle in a Brooklyn courthouse on December 27, calmly demanded that her son relinquish all control over Desti and Company and all financial interest in it. She was, in effect, firing him.

> I was aghast [he later wrote] at giving up the only business I knew, the only business I had ever been in, the only trade or profession with which I was familiar. I pointed this out to my mother, but for the first and only time in her life, she was adamant.

Mary's motives seem to have been mixed. For one thing, her marriage to young Howard Perch was effectively over (although they were not divorced), and she was eager to reestablish herself as sole head of her own business. She was also avid to reenter New York society through strategically placed press announcements. But another reason for Mary's sudden act of power may have been her resentment of Estelle, based on fear. In any case, she was no more successful with the business now than ever before — "[it] was run in its usual haphazard way," as Preston later wrote.

Preston and Estelle moved from Throop Street to a studio at 142 East Thirty-ninth Street. Then, after Estelle's half brother bought from her the family estate she had inherited in Rhode Island, Estelle and Preston took the profit and purchased a country house in Westchester

County, New York. Situated above Saw Mill River Road between Peekskill and Yorktown Heights, the hundred-acre property had a mill pond,
running streams with water wheels and waterfalls, a spacious farmhouse
and two cottages. By a pleasant coincidence that facilitated legalities,
they purchased the house from Edward Harden, whose brother-in-law
Frank Vanderlip was a friend of Solomon's. Vanderlip owned a small
community theater in Scarborough, a few miles distant.

And so, in an apparently flawless situation and setting, they spent
1924 through 1926 — still in their twenties but very comfortably situated, alternating their time between the country house and city social
life. For a while Preston tinkered with sketches for a few inventions: an
intaglio photo-etching process for which he received a patent, plans for a
vertically ascendant airplane for which he did not, and a design for a small
automobile with its power train in the rear. From none of these were there
concomitant commercial benefits, but they were satisfying creative pas-
times for a man with no occupation. His weeks were spent keeping house
with Estelle, attending parties and dinners with her in New York and
Westchester County, going to theater and often, as he later described it,
simply

> fishing the same sunfish out of the [pond] with barbless hooks and then
> throwing them back again, or swimming in the pond myself, and teaching
> people who were persuaded they couldn't swim, how to float.

He also cultivated the friendship of a neighbor, a New York judge who
provided a basic education in the byways of shady politics — ballot-
stuffing, official briberies and the like — and whose detailed stories would
later be useful in writing a screenplay. Otherwise, he was content to live
lazily, dependent on his wife's trust fund.

Winters in the country were "too cold for civilized living," according to Preston, and the primitive heating and plumbing systems sent
them back to Thirty-ninth Street. On March 17, 1927, Preston told
Estelle he might have a business opportunity with an acquaintance in
Paris, and asked her reaction to a possible voyage together. There followed one of the unforgettable dialogues of his life, one he recorded
verbatim:

"Why don't you go alone?" Estelle asked.

"What do you mean?" Preston rejoined. "How can you say such a
thing?"

Estelle paused only for a moment. "Because I really don't love you
anymore."

FIVE

Exit Laughing

FOREVER AFTER, Preston maintained — in his unpublished memoir as in conversation — that Estelle's departure was one of the deepest wounds in his life. Besides hurt male vanity, he may have vaguely realized that in fact a splendid opportunity for adult life had been missed.

Estelle had a vivid, inquisitive personality, and she was not without character. Neither churlish companion nor whining wife, she had a pert exuberance that leavened their marriage and a cheerfulness that matched her husband's. But she was in a frequent state of astonishment as she rediscovered herself and her shifting emotional needs, and over the next two decades she repeatedly left in her wake a number of husbands in similar astonishment. The pattern of her life after Preston — marrying and divorcing several more times in dizzy, rapid succession — suggests a yearning for security that perhaps no mate could fulfill.

Preston, in any case, was certainly not the one to answer anyone's emotional wants. Nothing in his own history — what he had seen or what he had experienced — had prepared him for the demands of an adult, committed relationship. The women he had known best (Mary and Isadora) were freelance lovers who never attempted fidelity to a single spouse. And once grown up, he, too, had apparently been quite content with serial romances, as he was satisfied with a succession of unchallenging, casual employments. He tinkered with inventions for fun, and in fact he was something of a tinkerer with all of life.

His emotional life, in other words, seems to have suffered from the accident of his peripatetic youth: life was a succession of quick visits to

56

one city after another, an exotic dinner here, a show there, some classes in one school followed by abrupt transference to another, a summer here, a shop there, a girlfriend in this port for one season, then on to the next and the next, with a man back in Chicago he fondly remembered, but a series of surrogate stepfathers in Mary's husbands and lovers. There was never any reason, time, inclination or encouragement for attachment or reflection. He was almost twenty-nine years old, talented, quick-witted, active, eager and hopeful — and utterly without stability. With Estelle as with his earlier girlfriends and acquaintances, he relished a good time, the comforts of home, social excitement and all the pleasures accompanying carefree youth. But the deeper requirements of adult bonding were beyond him.

After a visit to Solomon in Chicago, Preston returned to New York to find that Estelle had removed herself and all her possessions from their apartment. Mary was soon reconciled to her son for the first time since their cool separation, after Solomon wired her of Estelle's departure. She invited Preston to her new studio and residence on the second and third floors of a commercial building at 603 Fifth Avenue. She had been supporting her tapering cosmetics enterprise with yet another venture, the design and manufacture of hand-painted shawls, scarfs, and batiks with exotic flowers, birds and other patterns.

From 1920 to 1933 the manufacture and sale of alcoholic beverages were outlawed in America, but Mary had some homemade gin stashed away, and on his arrival she poured Preston a tumblerful. Then Mary told him that, as so often, practical assistance for both of them was forthcoming from Solomon. He offered Preston a thousand dollars a month to rehabilitate the Desti business, thus reestablishing his stepson's position and freeing Mary to return to her depressed friend Isadora, who, she felt, needed Mary's companionship after Essenin's suicide. Preston agreed to send her as much money as he could, and mother and son embraced, promising never again to allow estrangement — a pledge both kept.

On April 23, Mary departed for Paris (her journey subsidized by Solomon). Packing hurriedly, she took from her collection of exotic scarfs a gift for Isadora — an especially beautiful, bright red hand-painted batik shawl with a long silk fringe.

Preston moved into the rear portion of the upper floor at 603 Fifth Avenue, and in addition to his work at Desti's he paid for a mail-order course in piano playing. He then bought an old upright piano for eighteen dollars, began to compose a few simple tunes and add lyrics, and engaged a musician to provide orchestrations. The results were indifferent, but the composer and lyricist Ted Snyder, whom he had met at a nightclub, counseled Preston about song lyrics — how to avoid superfluity and how to arrange phrases for a specific melody and tempo.

At the same time, Preston's love life was thriving: he was in his own words "a bachelor again . . . and it's surprising how a young single male just happens to meet young single unattached females." Their identities remain unknown, for Preston, according to the dignified silence of an earlier era, did not offer written elaboration.

In Paris, meanwhile, Mary was encouraging Isadora in the completion of an autobiography. From her small apartment at 24 boulevard des Capucines, she fired off regular cables and letters to Preston begging for money, each more importunate than the preceding. But business expenses at 603 Fifth Avenue and his own expenses prevented him from sending her the sums she expected. "CABLE MONEY IMPOSSIBLE WAIT ANOTHER DAY LOVE MOTHER," she wired on May 24, and on June 3 she elaborated in a letter calculated to evoke guilt and pity; there was also perhaps a veiled threat that she might commit suicide:

> I hadn't a penny for nearly a week. I sent you a cable that I was penniless but it didn't seem to affect you very much as I haven't heard a word from you since. . . . I'm trembling with fear that you won't keep your promise. If you do this to me again, it's all off between us and I'll know you just mean to make me suffer as I'm quite sure you are not going hungry as Father is taking care of that. . . . You promised on your word of honor to send me $50 a week and I am depending on it and you fail me. I'm sitting in a little kitchen with a gas stove. . . . This is God's truth, Preston, don't take it as a joke. . . . I don't know what to do. . . . I know you are doing it for the business, but that won't do me any good if I die of starvation. *It's no joke.*

"I can't pay my rent tomorrow and don't know when I'll eat after today," she wrote on June 21. Next day — Preston having forwarded the June 3 letter to Solomon — she received two hundred dollars from her former husband's Chicago bank. By July 5, her rent and food bills were paid, and her mood had swung.

> I love and adore you [she wrote Preston], the one thing I have in all the world. . . . There is no suffering on earth, there are no heartaches so bitter

as a neglected mother. Life seems all empty and worthless when your child doesn't even care to write to you. . . .

Her epistolary style was akin to her unfortunate attempts at play-writing, and Preston knew the letters seldom bore much resemblance to her true situation, much less her true feelings. In addition, he was not easily moved to feel guilty by her manipulative tone. To be sure, Mary was not living in Parisian *grande luxe* — nor was he, in New York.

Of her true feelings in the letter dated October 3, however, there was no doubt, for they reported — with an atypically calm directness — the event that had shocked the world on September 14. That evening, Isadora Duncan was killed in a hideous accident.

The two friends were in Nice, and Isadora had planned an evening ride in an open roadster with a handsome young driver. Mary's letter to Preston described the event, and it is exactly as other eyewitnesses, the press and Isadora's biographers have related:

> I put Isadora in the car and before she had gone five yards, the fringe [of her shawl] caught on the side and wound about the wheel. It being several times wound about her, the jerk broke her neck instantly. . . . I ran and thought she had fainted but realized her head was caught in the folds of the red shawl she had taken from me and which she wore always — the painted shawl. . . . Writing this has almost killed me. I'm just shaking all over.

The funeral was held in Paris. Very soon thereafter, Mary began to endure a deep, protracted and debilitating languor.

In New York, Preston's love life continued as he kept what he called "various appointments with members of the fair sex." By the end of the year, Solomon had decided that putting money into the Desti Company was as profitable as tossing it into a bottomless well; he announced, therefore, that he would no longer subsidize a futile enterprise.

Preston went to Chicago for Christmas with his stepfather. He had, as he wrote later, "worked out a certain technique" about visiting Sol-omon, "part of which consisted of arriving in a horrifyingly old suit Father would not care to have me seen in around the University Club." On December 19, as Preston hoped, Solomon sent him to a tailor for a gift of new clothes. But that day Preston had severe abdominal pain, and by evening he was dreadfully ill, feverish and vomiting. A doctor pre-scribed bicarbonate of soda, saying the young man had simple indigestion and would recover quickly. But by Christmas Eve, Preston — mortally ill, barely able to speak — indicated that he felt he was dying. This time the physician was not so sanguine. Preston was rushed to Chicago's Presbyterian Hospital where surgeons performed an emergency appendectomy.

While hospitalized, he read the famous comic essay "Speaking of Operations," by humorist Irvin S. Cobb. Imagining it as a musical farce, he went so far as to sketch ideas and scenes, to contact Ted Snyder as prospective composer, and to seek Cobb's permission for performance rights. The project was abandoned not only because Preston was finally dissatisfied with the results of his own sketches, but also because Cobb wanted a half interest in the project and total artistic control over it as well. Also during his recuperation, he read James Brander Matthews's classic text on playwriting and dramatic structure, *A Study of the Drama*. By mid-February 1928, Preston had been discharged from the hospital and was quickly resuming an active life.

Before his surgery, he had had a romance with an aspiring actress (never named by him) who ended their affair when she told him that it had only been a way of her finding material for a romantic play she wanted to write. Hurt and challenged, he said *he* could write a better play than she, and with small effort. Back in New York, he locked himself away with Matthews's book, and within three weeks he wrote a comedy about a playwright who, as part of her research, seduces a young dramatist to learn how a man speaks and reacts in such a situation. The title was the easiest part: *The Guinea Pig*.

What had been planned as a brief winter holiday with his stepfather, then, had by happy accident become the prelude to a new career. Preston had, after all, always liked the theater — comedy most of all — from Paris farces to New York vaudeville. He had a keen sense of humor and (at least partly because of his life with Mary) a sense of the comically absurd, of the wild exaggeration and the zany non sequitur.

Building a play, imagining scenes and trying out dialogue, was in a way like tinkering with an invention, developing a cosmetic or a printing plate, designing a brochure or a painted box. And fancying a staged production was considerably more pleasurable than balancing Desti's accounts. Solomon cautioned him about the uncertainties of a theatrical career, but he had to admit that playwriting certainly could not be more precarious than his mother's business. Preston's first task, meanwhile, was to find a producer who could stage *The Guinea Pig* inexpensively — not a lunatic fantasy in 1928.

The professional and creative atmosphere Preston Sturges entered that year was the proverbial embarrassment of riches, singularly hospitable to new talent. By any standard of comparison with what has followed, the decade 1920 to 1930 remains an extraordinarily rich era in American theater history. In over a hundred Broadway theaters and forty small playhouses, more than twenty-five hundred productions were mounted during the decade — an average of two hundred fifty new shows per year. On any night in that pre-television era, a New Yorker could ordinarily select easy entertainment or high art from among sixty or seventy titles.

In the 1926–27 season, for example, there were almost three hundred offerings. Eighteen new productions opened during Christmas week of 1927 (*Show Boat* and *The Royal Family* were two of the most successful); there were eleven Broadway premieres on December 26 alone.

The numbers were, of course, no guarantee of consistently high quality. There were many silly, bland farces, bloated musical spectacles and homiletic soap operas. But there were also first-rate musicals that established America's primacy in that form, among them *The Desert Song* and *Funny Face*. The decade offered new works from Irving Berlin, Jerome Kern, Cole Porter, Richard Rodgers and Lorenz Hart, and regular performers included Eddie Cantor, Fannie Brice, Gertrude Lawrence and Helen Morgan. There were also seasonal presentations of the classics, and frequent visits from foreign theater companies.

The abundance of talent was indeed remarkable. Playgoers filled theaters to see established artists like Alla Nazimova and the Barrymores, but younger talent abounded, too — Katharine Cornell, Alfred Lunt and Lynn Fontanne, Tallulah Bankhead, Helen Hayes, Mae West, Spencer Tracy, Barbara Stanwyck, Bette Davis, Henry Fonda, the Astaires, the Marx Brothers and literally dozens of others who would soon be famous names on Broadway and in Hollywood.

In addition, it was relatively easy for writers to have their works produced, and there seems to have been a marvelous alchemy resulting in an unprecedented flourishing of new talent. Pulitzer Prizes were awarded that decade to Eugene O'Neill, Sidney Howard, George Kelly, Elmer Rice and Marc Connelly.

Preston submitted his play to a small summer acting troupe on Cape Cod, and with a cast of amateurs *The Guinea Pig* was presented from July

30 to August 4. The author lived in a boardinghouse near the ocean and spent five days before the premiere helping to construct the simple set and distributing handbills which announced, for seventy-five cents, a "new comedy."

The production was extremely simple and the performances were only adequate, but audiences were responsive. The biggest laugh of the evening, then and later, came when the aspiring lady playwright asks a man the words he would use to effect a successful seduction. "I wish I knew," replies the man wistfully.

Encouraged, Preston returned to New York in early August, and things happened quickly. At Pirolle's Restaurant on West Forty-fifth Street, he happened to meet his old friend, the actor Georges Renavent, who had shared his Long Island home with Preston during the winter of 1920, and who since then had only a few minor roles. Over the sixty-five-cent lunch provided for theater folks by host Alexis Pillet, Preston and Georges shared accounts of mutual hard luck. Renavent, however, had a suggestion. He was about to appear in a play by Ransom Rideout called *Goin' Home*, and he thought the production could use an assistant stage manager to handle the marching troops and special effects in the play about the American military and race relations in a French seaport town. Preston, eager to meet a prospective producer for *The Guinea Pig*, landed the job.

Produced and directed by Brock Pemberton, *Goin' Home* opened at the Masque Theater (later the John Golden) on August 23 and ran just under ten weeks, during which Preston befriended the cast with his casual cultivation and urbane manner, giving commands so they sounded like charming invitations. He was adept at issuing orders backstage, giving actors cues, supervising scene-changes and managing the general chaos.

Several afternoons weekly, Preston met Ted Snyder for regular lessons in rhythm and counterpoint, and in September he wrote, among other songs, a fox-trot called "At Twilight." After evening performances, Preston and the show's senior stage manager, Jack Gilchrist — also an aspiring playwright — joined others at local cafés and bistros. Jack had a dark-haired and attractive, brightly articulate wife of Spanish-Jewish ancestry named Bianca Fernandez. She usually came along for late-night drinks, joining what Preston and Jack called the "Broken-Down Stage Managers Club."

*   *   *

During that summer, there were developments in Mary's life, too. On August 10, she signed a contract with publisher Horace Liveright for a book about her friendship with Isadora Duncan.

"She was a charmer," recalled Sidonie Lederer years later; she was a secretary and freelance editor who worked with Mary as she tried to sort through her memories for a manuscript. Preparing the book was no sacrifice of business time for Desti, according to Lederer, because "the business slowed to a crawl even before the Depression, and it was never exactly booming in any case." As for Mary's working style:

> She didn't work from diaries, she just spoke aloud and I tried to take notes, type and edit them. And then she would review them and make her own changes and recast them in her own style. . . . She was very attractive and not fat, but certainly substantial by 1928. She had a rather complicated sex history, and she was altogether a very bohemian character. She was also an improvident lady, chronically out of funds and not very good at paying bills. When it came time to pay me for my work, she gave me scarfs and large pieces of material, so I was rather exotically clothed for many years.

According to Sidonie Lederer, virtually the entire Russian colony in New York found its way to 603 Fifth Avenue, where each week Mary put out a buffet of hors d'oeuvres. It was as if through them she was keeping contact with Isadora's last professional achievement, the dance school in Moscow.

But as the summer progressed, it was clear that Mary was not merely fatigued and depressed, but ill. The lassitude that had afflicted her since Isadora's death seemed worse, but doctors were in conflict over the precise nature of her illness. Preston later recalled meeting her for lunch one day; he sensed that she was not well, for she refused to look at herself in the mirror — and not only for vanity's sake.

Mary then shook her head ruefully and said: "There's no doubt about it, Preston, I'm breaking up after a hard winter." Then her expression changed and she added with great sincerity and good humor, "If only I'd known what a heavenly period of a woman's life this is — without husbands, without lovers, without jealousies or stupid angers. Believe me, I wouldn't have fought it off as long as I did!"

Estelle, who at this time initiated occasional correspondence with Preston, wrote to him with the announcement of her marriage on July 12 in Tucson. Her third husband was a strange man named Draper Daugherty, son of the former attorney general under President Harding. Daugherty had been committed to an alcoholic asylum in 1923 but escaped after six weeks. In 1924 he had sought a movie career but had only worked as an extra in crowd scenes; the following year he was consigned to a mental hospital, from which he was released in 1926. Since then he had worked only occasionally and relied (like Estelle) on family funds. Anxious about her former mother-in-law, Estelle wrote from Peekskill on July 23: "I hope most sincerely that the new doctor is right about your mother and that she will recover and live for many years — she is too nice and too amusing to die."

Still hopeful for a major production of *The Guinea Pig*, Preston cultivated theatrical attorneys and producers. One cheerful, friendly lawyer who hoped to back plays was Charles Abramson, a handsome, sophisticated bachelor with a long list of past girlfriends and never without a current one. Immediately, he and Preston formed an easy friendship that lasted three decades.

In response to Preston's query, Abramson replied that the playwright himself could produce his simple comedy for as little as $2,500 — plus theater rental. Preston was given that sum by a wealthy friend of Mary's. He was now, he told his mother, a theatrical producer.

While Abramson sought a theater, Preston (on October 18) signed with producer Brock Pemberton, to repeat his backstage duties for *Hotbed*, the first play by Paul Osborn (who later wrote *Morning's at Seven* and *The World of Susie Wong*). Preston also rehearsed a walk-on role in the play; both jobs paid him eighty-five dollars a week. The director was Antoinette Perry, a former actress and Pemberton's associate and lover.

The autumn of 1928, Preston was thirty and optimistic about *The Guinea Pig* and its commercial potential. He was also widely expanding his social and romantic life. His presence was commanding, his tone and diction just baronial enough to be impressive; his intelligent expression, his attentive, seductive gaze and his courtly manner were appealing to women, and he never had to spend time without their company. Welcome in any social circle, from his mother's band of eccentrics to the businessmen of Broadway, Preston was "a young man of enormous *joie de vivre* and unfailing courtesy" — thus he was described many years later by Sidonie Lederer, who remembered meeting him many times that year.

> He was a very gracious young man, tall and slender, entirely outgoing. He read sections of his play [*The Guinea Pig*] to me and asked reactions, which

I thought was very generous, since after all I was just working there for his mother.

After three days of tryouts in Westchester County, at the New Rochelle Theater (which was, as George M. Cohan had it, a mere "forty-five minutes from Broadway"), *Hotbed* opened at the Klaw Theater on November 8, where it played for nineteen performances. Osborn's drama concerned a bigoted clergyman who resents the freedom of local university students and obtains the dismissal of a young professor who has invited a woman to his apartment. The Reverend learns, however, that the woman is his own daughter, quite pleased to be quit of her father when she departs with her boyfriend. As Lawrence Binnings, a student whose baseball playing results in a broken window, Preston had only one brief moment in the play and very few words. He was ignored by the unenthusiastic press who reviewed *Hotbed*.

He was not, however, looking for stellar acting notices, but for news from Charles Abramson about a theater for *The Guinea Pig*. An ingenious solution, in fact, had been found to the problem of rental cost. Abramson's friends the Leone brothers, proprietors of a restaurant on Forty-eighth Street, also owned a 250-seat theater, the Edythe Totten. Virtually cursed with a run of failures, it was renamed the President Theater (after the hotel nearby) by Abramson, and rehearsals were scheduled for December — with Preston as producer and Walter Greenough directing.

By this time, Preston had revised *The Guinea Pig*. The comedy in its final state concerned Sam Small, a businessman-producer who advises a young playwright that she must complement her talents with life experience in order to write about a seduction. To that end, she seduces a young male dramatist as her guinea pig. The lady's motives are exposed, subsequent comic obstacles are overcome and the woman and her human experiment fall in love. (*The Guinea Pig* does not, unfortunately, survive in its complete form: the text was never published and the Preston Sturges archives contain only scene fragments.)

Casting was accomplished without difficulty. As Sam Small, Abramson and Sturges were able to engage Alexander Carr, who had played in the long-running *Potash and Perlmutter* cycle of Jewish dialect farces about feuding business partners. Mary Carroll, the ingenue who had played 245 performances in the romantic comedy *The Potters* in 1923 was signed for the role of playwright Catherine Howard (a name perhaps intended as an ironic reference to the penultimate wife of Henry VIII, who was judged a manipulative seductress and lost her head). And John

Ferguson made his Broadway debut as Wilton Smith, the eponymous hero.

With Charles Abramson as his friendly counsel, Preston drew up an agreement that would give him (in addition to a nominal producer's salary of fifty dollars a week) five percent of the first four thousand dollars taken weekly at the box office, seven and a half percent of the next two thousand and ten percent of income over six thousand. But it was too early to think of making a killing in the theater, for the production company was dry of operating funds before the scheduled opening night of January 7. To measure audience response in tryout performances, Preston contacted his old acquaintance Frank Vanderlip, who owned the small Beechwood Theater in Scarborough, Westchester County. There, on the evenings of Friday and Saturday, January 4 and 5, 1929, *The Guinea Pig* was presented to great applause.

The following Monday, January 7, Preston had his Broadway premiere, which (he told the press two weeks later) was

> an evening of delightful torture. All of us [in the production company] were young, all of us [were] poor. . . . Charley Abramson [was] wringing his hands in the empty balcony. My mother, sitting proudly in the third row, [was] laughing gaily with trembling lips.

There was, however, no need for anxiety, and next morning he was able to write in his dairy, "Very good notices from every paper — except the Post, Mirror and Journal." Typical was the unsigned review in the *New York Times* (written by no less a craftsman than playwright George S. Kaufman), which called the play

> miles from sure about where it is going and how it is going to get there, but with quite a little simple and entertaining humor in it, and so completely unpretentious that time and again you are drawn to it.

At the box office, the first week's receipts totaled $3,200, a tidy profit for the modestly mounted play.

On February 16, halfway through its New York run of sixty-four performances, Preston decided (in a send-up of old-fashioned melodrama titles) to give the play an alternate title, and the President's marquee announced *The Guinea Pig, or Passion Preferred*. On March 2 it closed. The attentive Charley Abramson, who took only a nominal fee as general counsel for the production (and who saw sixty-three of the performances), had the immediate answer: he had booked the play for a week's run at the

Broad Street Theater in Philadelphia beginning March 4 and then for a second week at the Walnut Street Theater in the same city.

Grateful for the role in Preston's play, Alexander Carr advised Preston to contact A. H. Woods, the producer of his old *Potash and Perlmutter* farces. Woods was about to assemble a cast and crew for *Frankie and Johnny*, a play with raw language and indelicate situations by Jack Kirkland (who later gave Broadway its longest running drama up to that time, his dramatization of Erskine Caldwell's novel *Tobacco Road*). Preston signed with Woods, not only to be assistant stage manager (supervising costume and set changes), but also to appear in the small role of John Walsh, a gambler. His salary would be eighty-five dollars a week.

The play appealed to Al Woods, one of the most colorful characters in the theater, an uncultivated, somewhat crude Hungarian immigrant and former garment worker on Manhattan's Lower East Side who began his theater life as an agent for traveling shows. Known as the king of melodramas, he produced dozens of bedroom and ethnic farces and scores of lurid melodramas over a career that eventually spanned half a century. His normal greeting in person as in letters and telegrams to employees, friends, associates and strangers was "Hello, sweetheart!" and thus he addressed theater patrons, between puffs of his cigars, each night during his productions.

Woods and Preston compared cigar brands and bottles of bootleg gin, and Preston was amused by Woods's rhinestone-in-the-rough quality. Typically, however, he never patronized less cultivated men like Woods, never boasted of his own broader cultural exposure; to the contrary, he always put people like Woods at ease, without condescension.

On May 2, rehearsals for *Frankie and Johnny* began in New York. Preston's major duty as assistant stage manager was to blow a policeman's whistle offstage. In the role of a professional gambler, he made a first act entrance dressed entirely in black, saying, "Thirteen thousand dollars will change hands tonight, Johnny." He later returned to gamble, saying "Something tells me I'm digging my own grave, Johnny — but you got to promise to be kind to me. . . . We'll make it sort of a friendly game." And that was the extent of his role. (Johnny was played by the handsome blond actor Louis Jean Heydt, then beginning a career which would later intersect Preston's at important junctions.)

A brief tryout in New Rochelle was followed by a run at Chicago's Adelphi Theater prior to a projected New York premiere in June. But there were problems at the Adelphi. First, Preston became furious and made a scene when his paycheck for one week was ten dollars less than the contracted amount. On June 1, the error was corrected, and he was also given two weeks notice, ending his job.

But the management was not being vindictive about Preston's outburst over the miscalculated paycheck. In fact the Chicago police were threatening to close down the show because of its salty dialogue, and Woods decided temporarily to withdraw the play for revisions. Every *damn, hell, God, Jesus, Christ, bitch* and *whore* was excised, but the play then sounded artificial, as if the unpolished characters had swiftly been trained as country-club waiters. But in spite of the new and expurgated version, the police successfully petitioned to close the show on grounds of public immorality. On the night of June 13, the company returned to New York on the Erie Railroad's 11:20 express.

Preston was not onboard, however. He was at Solomon's apartment on East Goethe Street — not hoping for a new suit, nor on holiday. He was there to take over the dining room as a work space. For the previous two weeks, he had been preoccupied with an idea for a new play, and he seems to have been sufficiently confident about it, for he wrote a simultaneous account of his extraordinarily fecund achievements over the next three weeks.

Because the result was *Strictly Dishonorable* — one of the great comedy hits of the decade, establishing Preston Sturges as a leading writer — his daily record is worth generous citation. This marks the first time he embarked on a fiercely demanding, entirely self-imposed writing schedule, oblivious to the hours, often working through the night, sustaining himself with coffee. The idea was there, and he responded to it with an almost manic ardor. He wanted desperately to succeed, and he wanted his adored stepfather to see the inchoate stages of that success. (Driven and euphoric, he also began yet another new play as soon as *Strictly Dishonorable* was shipped to Brock Pemberton.)

June 14, 1929: Beginning work on *Strictly Dishonorable*. Promise myself to do five pages every day, not average. Which means if I do 20 pages one day I must still do 5 the next. Had breakfast with Father at 7.45. The play should be finished inside of a month. Later: 5½ pages finished at 11 P.M.

June 15: No work to-day.

June 16: Or to-day either.

June 17: Did 11 pages today. Pretty good. According to schedule I should have 20 done but I have 16½. Finished 3 A.M.

June 18: Worked very hard — not really, as the play is beginning to move at last. It's like getting a regiment out on the march. Got a lot of good stuff in. Think the scene with the policeman will lay them in the aisles. My schedule calls for 25 pages completed by now, when, as a matter of fact, I've done 30¾. Finished 3 A.M.

June 19: Wonderful progress to-day. Finished first act, 37 pages, and did 6 full pages of Act II. Schedule calls for 30 pages finished, and I've completed 43. Did 12¼ pages to-day alone. And it's GOOD. Hooray! Finished 3 A.M.

Mr. Schoolcraft [a friend of Solomon Sturges] came to dinner here. We had a long discussion about philosophy, history, the Papacy and many other things. The conversation was mostly a monologue, with this charming and erudite old gentleman answering questions of mine. I believe he was formerly professor of history at the University of Chicago. How little I know.

June 20: How did I work to-night? Felt rotten and headachy all day. Had dinner and too much to drink at Tip Top Inn. Came home sleepy and dizzy at 9.30. Took a nap until I heard Father come home at 11. Staggered into dining room without a thought in my head — looked vaguely at the typewriter — forced myself to write a couple of exchanges and then — I

FINISHED ACT II.

Got through at 7 A.M. That means 20 pages of dialogue and I think it's good stuff. Schedule calls for 35 pages completed and I've done 63 — that's in ONE WEEK! I can't believe it.

June 21: Slept from 1 to 6 P.M. Worked all day and till 5 A.M. of the next [22nd]. Did 21½ pages — could have finished — but I've suspected something was wrong for the last couple of hours — not dialogically, but mechanically. Will probably have to rewrite from Act III page 15 to the end as I seem to have evolved one of those tragic endings which is a snarl of entrances and exits, with the playwright hastening to tie up the whole bundle. Schedule calls for 40 pages and I've done 83 in 6 working days. To hell with the schedule.

June 22: No work to-day. Am resting up for a strong finish. To bed about 1.30.

June 23: *Strictly Dishonorable* finished 5.40 this afternoon. Will polish tonight. Later: Did so and drew set plans. Wrote to Pemberton.

June 26: Got letter from Pemberton asking me to send on play as soon as it was finished. Will send carbon copy right away. Later: Did so.

June 28: Play to Pemberton returned for insufficient postage. Mailed it again, special delivery.

June 30: Diary, prepare for a surprise. To-day, beginning at 9 A.M., I planned the sets and then did 18 pages of the first act of *Recapture*. Some very funny stuff and some moving stuff. I think it's going to be a FINE play. So far ahead of *Strictly Dishonorable* it makes me ashamed. Intend to keep my schedule, 5 [pages] a day, as before. F[inished] 6 A.M.

July 1: Changed second act set plan [of *Strictly Dishonorable*], then finished act 1, 37 pages [of *Recapture*]. Did 19 to-day. Some good stuff. Schedule calls for 10 completed and I've done 37. Am I, perhaps, learning to write? Finished 6.40 A.M. Pemberton probably received *Strictly Dishonorable* this morning.

In the course of a thirty-year career, the gentlemanly Pemberton had several successful productions: *Enter Madame* (1920), *Personal Appearance* (1934), *Kiss the Boys Goodbye* (1938), *Janie* (1942) and *Harvey* (1944). His associate producer, who staged all these but the first, was his great love, Antoinette Perry. Energetic, slightly imperious and enigmatic, Perry was a demanding but highly respected director. Together, they were known to accept a script for production only if the author agreed to do all revisions they deemed necessary.

Pemberton, who had not seen *The Guinea Pig*, could hardly have expected a polished play from a member of his backstage crew, his former assistant stage manager on *Goin' Home* and *Hotbed*. Nevertheless, he and Perry read *Strictly Dishonorable* and sent Preston a telegram he received on July 2:

CONGRATULATIONS — IF YOU ARE WILLING TO DO A LITTLE WORK THINK YOU HAVE FINE COMMERCIAL PROPERTY — FIRST ACT ONE HUNDRED PERCENT — SECOND AND THIRD SKIMPY — NEED DEVELOPING — PLAY TEN MINUTES TOO SHORT BUT CONTAINS WORLDS SWELL MATERIAL — CAN YOU COME FOR CONFERENCE AND WHEN — WOULD LIKE TO TRY FOR AUGUST PRODUCTION.

Preston did not, however, think this good news warranted respite from his schedule. On July 2 he wrote:

I was very bad to-day. Did only 2 pages and drawing for second act set. Very tired, also excited. Answered B.P.'s telegram, saying I wanted to stay here one week longer to finish *Recapture*. Schedule calls for 15. Have done 39, but it's very hard just the same.

July 3: Nothing to-day. Simply could not concentrate. Schedule calls for 20. Have done 39.

July 4: At last I was able to concentrate again. The second act, which seemed impossible, simply melted away when my brain started working. Began by tearing up page 2 of Act II and then wrote 20 more — some of it absolutely hilarious. Got my tag line: "Never mind, Auguste, s'alright." Schedule calls for 25, have done 58. Finished 6.05 A.M. Letter from Pemberton telling me to stay my week if I liked.

July 5: Finished Act II and did 4 pages of Act III. Eight pages to-day. Fair, but nothing remarkable. Schedule calls for 30. Have completed 66. Will take train for New York Monday. Finished 5 A.M.

July 6: Did a complete synopsis of the rest of Act III. Finished 6 A.M.

July 8: Leaving for New York — Lake Shore Limited, 6.30.

And then, a week after he arrived in New York:

July 17: Signed Authors League contract with Pemberton for *Strictly Dishonorable* and received $500 advance.

Thus ended the struggles of his private creative work on the play (and his journal-account of them). Now began the conflicts of cooperation with producers, crew and cast, to enliven the work for audiences.

SIX

The Romantic Well

PRESTON had first thought of *Come, Come, Isabelle* as the title of his play, but the day he began writing in Chicago he recalled something he had said to a girlfriend several years before. She asked his intentions during their romance, and he replied in two words that became his play's new title.

The first act of *Strictly Dishonorable* begins in Tomaso Antiovi's speakeasy on West Forty-ninth Street, Manhattan, late one Saturday evening in autumn; acts two and three are set in an apartment above it, later that night and the following morning. "I laid [the action] in Tomaso's," Preston wrote years later of the favorite New York hangout that inspired the locale, "and the lovely set by Raymond Sovey was an exact duplicate of the little joint."

To the illegal bar come (by mistake) a young couple — priggish and dictatorial Henry Greene and his fiancée, lovely and innocently unpretentious Isabelle Parry (a character named after the author's paternal grandmother). Isabelle's family, in Yoakum, Mississippi, lost a fortune on their plantation, because "just when the cotton got high, women stopped wearing underwear." She finds northern city life exhilarating and resents Henry's insistence that they live "in the heart of a restricted neighborhood [i.e., forbidden to Jews], near a playground . . . half a block from Mother's."

Also at the speakeasy is Judge Dempsey (named after the playwright's mother), a tippler who blinks at the Prohibition laws ("I'm on the wagon — not drinking anything except a few Old-Fashioneds"). The judge lives in a room above Tomaso's, where another tenant is Augustino

("Gus") Caraffa, the Count di Ruvo, a handsome opera star and a notorious womanizer.

When Henry exits to move his apparently illegally parked car, Gus — eager to make a new conquest — dances with the unworldly but star-struck Isabelle. Henry returns, humiliates Isabelle and hurls ethnic slurs at the Italian singer; defying her fiancé, Isabelle refuses to depart with Henry and gives back her engagement ring.

Another participant in the action is a local patrolman named Mulligan ("How many times do I have to tell you," he asks Tom, the speakeasy proprietor, "I don't know what this place is?"). Mulligan shares a drink of liquor with Judge Dempsey:

MULLIGAN (*raising his glass to the judge*): Well, here's to Prohibition, sir — a noble law.

JUDGE: Experiment.

MULLIGAN: Whatever it is.

Gus invites Isabelle to spend the night on his living room sofa upstairs:

ISABELLE: What are your intentions toward me?

GUS: Strictly dishonorable.

In Gus's apartment, he tries to conceal his real character from her:

ISABELLE (*picking up a hairpin on loveseat*): I didn't know women used hairpins any more.

GUS: Probably my cleaning woman dropped it.

ISABELLE: Probably. Is she blonde?

GUS: I never noticed. She wears a dust cap.

ISABELLE (*pushing cigarette end from tray*): Well, you ought to tell her to stop smoking your cigarettes. It doesn't look nice to see the ashtrays all full of cigarette butts with lip rouge on them.

GUS: Darling — are you jealous?

ISABELLE: Me? No, just neat.

One of his many girlfriends then telephones, and Gus prevents her arrival by saying he's "in conference — I wouldn't come here, it would not amuse you." He then makes his move to seduce Isabelle, but the judge enters, claiming it's his birthday and everyone must have champagne. When Tom pours champagne for everyone, Isabelle objects that Officer Mulligan cannot have any:

ISABELLE: But policemen never drink on duty!

MULLIGAN: It just seems like never.

Isabelle then confides to Dempsey that she has fallen in love with Gus, but the judge — to save her from seduction — advises her to go to an hotel. Isabelle protests:

> If I want to be foolish, let me be foolish for once. I've always been sensible and good — you know it isn't much fun to be a girl, sometimes — and now I'd just like to drift with the current and not struggle any more, and for a little while, be happy.
>
> JUDGE: Suppose you have a baby!
>
> ISABELLE: Suppose I don't! They're compulsory only in the movies.

Unable to dissuade her from remaining with Gus, the judge departs. The opera singer then reenters with pajamas for Isabelle.

> GUS: Here are the p.j.'s and things. May I help you?
>
> ISABELLE: Uh-huh.
>
> GUS (*looking dress over*): Where does it unbutton?
>
> ISABELLE: You see where it unbuttons.
>
> GUS: Shall I, then?
>
> ISABELLE: Uh-huh.

He starts to unhook the dress. When she lifts the dress over her shoulders:

> ISABELLE: I used to love to have my clothes taken off when I was too little to know how.

Gus hangs up her dress. Isabelle is now wearing her teddy (an undergarment with a camisole top and loose-fitting panties). Gus helps remove her stockings and shoes:

> ISABELLE: I used to wear a lot more clothes when I was little, and Mama wore more than I did, and Gramma wore more than all of us put together. . . .

Gus puts pajama top over her head, and as it slips down her teddy falls to the floor:

> ISABELLE: I'll bet the men back in Gramma's day used to get awfully impatient waiting for the women to get undressed — to go swimming.

Gus holds the pajama trousers for her, and she slips into them; he draws them up and over the top.

ISABELLE: No, no, no — the top goes on the outside!

GUS: I must patent this.

And then, as he is about to complete the seduction, Gus sees in a flash that she is really a sweet girl, and that to take advantage of her as a passing conquest is beyond even him. He puts her to bed, and to avoid temptation he leaves to share the judge's quarters. Isabelle, however, is very much disappointed by his sudden valor.

Next morning, Isabelle learns that, to protect her reputation, Gus told the judge that *she* sent *him* away. Isabelle protests to the judge that she is not that good: "Maybe good women are good only because it takes two to be bad, and they can't find anybody." Gus then admits that during a sleepless night he realized that he loves Isabelle as much as she loves him.

Henry returns for Isabelle, suspicious about her conduct overnight:

ISABELLE: I *still* have my virginity, if that's what's worrying you.

HENRY (*shocked*): *Isabelle!*

ISABELLE: Don't be a hypocrite — that's what you were
    thinking — though why they make such a fuss about it is more
    than I can understand.

HENRY (*thunderstruck*): *Fuss about it!*

ISABELLE: You heard me. As if it mattered to anybody but me. By
    the way, I forgot to ask you — are *you* pure?

HENRY: *What?* Why —

ISABELLE: You needn't bother to answer. I'm not curious.

HENRY: It's *entirely* different, anyway.

ISABELLE: Well, I don't *really* know anything about it, so you may
    be right.

Left alone with Isabelle for a moment, Gus asks her to marry him, reminding her that this would mean a life of ceaseless travel to places like Milan, Barcelona, Madrid — even to South America; Isabelle "listens to this itinerary breathlessly, dreamily contemplating the wonders of such trips." After some hesitation and a momentary return to the waiting Henry outside, Isabelle rushes back to Gus:

ISABELLE: I do love you.

GUS: But I warn you — I must have four sons and seven daughters!

JUDGE (*starting to exit*): In that case I'll tell Henry not to wait.

The final curtain falls.

* * *

Strictly Dishonorable has all the characteristics of Preston Sturges's best achievements for the stage and screen: the witty, pointed conversation; the acute sense of social satire; the deftly developed characters; and action as well as dialogue that derives typically from those characters — never from an imposed theme or labored thesis. The situations are economically presented, the motivations recognizably adult and the tone brisk without being murky, sometimes ribald but not coarse or prurient. In that regard, the humor is never merely bold, never strains for provocation.

The characters are sharply etched. Individual hypocrisy is punctured in the character and fate of Henry, and social folly — in this case, Prohibition — is mocked in the warmhearted and protective Judge Dempsey, who is both victim and challenger of the ban. Gus, the modern Casanova, is reformed by discovering his love for a candid and unaffected woman, while Isabelle's rejection of the easy security Henry offers is rewarded by a life of travel with Gus and the concomitant exposure to world culture. The fertility of this union (suggested by the play's closing lines) — between an experienced man who needs love and an innocent woman who needs sophistication — is a recurring motif in Sturges's writings. The deliberate abundance from the relationship will be the converse of the accidental (and apparently punitive) birth that is "compulsory only in the movies."

The surviving script is, of course, the final draft as it was staged, but this form was achieved only after more than two months of daily revisions. Against Brock Pemberton's and Antoinette Perry's demands for numerous changes (they were co-directing) Preston fought loudly, and certain delicate negotiations had to be finessed involving both rewriting and casting.

First, Perry wanted Muriel Kirkland for the role of Isabelle — a lovely, petite brunette who had appeared as a waif in a forgotten melodrama called *Brass Buttons,* and in *Cock Robin,* a murder mystery by Philip Barry and Elmer Rice. Preston, however, argued on behalf of his current girlfriend, a fragile, dark nineteen-year-old beauty named Sidney Fox, twelve years his junior. When Pemberton and Perry held fast and signed Kirkland, Preston threatened that he would make some crucial dialogue changes only if Fox replaced Kirkland. Calling his bluff, Pemberton summoned the cast in late August and announced that because of the playwright's intransigence *Strictly Dishonorable* would be canceled. Preston relented and Kirkland continued, but he did not in fact yield to all the changes required.

By September 9, the play was ready for a pre-Broadway tryout. Standing at the rear of the Boulevard Theater in the New York City borough of Queens, Preston was outraged to hear the cast speaking lines he had not written. His friends Bianca Gilchrist and her husband, Jack (who was stage manager), tried to calm him: the producer and director were renowned for doctoring a play before Broadway, and this was to be no exception. Despite his protests, *Strictly Dishonorable* was moving toward the Wednesday, September 18, opening at the Avon Theater with what he considered an unconscionable, ruinous set of script changes he neither provided nor authorized.

The night of the premiere, Mary sent Preston a telegram at the Avon:

I KNEW YOU WOULD MAKE GOOD. HERE'S TO A LONG
RUN. I ADORE YOU. YOU ARE MY SUCCESS.
YOUR FOOLISH MOTHER.

But when she went backstage before the curtain rose, Mary was told Preston had not come to the theater. Before taking her seat, she sent a second telegram to him at their apartment:

GOD BLESS YOU. MAY THIS BE THE FIRST OF MANY
HAPPY SUCCESSES.

Neither in the audience nor at home, Preston was so convinced that the play had been mutilated beyond repair that he took refuge in every neighborhood speakeasy that day, and by curtain time he staggered home. Next morning, Thursday the nineteenth, he awoke with a blinding headache when Mary, the Gilchrists, Pemberton, Perry and a score of friends crowded into the apartment with the news.

The first-night audience had left the theater in high spirits, after offering prolonged applause. Hours later, the crucial *New York Times* review had appeared, and Brooks Atkinson had assessed the play as

> a well-nigh perfect comedy [by] a fresh talent for gay, buoyant comedy. For no one could write such deft, amusing lines and describe characters with so much understanding who did not have genuine talent for the theatre. . . . [The play] is not only a rippling comedy but [also] an affecting romance. . . . Mr. Sturges has not only an extraordinary gift for character and dialogue, but for the flow and astonishment of situation.

Detailed praise was also offered to every one of the eight-member cast, including the singer and actor Tullio Carminati (who had acted with

Duse) as Gus, Muriel Kirkland, Carl Anthony as the judge and, in the role of Henry, Louis Jean Heydt (who had played Frankie's Johnny in Chicago).

Nor was Atkinson alone; the New York daily press was unanimous in its praise, as were the weeklies. Four months later, Preston was still the favorite new playwright celebrity. The *New York Times* commissioned a drawing of him for its edition of January 26, 1930, with the caption: "The Author of 'Strictly Dishonorable,' and by That Token, a Person of Consequence in the New York Theatre."

Ticket lines had formed round the block of the Avon Theater before Preston was awake, and by Friday afternoon, September 20, the box office had $19,028 in receipts, a staggering advance sale when ten dollars was a scalper's price. Suddenly, the penniless Preston Sturges was a wealthy man: he received $1,500 cash from Pemberton within the week.

The stock market crash and the beginning of the Great Depression on October 29 did not affect Preston Sturges, for *Strictly Dishonorable* was only at the start of a 557-performance run. While most other Broadway theaters were half-empty that winter (due to harsh weather and the economic crisis), the Avon Theater sold every one of its thirty-two standing room tickets each night. From Chicago, Solomon wrote congratulations on November 18.

> I can well imagine your mother is delighted and I'm more glad for her, almost, than for you. She has done a big lot for you, Preston, in your youthful life. She worked hard to give you an education in France, in Switzerland, in Germany, in England, and you should be wonderfully proud to have a mother who has done so much.

Regarding the stock market, Solomon was grateful to have "escaped the pit so many tumbled into. The things I had were paid for and all I suffered was a depreciation in value and some of this will come back, if not all." The letter was signed "Your delighted Father."

In reply two days later, Preston sent Solomon his first month's profit on the play, a check for ten thousand dollars — "to invest for me in any way you see fit. . . . I will send you at least $90,000 more." This, however, turned out to be an exaggerated expectation of his ability to save. From more than one hundred thousand dollars' income over the next several months (his share of the profit plus that from the sale of the film rights), Preston sent Solomon only fifteen thousand to invest.

Untouched by the nation's economic collapse, the most popular new playwright in New York was dining at New York's best restaurants, ordering fine bourbon and champagne, dating pretty ingenues like Sidney Fox and pricing automobiles and yachts. But he was also paying his mother's bills and her mortgage on a small house she had taken upstate in Woodstock, New York — aptly located on Maverick Road. Within three weeks of the play's opening he also bought a slightly used Renault.

As later, successful Broadway playwrights in the 1920s were routinely engaged by film studios to collaborate on scenarios. Monta Bell (who had directed Greta Garbo's first American film in 1926) was then in charge of production at Paramount's New York City studio in Astoria, just a short ride over the Harlem River. He offered Preston the handsome sum of ten thousand dollars to polish a few lines of dialogue in *The Big Pond,* which in 1929 was planned for Maurice Chevalier and Claudette Colbert. Robert Presnell and Garrett Fort (among others) had already drafted a script for director Hobart Henley — in it, Chevalier would sing "You Brought a New Kind of Love to Me" — and Preston had only to add a few bright lines; this he easily did at home in a few days.

While *Strictly Dishonorable* continued to play to capacity crowds, Preston — eager to repeat his success — worked several nights on the completion of *Recapture.* When Pemberton twice rejected it for production, Sturges left the manuscript with producer A. H. Woods. By November 17, Woods offered a contract that gave Preston ten percent of the first fifteen thousand dollars gross receipts and twenty percent of everything beyond. Rehearsals began on December 18 at the Eltinge Theater, but Sturges — perhaps after the great success of *Strictly Dishonorable* — was not keen on accepting the producer's or the players' suggestions for revisions. Further tension derived from last minute cast changes and fervent arguments between director and crew backstage.

"I think you will like it," he wrote to Solomon on November 20. "Most of it, also, was written on your dining room table." But as it happened, no one liked the play very much at all. Its premise was remarkably like that of Noël Coward's comedy *Private Lives,* which premiered in London in September 1930 and in New York the following January. Both plays concern a separated couple who accidentally reunite, only to discover that their love may indeed not be forever past. Sturges's tone, however, was far grimmer, and with a tragic ending — an elevator crashes and the leading character is killed.

After several weeks of strained rehearsals and revisions, Woods began out-of-town tryouts in Atlantic City and Philadelphia prior to a Broadway premiere at the end of January 1930. By this time, however, Preston was preoccupied with his own new romantic negotiations, and *Recapture* had nothing like priority in his life.

While visiting Palm Beach, Florida, in December, Preston was invited to a formal dinner party. There he met one of the most desirable young ladies of the time, the beautiful and charming Eleanor Post Hutton. The unmarried daughter of heiress Marjorie Post and Edward Close, she and her sister Adelaide took the surname of her mother's second husband, E. F. Hutton, for whom wealthy is too weak a description.

A graduate of the genteel Miss Porter's School in Connecticut, Eleanor had been formally presented to society in 1927, at a ball at the Ritz-Carlton, New York. The following year she was presented to the king and queen of England.

Cultivated, gracious and hopeful for a career as a concert and opera singer, Eleanor turned twenty that December of 1929; Preston was thirty-one. Winsome and fair, with a quick, warm smile, bright eyes and an immediate charm, she was exactly the age at which Estelle had met Preston. In fact she rather resembled her predecessor: both were vivid and energetic, playful and well-bred, both wanted to escape the limitations (however privileged) of their families and both were intensely feminine, unpuritanical and attracted to Preston's dashing grand style and commanding gestures. Eleanor was also affluent (much more so than Estelle); she would, then, share his appreciation of elegance and luxury but need not depend on him to provide for her.

An intense, whirlwind courtship began, complete with clandestine telephone calls and quickly repeated train journeys between New York and Palm Beach. Nominally Catholic and suspicious of a New York playwright with the reputation of a roué, Eleanor's family was unhappy at the prospect of a marriage. By Christmas, the press reported the romance between the very wealthy young heiress and the merely rich divorced playwright. News wire services noted, alongside weekly suicide counts of the Great Depression, that Eleanor Post Hutton's personal jewelry was valued at over one hundred thousand dollars. And she had not yet received her major inheritance, due on her twenty-first birthday.

The troubled *Recapture,* meanwhile, limped along its doomed way. On January 7, it began a week's tryout at the Apollo Theater, Atlantic City.

Preston, reported the *New York World,* was busily rewriting lines, and was "a mysterious figure in a green hat on the boardwalk." By January 20, the play had settled in for a final week of previews at the Flatbush Theater, Brooklyn, where that borough's *Daily Times* found the play's ending "dramatic but not particularly realistic or convincing, [merely] extricating the author from the impasse in which he seems to have placed his characters." On the twenty-second, Preston wrote to his stepfather, "This play won't get the notices the other one did."

He could not have been more accurate, and he later wrote to Solomon that he received, after the New York premiere,

> the most violently destructive notices I have seen in years. The critics boiled me in oil and then danced a swan song on my corpse. . . . [From] the next play they will expect nothing and I may be able to surprise them a little. It was a perfectly natural reaction: *Recapture* is not a bad play, but I took a few liberties with the dramatic construction — which they might have forgiven [Eugene] O'Neill but which, in me, they consider only impudence.

The problem with *Recapture* is not only one of conclusion, however: the dialogue is creaky and heavy with artificial speeches. Although Preston seemed to have been drawn to the romantic situation of his story, he did not know the inner lives of the characters. At sprightly repartee he was an expert, but not at fashioning serious drama with fully realized adult roles. Romance had an hypothetical appeal, but deeper sentiments somehow still eluded him. He could do no more in his craft than he could in his life, and in a sense *Recapture* was an unwitting attempt to explore — perhaps even to construct imaginatively — what he had not achieved with Estelle. In this regard, the tragic ending was not simply gratuitous; it signaled an awkward creative blockage.

The failure of *Recapture,* however it may have disappointed Preston, was not much of a setback in early 1930: professionally, financially and emotionally, he seemed unassailably blessed. The Broadway production of *Strictly Dishonorable* was bringing him a tidy fortune and considerable fame, he was soon contracted to collaborate on a comic operetta, and he was in love.

That year, he won the Megrue Prize of five hundred dollars, awarded by the Dramatists Guild of the Authors League of America for the best work by a new playwright; he accepted the honor but returned the cash as a contribution to the authors' loan fund. In addition, *Strictly Dishon-*

orable was included (with Marc Connelly's *Green Pastures,* John Balderston's *Berkeley Square* and others) in Burns Mantle's *Best Plays of 1929–1930. The Nation's* honor roll for 1929 was announced, too, and that periodical cited Preston

> for enlivening an otherwise dull season with . . . a delightful trifle which approaches the ideal of pure comedy without ceasing to preserve the flavor of contemporary American life.

Redbook, that summer, presented people "in tune with our times," and Preston was included with Maurice Chevalier and with Ginger Rogers. His play was also given free advertisement by the Talon Hookless Fastener Company, which hawked its wares by running a photograph of Carl Anthony buttoning Muriel Kirkland's dress and suggesting the buttons be replaced by a zipper.

The Avon Theater continued to sell tickets for all seats, and by July 1 the play was the longest running nonmusical on Broadway. By September 1930, Sturges had realized more than one hundred thousand dollars from *Strictly Dishonorable* and one hundred twenty-five thousand dollars from the sale of its film rights at a time when former Wall Street businessmen sold apples two for a nickel near their Central Park shanties. By then his comedy had played more than seven hundred performances in ten American cities, where the road company brought the author several thousands more in monthly income. Brock Pemberton was sufficiently delighted to give the entire New York audience individual birthday cakes as they entered the Avon on September 18, 1930 — cakes commissioned from Alexis Pillet at Pirolle's, where formerly Preston was limited to the sixty-five-cent lunch or begged credit.

On November 15, *Strictly Dishonorable* became the thirtieth play in Broadway history to have five hundred performances, and when it closed on January 3, 1931, it had been presented 557 times and was still bringing in profits from tours in thirty American cities as well as stagings in Canada and England. During the following decade, Solomon Sturges kept Preston's portfolio of stocks in safe order, and there was always an income from Standard Oil of New Jersey and from the Baltimore and Ohio, the Chicago and Northwest, and the Pennsylvania railroads. For Preston, the profits were to be enjoyed.

Mary — whose book *The Untold Story* was published that season, but without arousing critical or popular excitement — was then virtually a permanent resident of Woodstock. Her son, therefore, continued to

Mary Dempsey —
Chicago, 1897.

Edmund Preston Biden about
1902, adopted by Solomon Sturges
and known thereafter as
Preston Sturges.

Mary and Preston (Chicago, 1904), dressed in the style favored by her friend Isadora Duncan.

Preston (seated, left) at the Lycée Janson de Sailly — Paris, 1910.

At East Ninth Street, New York, age seventeen.

During advanced flight training in Tennessee —
autumn, 1918.

Mary, then known as Madame Desti, in her Fifth Avenue studio,
New York, about 1921.

Portrait of Estelle de Wolfe Mudge (artist unknown) about the time of her marriage to Preston Sturges (1923).

Mary (left) with Isadora Duncan, on the French Riviera not long before the dancer's death in 1927.

At the time of the Broadway success of
Strictly Dishonorable. 1929.

Eleanor Post Hutton, at the time of her marriage to Preston Sturges, 1930.

Mary Desti — New York, 1931.

Margaret Sullavan and William Wyler (front center and right) within a
week after their elopement, on the set of *The Good Fairy,* November 1934.
Behind them, Bianca Fernandez Gilchrist, Preston Sturges and (at left)
actor Henry Hull.

Louise Sargent Tevis, at the time of her marriage to Preston Sturges, 1938.

Preston and Louise at the Academy Awards (March 1941), moments before he received the Oscar for Best Original Screenplay. Behind them, David O. Selznick and Alfred Hitchcock.

Preston, Louise and their son Solomon (Mon) with nursemaid
Mary Merrow, at Ivar Avenue.

At Paramount Studios, 1940.

Solomon Sturges with Preston in
Los Angeles, 1939.

Outside his restaurant,
The Players, on
Sunset Boulevard . . .

. . . and preparing a dinner
party at Ivar Avenue.

During the editing of *The Great McGinty*, 1939.

Sturges's cameo appearance in *Christmas in July*, 1940.

Sturges (left) directing Dick Powell and Ellen Drew in *Christmas in July*.

Hopping across the Paramount back lot, 1941.

occupy her modest fifth-floor quarters at 603 Fifth Avenue, where — due to the economic madness of the time — his rent leaped in one month from fifty dollars to one hundred fifteen. His grocery bills arrived from Sommer Brothers and from T. Henry Lohsen, the most expensive New York markets, which submitted invoices with monthly totals of several hundred dollars when bread was twelve cents a loaf. In March 1930 he bought a fifty-two-foot yacht, christened it *Recapture,* insured it for ten thousand dollars, and took it from New York to Palm Beach and from its Hudson River dock to destinations in Long Island and New England. He also joined Manhattan's Riverside Yacht Club.

The invitation to write the book and lyrics for a comic operetta came from H. Maurice Jacquet, once a pupil of the French composer Jules Massenet and former musical director of the Théâtre de l'Odéon, Paris. He had written thirty musicals in Europe, and after coming to America he wrote the incidental music for a 1920 play called *Spanish Love,* remarkable only for the acting debut of William Powell.

Jacquet's operetta *The Silver Swan* was a thundering failure when it closed in December 1929 after twenty-one performances, but he had the unfortunate idea to salvage the sets, costumes and orchestrations and rework them as a (more or less) new work for the following season. Through Ted Snyder, he met Preston and learned that the author of *Strictly Dishonorable* was also a closet songwriter who had written the lyrics for a score of melodies, all unpublished. A contract was drawn up in January for Sturges to write not only the new words for the rehabilitated tunes but also a libretto for something to be called *The Well of Romance.*

By March, Preston had completed only twenty-five pages of the first act, and his story and lyrics vacillated between standard Viennese confectionary kitsch (officers in full dress, romantic escapades at an Alpine inn, a love triangle) and a merciless parody of that genre. The tale was set in the mythic kingdom of Magnesia, which indicated straightaway that Sturges intended something more in the tone of Chaplin than Romberg.

The major reason for Preston's creative languor was Eleanor Post Hutton, who easily upstaged every practical professional concern. Instead of keeping his promise to Solomon Sturges to attend the Chicago premiere of *Strictly Dishonorable* on February 10, Preston at the last minute fled to Palm Beach, on the pretext of working on *The Well of Romance.*

By March, newsmen were predicting an imminent marriage. At that time, he was summoned by Eleanor's stepfather and asked if he could support her in the style she already took for granted. "I would hope in better taste," Sturges replied without flinching. Alluding to private investigators sent by the Huttons to report on his private life in New York, Preston wrote to Paris Singer on March 10:

> I have already denied it to two of the newspapers, but it was mentioned in one paper last week and in another paper this morning. . . . It's all over New York, of course, thanks to Hutton and his detectives.

He was more explicit to Solomon, writing on the thirtieth that he had asked Hutton's permission to marry Eleanor, and that they had hoped to marry on June 3:

> The family promptly decided that I was a fortune hunter, a bum, a drunkard, and everything else they could think of to say. Hutton had detectives put on my trail, to dig me up a bad reputation, if possible, but so far they haven't succeeded. They have promised to cut Eleanor off without a cent if she marries me without their consent, and when I still wanted to marry her, it knocked the fortune hunter theory for a loop. They also object to the fact that I was divorced, although her mother has been too. They also feel that the difference in our ages is an insurmountable barrier, although I don't think my eleven years' seniority makes it exactly a May-December romance.

The affair was, in fact, interrupted by Mary's debilitating illness, which had just been diagnosed as leukemia, and for which there was at the time no treatment. She had to be hospitalized in January in New York where, Preston wrote to Solomon, she was "quite weak and crying all the time, which is not like her." Later, because Preston was virtually a commuter to Palm Beach from New York, Solomon brought Mary to Chicago, where her condition deteriorated even further. In spite of their estrangement and her other marriages, Solomon had never stopped sending Mary at least a hundred dollars each month — perhaps because he still loved her, perhaps also because by supporting her he assured himself a place in the affections of her son. In any case, now he also assumed her medical bills.

While Mary was at Presbyterian Hospital, Chicago, Solomon also fell ill and eventually needed a series of operations for an enlarged prostate. Both of the patients (Solomon was almost sixty-five, Mary almost fifty-nine) were lovingly attended by Estelle, whose mother and husband had died within a week. She had arrived in Chicago in mid-February for a friendly visit with her former father-in-law, but when he and Mary needed care she demonstrated both her gratitude and her essential sweetness by remaining to assist them for several weeks. On February 18 she wrote to Preston, "I wonder if I shall ever see you again. It would be rather nice to talk over old times and all the silly things we used to do." In a postscript she wrote that neither she nor her late husband "had a drop to drink in two years." That was one way, she added, in which she was reexamining her approach to life and trying to live more seriously.

Preston's reply to Estelle, after thanking her for attending Mary and Solomon, was frankly condescending:

> I am glad you are beginning to think a little on the vagaries of life and ask yourself questions about them, because in answer to these questions will come philosophy or understanding, which is the greatest happiness intelligent people can hope for. You have a good head and I don't see why you shouldn't be somebody of importance before you get through.

Estelle could not ignore his patronizing attitude, and she fired off a reply:

> Do you really think it is possible to have had the kind of childhood you know I had, to have left one husband [Godfrey] because of senility, another [Sturges] because of laziness and to have lost the third [Daugherty] by death *and only be just now beginning to think a bit on the vagaries of life?* . . . As to my becoming "somebody of importance," don't think that just because of a slight mental advantage you have a God-given right to be high and mighty and lord it over all the rest of us who are less fortunate.

There is no record of a reply by Preston.

By March, it seemed as if Mary's death might indeed be imminent, but then — with the typical unpredictability of both Mary and her illness — she rallied: "We're sitting on top of the world," she wrote to Preston after returning to her home in Woodstock after leaving Chicago, and where she now had a nurse-companion. "I'm getting well again."

She was not recovering and she knew it, but on a recent visit Preston had been so ecstatic about Eleanor that Mary did not burden him. No longer eager for constant social stimulation, Mary was in a sense being transformed by her sickness; she was usually desperately tired, quiet and withdrawn — not, it seemed, unhappy or in very much pain, but perhaps for the first time in her life reflective, and even sometimes peaceful. The lines and shadows of tension that had been drawn onto her features after the death of Isadora were not so pronounced now, and she was grateful for the small pleasures of life in her Woodstock cottage, and for such visits as neighbors and New York friends made. She was, as she wrote repeatedly to Preston and to Solomon, gleamingly proud of her son. But she was also terminally ill.

Just then Preston's natural father suddenly emerged from obscurity. From the Hotel Hough in Schenectady, Edmund Biden wrote for the first time since 1914, reminding his son that he had paid for a childhood operation on a gland in Preston's neck — surgery that had cost five hundred dollars, he claimed.

> Now I am 60 and I have angina pectoris and my years are numbered. . . .
> Your present position and happiness is directly due to my most unselfish
> efforts to keep you alive. . . . If you are not inclined to give me a square
> deal I shall forget you are my son and lay the entire matter before Mr.
> Hutton and give him in detail your mother's terrible record as a *Harlot*
> [*sic*]. . . . I have in my possession a witnessed confession written by your
> mother admitting adultery with eight men previous to her marriage with
> me. I insisted on this to stop her constant attempts to see other men. . . .
> Now, my boy, which is the easier way out in your estimation? To pay to
> me only what you owe me for your being, life and happiness or to have
> dragged out of the cesspools of filth the history of your mother, much of
> which would reach the press? I ask for nothing but what is due me in cash,
> leaving out and making no charge for the intense worry I underwent
> through it all. . . . I will [give you] a week. The payments end absolutely
> any further communication between us.

The letter was signed "Your affectionate father, Edmund C. Biden."

Enraged, Preston made no reply. A second letter then arrived from Biden:

> I shall give out the whole wretched story if you refuse to reimburse me for
> saving your life. . . . Let me hear from you and if you have any reasonable
> counter proposal, we can get together.

He again signed the letter "Your affectionate father." And with it he enclosed a second letter, addressed to Eleanor; it warned her against marrying into a family that had a wanton mother and an ungrateful son. Preston did not, of course, transmit the letter to her.

In the face of continued opposition from the Huttons, Preston and Eleanor followed a venerable tradition. Risking her disinheritance, they eloped and drove north from New York City to Bedford Hills in Westchester

County, where on April 12, 1930, they exchanged vows before Justice of the Peace Leo L. Hunt. Onto her finger Preston slipped a plain wedding ring for which he had paid $3.50 at Betteridge's, on Fifth Avenue. They spent the wedding night at Mary's Woodstock house and next day they proceeded north to Eleanor's uncle and aunt, Mr. and Mrs. H. B. Close, where they were also warmly welcomed and embraced. From there they wired the news to Solomon Sturges and their New York friends.

The reception back in Manhattan next day was not so cordial as the Closes had provided. Preston and Eleanor moved into small rooms at 603 Fifth Avenue while the press lurched into high gear, detailing every snarl and smirk from Palm Beach.

> In the face [reported the Associated Press on April 14] of opposition to the match by her mother, the former Marjorie Post, and her stepfather, Edward F. Hutton, the couple eloped Saturday and were married. Members of the Hutton family have declined to say where the marriage took place or reveal the whereabouts of the honeymooners.

And then, less than three weeks after their elopement and just after Eleanor and Preston returned from a few days aboard the *Recapture* and left for a visit with Solomon, a very interesting coincidence occurred.

On April 30, Estelle de Wolfe Mudge Godfrey Sturges Daugherty, twenty-nine, came before the same Bedford Hills justice of the peace with Myron Davy, a thirty-six-year-old, freshly divorced mining engineer she had just met in Nogales, Arizona. It seemed to have been something of a surprise even to herself that she was remarried, as she wrote next morning to Solomon:

> . . . I wish you were all here and could have been at our wedding, which was very jolly. Judge Hunt married us and we all had some very good cognac afterwards. Judge Hunt is now an old friend. . . . Before I had any idea of getting married, I invited more people [to her home in Connecticut] than the house will hold, so they are all coming anyway, and I think it is a very good idea to have lots of people on a honeymoon, then you don't get lonely. Myron said after all, if we didn't take them along we would be bound to run into some sooner or later so we might just as well have some hand-picked ones.

Myron, she added, was soon about to depart for Arizona on business. "He is very amiable and has a grand sense of humor, which would almost be a necessity living with me — it makes me less difficult. . . . He was a track man at Princeton and can jump 6 feet 4 inches, so I better look out not to make him nervous or he might hit the ceiling." She was also about to be the occasional mother to Myron's two children, who would mostly live with his former wife: a good thing, she felt, "as I can't quite see myself seriously in the role of a mother."

Her conclusion reveals the same Estelle — rather poignantly fragile beneath her humor — and also the esteem in which she held Solomon Sturges:

> God bless you and please keep on loving me, it is the one dependable thing in my life which gives me a sense of security.
>
> Always your devoted Estelle

Preston and Eleanor, meanwhile, were feeling the first dilution of their dizzy romance. His work area overflowed most of the living room at 603 Fifth Avenue, the closets could not accommodate her extensive wardrobe, the rooms were dark and cramped, the atmosphere almost morbidly variant from the luxury of her Florida estate. But space limitations were not the most severe problems, for the truth is that Preston's and Eleanor's styles, habits and expectations about life and relationships were widely incongruous.

Although she was accustomed to elegance and luxury, Eleanor's increasing dismay in 1930 and 1931 was not because of a suddenly simpler life, nor because of any unwillingness to undertake household duties, nor because she felt she deserved pampering. Quite the contrary: she wanted a career, too, like her husband. Always fond of music, she hoped to refine a pleasant voice and an appealing manner to some kind of professional level. Sidonie Lederer recalled that Eleanor was

> interested in everything, liked to discuss everything, and was not afraid to have very radical ideas about what was wrong with the country in 1930. Sometimes I thought she was just a socialite, but then I realized she was curious and intelligent.

As Lederer suspected, Eleanor was more than the sum of her heritage. When she was dropped from the New York Social Register — an event headlined in the *New York Daily News* on November 26 and certainly due to her marriage to a playwright and defiance of her famous family's wishes — she was genuinely indifferent.

Preston, on the other hand, was a man tinted with a traditional European bias about a wife. Eleanor, he expected, would be gracious, patient, the perfect lady to escort to his favorite nightspots and a willing, bright listener to dialogue excerpts he needed to read aloud. They would have fun, and she would be available to him, the lovely wife of a successful playwright. She would leave him alone when he needed to work, to meet with cronies, to make decisions about his career or their social plans.

He could not, however, imagine that it might be important for her to be more than an element in his life. He was amusing, and he expected her to be an amused wife. Like Estelle, she should be socially adept but passive, frolicsome but ladylike, always supportive of her husband and his needs. He had chosen her for her loveliness, her charm and her style; but perhaps he had not sufficiently accounted her needs, nor did he think there might be more to her character. Like the polished and gifted Gus Caraffa in *Strictly Dishonorable*, he could be gentle and respectful, urbane, persuasive and responsive to innocence; but he was also partly like Henry Greene, slightly imperious, benevolently presumptuous of his manly primacy. He thought of himself, in other words, as a "proprietor," as he wrote later to his stepfather.

Preston Sturges was, then, exactly the *belle époque* gentleman his experience prepared him to be. He was also the son of Mary Desti, who for him had confirmed that women were only capricious, willful dilettantes, polished and polite, harmless, energetic and exuberant but requiring a firm control — and, he felt, ordinarily not to be taken very seriously. It is interesting, in this regard, that in correspondence and conversation he ordinarily addressed his wives as "my sweet child," "dear child" or "dear little thing."

From their busy Long Island production studios, Paramount Pictures offered Preston a second assignment on June 11: he agreed to write the dialogue for a film based on the moderately successful 1924 comedy *The Best People*, by David Gray and Avery Hopwood. Jack Kirkland (who had written *Frankie and Johnny*) had already drafted a screenplay but was on to a new project, and he suggested his old acquaintance for dialogue revisions. Exactly four weeks later, Preston delivered his manuscript and was paid ten thousand dollars. (Directed by Fred Newmeyer and released as *Fast and Loose* on November 29, it marked the screen debut of Miriam Hopkins.)

By late summer, Mary was desperately ill and clearly moribund. Preston spent more time with her in Woodstock, racing back to Manhattan for story conferences on *The Well of Romance*, which was also unhealthy. To him it seemed more and more a futile enterprise, merely stage sets in frantic search of a story. Preston seemed unable to focus long enough to develop an attitude about operetta, and Jacquet's indifferent pastiche of a score was no help in the decision. Two stars from the landmark *Show Boat* were engaged (Norma Terris and Howard Marsh) but they, too, felt the confusion of realms. The premiere, originally announced for October 20, was delayed several times.

A sorry production of a wan tale, *The Well of Romance*'s thin story concerned a prince (masquerading as a needy poet) who meets a lonely princess over the waters of a magical well. After parental and political obstacles are put in the way of the young lovers, they live happily ever after; there is very little more to the tale except the frequent intrusions of unexceptional songs and chorales.

A tryout at the Nixon Theater in Pittsburgh the week of October 27 was disastrous, the general anxiety exacerbated by Eleanor's temporary loss of a $10,500 bracelet. "Jewels Gone; Heiress Calls Police" shouted the headline in the *Post-Gazette* on October 30. The bracelet was found several hours later: a hotel clerk had spotted it on a foyer table and, thinking the 476 diamonds could certainly not be real, gave the "fake" jewelry to his small daughter. When the poor man read the headlines, he telephoned police, who believed his account only after hours of protest and interrogation.

About the show, the Pittsburgh press was not encouraging, and the New York reaction to the November 7 opening at the Craig Theater was unequivocally dispiriting. After the disappointment of *Recapture*, some critics were now beginning to wonder if Sturges's first hit (still a successful Broadway resident) was anomalous: "There was little to suggest the author of *Strictly Dishonorable* in either book or lyrics," observed the *Herald-Tribune*. The show closed within a week, leaving Robert Benchley to wonder in *The New Yorker*, "The more young Mr. Preston Sturges continues to write follow-ups to *Strictly Dishonorable*, the more we wonder who wrote *Strictly Dishonorable*."

The Well of Romance lost its $125,000 investment — $45,000 of which had been contributed by Preston and his wife. In December, she was scheduled to inherit three million dollars from her grandfather's cereal fortune on her twenty-first birthday. For that occasion, and because he hoped for better luck next time, Preston presented her with a new Mercedes-Benz.

On January 4, 1931, Solomon Sturges wrote a long letter to his former wife Mary Desti, inquiring about her health and offering continuing

90

financial support in her need. He then turned to the subject of his son's marriage to Eleanor Hutton.

> I am rather fearful of that combination. . . . She has not been brought up to stand poverty and although Preston must be making something still on *Strictly Dishonorable*, she has been accustomed to millions and large abodes and perhaps she will find three or four rooms rather small after the first flush wears off. I sincerely hope not. Divorce is a fearful thing. It wrecked my life and I shall never get over it.

At the same time, Preston and Eleanor were in fact planning to move from the cramped rooms at 603 Fifth Avenue to more capacious quarters at 125 East Fifty-fourth Street — as extreme a transfer as could be imagined. From Charles C. Goodrich (the tire baron) they bought a house valued at $250,000, each paying half. Designed by DeSuarez and Hatton, the 34-by-101-foot residence was in the style of a European city house or *hôtel particulier*, decorated within as a Venetian *palazzina*.

The thirteen rooms were approached through a central foyer, its vaulted ceiling twenty-four feet high. On the first floor were the kitchens, pantries and workrooms; on the second was the dining room, decorated in white stucco and red Verona marble, which led through to a main staircase to the upper hall, from which there was access to a library and two living rooms twenty-two feet high with Tuscan vaulting. The third floor had connecting master bedrooms overlooking an enclosed garden court, with guest suites and servants' quarters on the top floors. An elevator facilitated access. There were echoes in the long, stone-cooled corridors, and if there were not forty at dinner, the dining room seemed forlorn and empty. The house did not exactly invite cozy suppers by the fire. The Sturgeses spent the first months of 1931 supervising improvements, selecting new furniture — most of which, according to the custom of that time, they rented, the better to see if they wanted to live with the pieces permanently.

In addition, they brought Mary back to New York and moved a hospital bed into her room at 603 Fifth Avenue, for she was rapidly losing weight and running high fevers as the final stages of leukemia ravaged her body. Although she had enjoyed spectacular health almost her entire life and been accustomed to having virtually every demand met by some man or another, she endured her suffering with an almost heroic calm and tolerated the indignities, bleeding and incontinence with a dignified resignation that astonished her nurses.

For the first time, too, she seemed to open her heart to Preston, calling on her old culture-maven creed to encourage him even while she offered praise:

> Never forget, dear [she wrote to him from Woodstock on January 31] that God has given you his most precious gift — *talent*. . . . You have a marvelous talent, and I beg of you to let nothing interfere with it — *nothing*. You are an artist — and for art one gives his all. Only she is a jealous mistress and will permit no other gods. . . . Your talent belongs to the world, so more courage is demanded of you than of an ordinary being. You have work to do — and are one of the few young Americans *truly gifted* — so up and to work. . . . God bless you — I have the deepest faith in you.
>
> Yours devotedly, Mother

It turned out to be her last letter. Mary lingered quietly through March, and by early April Preston was at her bedside around the clock, alternating watch with the nurses. Eleanor visited occasionally, but she had really never known her mother-in-law and she felt her presence might somehow be an intrusion on the intimacy of death.

On the evening of Saturday, April 11, Mary awakened and turned to her son. "I know," she whispered, "that you don't approve of very much in my life. But believe me, I was only trying to find happiness. There's no tragedy in dying, Preston — the only tragedy is never to have lived." She smiled, pointed to herself, pointed to him. As he later said, he knew exactly what she meant — her last advice was an injunction to live.

Early next morning — her son's first wedding anniversary — she pointed to her old bed, pushed into a corner opposite her.

"Always keep this bed somewhere in your house," she said, taking her son's hand, "and if you're ever heartsick or weary, lie down on it and I'll come and put my arms around you, and everything will be all right." She then seemed to sleep, but throughout the afternoon her breathing became more labored.

Finally, without any grand dramatic gesture or display of staged bravado, and just as the spring twilight cast an angular shaft across the quiet room, Mary Dempsey — a good-hearted, often foolish woman who had lately assumed a kind of tragic and courageous grandeur — slipped peacefully away.

SEVEN

The Call of the West

S HE CERTAINLY had a full life and at times a very hard one,"
Solomon Sturges wrote to Preston about Mary,

> but since she had her little place in Woodstock and saw your success, I
> think she was comparatively happy, outside of the times she was so ill.
> God rest her soul in peace.

Although he had certainly been hurt by Mary's life of capricious passion,
Solomon was always a man slow to judge, quick to temper understanding
with compassion and to demonstrate that compassion by unceasing acts of
generosity. He was, as Mary wrote not long before her death, "the
kindest, truest friend a woman ever had" — a fact clear even to her
quicksilver judgment.

Solomon's difference from Edmund Biden was never so clear as in
the notices of condolence to Preston. From (noteworthily) The Temper-
ance House, Niagara Falls, Biden wrote to Preston immediately after
Mary's death, again demanding money for Preston's care as a child and
again adding threats if the money were not forthcoming. The letter may
not, in fact, be from a rational mind:

> I seem to hear the Anvil Chorus rising from hell as that soul of hers reached
> its destination, where, until the end of time, her screams for mercy, for
> just one drop of water will echo down the corridors of the inferno until
> there is no time. You have my most sincere sympathies in this your most
> and perhaps greatest harassment. But cheer up, Son, you still have your

loyal Father who will keep close in touch with his dear Son. . . . If you saved her false teeth, send them to me as a loving remembrance of my former dear wife.

The conclusion is viciously sarcastic:

Your affectionate Father Edmund C. Biden, to his heart-broken son Edmund Preston Biden, alias Preston Sturges.

Sturges never forgave this "insane and sadistically imaginative letter he wrote, expressing his great joy at my mother's death."

Biden did not stop there, but continued in a letter dated April 13 to Howard Perch (for whom this may have been the first news of his former wife's death) in which he mentions persons for whom no connection with Mary can be discovered:

Possibly you are grieving over the death of your wife who called herself Mary Desti. Save your sorrow for someone worthwhile. . . . You were her seventh husband and I her fourth. In between she was the mistress of ten men — Baron Schillembach, the Russian Consul of Chicago, and the notorious confidence man in New York, Frankie Dwyer. . . . She led a worthless and rotten life, I fished her out of a brothel and she was drunk when I married her in Milwaukee. . . . She was one of the foulest women that ever lived . . . this filthy bitch . . . I only wish she had been burned alive. That boy my son is a rat.

Yours truly,
Edmund C. Biden

Within a week of Mary's death and cremation, Preston and Eleanor were trying to put the sadness behind them. Shopping at Henry Wellen's on East Forty-ninth Street, he bought her a pair of Japanese pearl earrings mounted in platinum and — one of the rare times he bought a gift for himself — a fourteen-karat gold bill clip set with carved coral. That year the Sturgeses bought a Lincoln automobile, and they continued to dine out often. But there were problems, some of them relative to Sturges's spending. That year, Preston earned seventy-five thousand dollars, but in December he had only six hundred dollars in the bank, and he was in debt for fifty thousand dollars.

Their life was indeed luxurious in that spring of 1931, and by June, Preston had to admit in a letter to Solomon that he had grown "awfully fat . . . 209 [pounds], which is awful. Incidentally, I've grown a long, flowing moustache which makes me look about fifty years old." Solomon had already been concerned for Preston's health. "I think you are probably smoking too many cigarettes," he had warned earlier, "and that will cause nervous indigestion. . . . Cut it out and take your meals regularly."

The extravagance of the rich life, however, was no security against a marriage that was unraveling as quickly as it had been stitched together. Emotional support for Preston during that time came from Bianca Fernandez Gilchrist, the wife of Sturges's friend and former backstage colleague Jack Gilchrist. Toward the end of 1930 she had begun working occasionally as Sturges's private secretary. By the spring of 1931 — while Jack was with the London company of *Strictly Dishonorable* playing the small role of the speakeasy lookout — Bianca and Preston were good friends. Soon they would be lovers.

During several periods of his life, tricky and passionate entanglements interrupted the concentration Sturges needed for any kind of serious writing. The interferences were especially distracting when these affairs were conducted during a marriage, with the accompanying problems philandering invariably creates. But Sturges was a fervent romantic, and the women he chose for affairs were sometimes (like his Paris attachments, and like another in later years) highly strung, tempestuous beauties capable of highly melodramatic scenes.

For seven years, Bianca Fernandez Gilchrist occupied center-stage of his emotional life, and the relationship gradually became ever more complicated and dramatic. Fair-skinned and slim, with dark hair and flashing hazel eyes, she was intelligent, energetic and polished; he could never, after all, be attracted to a slow or unsubtle woman. She was attracted to Preston's stylish confidence, his cosmopolitan charm, his grand gestures, his ability to control a situation and to make a woman feel absolutely central in his life.

Bianca was also fiercely protective of him — and extravagantly jealous. She had a wild temper, which frequently led her to throw chairs or hurl pots if she thought that he found another woman attractive. She also liked to break dishes if she disliked the way he spent his free time. To everything, she offered an unambiguous, enthusiastic response. Preston always knew where he stood (or dodged) in her presence.

He seems in fact to have been attracted to her earthy, direct emotionalism perhaps precisely because so much of life with Estelle and Eleanor had been very *comme il faut*, highly ordered by social convention and its regulations. After he and Eleanor separated, Bianca was the first woman he lived with continuously and openly, with no apparent intention of formalizing the bond in marriage. And it is important to recall that such arrangements were not at all so common in American society in the 1930s, nor so blithely acceptable among polite professionals.

Her passionate outbursts he considered either feminine wiles or signs of singular devotion to him, and he could ignore the first and luxuriate in the second. In pleasanter moods, she was quite mellow and frisky, curling up to Sturges and addressing him (in letters and conversation) as her "honey child" and her "baby boy" — neat revenge, perhaps, for his "dear child" habit, which she resented. Most important of all, however, was the fact that she appreciated his talent, and she forced him to work. Like many in his craft, he avoided its demands whenever possible. Bianca would not tolerate his indolence for long, for by sheer persistence — and by being a first-rate secretary and editor — she got him working when he might otherwise have indulged his preference for a protracted lazy period.

Eleanor, meantime, confirmed her plans to pursue her own career and booked an extended European tour. No sooner had his wife left in June 1931 than Sturges began what he called "a mild little play of not much importance," a comedy about American business titled *A Cup of Coffee;* it was finished in August. For the first time, Sturges did not work alone. He dictated at night, speaking the parts aloud while pacing his rooms. Bianca was his recording secretary and constant companion.

The play, to be sure, lacked the sharpness and focus of *Strictly Dishonorable.* A romantic comedy involving a young man who enters an advertising slogan contest, *A Cup of Coffee* did not have the bite of Sturges's earlier hit. The play was immediately rejected by Brock Pemberton, John Golden and three other producers to whom Sturges submitted it.

That summer of 1931, there had been an unusual gap in Sturges's normally attentive correspondence with his stepfather, whose letters he had ignored for almost five months. "I guess," Solomon wrote, "being so important has rather made you a bit careless." But an explanation was forthcoming, and it suggests that Preston was attempting to reorder his life, to write what he hoped would be a "sensational, probably a smash hit" after *A Cup of Coffee.*

Preston also wrote to Eleanor ("Dearest Darling") on August 2; the ardent letter suggests he may not have been hostile to the idea of a reconciliation, nor to something that later was termed an "open marriage." Significantly, he also referred — as he had to his stepfather — of his awareness of acting like a "proprietor" of women.

> This is my first letter to you since, on June 5, we said good-bye. I knew then, and you must have known too, we had ended something. I thought then, and I have thought many times since, that we had ended love; but now I don't think so. I think we ended only something that was making us both unhappy, something we would be better off without, something I would call a Ready Made Conception of Marriage in which the wife plays the role of chattel and the husband the role of Proprietor . . . although I had always been well considered and smiled upon as a lover, platonic or otherwise, *no one* had ever enjoyed me for a single minute as a husband. A year ago you told me you would rather be kept by me than be my wife. I didn't understand you then, but I do now. . . . I am not your proprietor. I would like to be your favorite man. It is so long since I have been nice to you that you may have forgotten that I ever was, and yet I think I can be.

And at the same time, he wrote to his stepfather:

> I love my wife with all my heart and soul. We had a terrible year — in a tiny apartment, and we had got very much on each other's nerves. We decided to separate for a few months to *save* our marriage. I was terribly unhappy when Eleanor first sailed — I thought we'd reached the end, although she told me I was a fool. . . . I'm going to be a much nicer husband than I was before. . . . From now on I ask only to be the Favorite Man — a sort of Lover-in-Law . . . [this] means that one can't sit back and rest on one's laurels, but on the contrary continue to put the best foot forward and be at least as gentle and nice to one's wife as one was to one's fiancée. However well everyone else may know all this, for me it has been a discovery.

He was also discovering the pleasure of writing alone again — this time, a seriocomic play he first titled *Consider the Lily* (and eventually *Child of Manhattan*), describing it to Solomon as

> one year in the life of a little New York girl. We meet her as a taxi dancer [a ten-cents-a-dance girl in a public ballroom] and leave her a year later beautifully arrayed and the mistress of a multimillionaire. The story has no moral but a lot of drama and fun. It's all fire and ice.

Preston worked on the play until September, and then, never much good at sustaining protracted solitude, he longed for life with Eleanor.

Absence had made the heart very much fonder, and he wrote to her almost desperately on September 11:

> I no longer resent your career. So long as you will try to love me a little in exchange for my loving you a great deal, you can be a tight-rope walker or a dame des lavabos [a ladies' washroom attendant], and see if I care. All joking aside, I want you to sing very well and become very famous and quench your thirst for achievement.

The closing is with "all my love to you, sweet child."

But there was no reply, and so Preston sailed for Paris aboard the *Mauretania* on September 23. He found Eleanor at the center of a busy and glamorous international crowd, and this worried him; he wrote to Charles Abramson that "every man in Europe is in love with her and wants her to divorce me and marry him."

She did, however, come back with him on October 24 from Cherbourg to New York, for reasons that are unclear but do not seem to have derived from her hope of a reconciliation (she had already booked her return). They moved some furniture from the house on East Fifty-fourth Street back to 603 Fifth Avenue, sent back most of the rentals, and then changed their minds and reordered more rental furniture back to East Fifty-fourth; the confusion reflected their uncertain future together. ("It seems a little stupid," he wrote to Solomon, "to have [the new house] just at the moment, as Eleanor's plans call for her staying in Europe at least another year.")

While he was meeting with the producer William Harris, Jr., about plans for *Child of Manhattan,* Eleanor was rushed to Doctors Hospital for an appendectomy, and before Christmas she sailed back to Paris. Her husband was to follow after the play opened.

But the premiere was postponed several times — not only for revisions, but because Harris withdrew after disagreements with the author over cast and script. Gilbert Miller then agreed to be the producer, but similar conflicts occurred. Finally, an agreement was drawn between Sturges and A. C. Blumenthal, a theatrical broker and friend of New York's Mayor Jimmy Walker.

The film of *Strictly Dishonorable,* meanwhile (without any creative contribution from Sturges), had opened on November 10 at Manhattan's Criterion Theater. Preston was genuinely pleased with the movie and said so in an amusingly ironic letter he sent to Carl Laemmle, the German immigrant film distributor and independent producer who had become the founding president of Universal Pictures.

> I have just seen the celluloid version of *Strictly Dishonorable* and want to tell you how disappointed I am. I thought the screen play would begin in a colonial mansion with sixty-four columns and an army of liveried flunkies and progress luxuriously through Roman baths and gin parties to a thrilling automobile chase ending on a mountain top with the golden dawn bathing the features of the two lovers ensorcelled by each other's beauty. . . . Instead, I saw only my play. Granted that you did it beautifully; granted that your cast is magnificent; granted that you used taste and discretion; and granted that little Sidney Fox can charm the birds out of the trees and back again, your production left me sad and disillusioned. . . . I arrived in the projection room with a very superior feeling . . . and presently found myself deeply interested and admiring my own play. Nothing could be lower than this. I am greatly disappointed.

Child of Manhattan, after lurching through rehearsals and tryout performances in Newark, opened at the Fulton Theater on March 1, 1932. Trying to achieve a counterpoise between romantic melodrama and satire, *Child of Manhattan* failed on both counts, taking an oddly dichotomous attitude regarding the title character, whose integrity as a simple dance-hall girl the play hails but who is also an object of condescending satire for her ignorance and lack of social polish.

The play fared poorly both critically and financially and closed in May after eighty-six performances. The failure of his third consecutive effort (after *Recapture* and *The Well of Romance*) depressed Sturges markedly, as he wrote to his stepfather in March. And his spirit was not much leavened by the reemergence of Edmund Biden in his life. Arrested and held in a Buffalo jail, he first wired E. F. Hutton (Eleanor's stepfather) to bail him out, then wrote of this to Sturges and demanded enough money to move from New York to the West. Sturges ignored the humiliation and the lunatic blackmail by his father. "I probably should have forgiven him to the extent of sending him money," he reflected many years later, "[since] I had so much and he had nothing at all, but I didn't, so that is that."

By springtime, Preston eagerly hoped for a reconciliation with Eleanor.

> Life to me is very futile, dull and purposeless [he wrote to her in March]. I have a great deal, and yet nothing at all — no contentment, no satis-

faction. The circus is swell, but I'm on the outside of the tent. Possibly this is because you are far away from me. . . . I like to think that I have your friendship.

On Saturday, April 2 — perhaps in an attempt at making one project successful — he departed for Paris to win back his wife. After several cordial but ineffectual meetings with her, however, he was formally served papers by Eleanor's attorneys; at the time he was at Harry's Bar on the rue Daunou. Coudert Brothers notified him of an "action for annulment," alleging that at the time of his marriage to Eleanor, a Mexican divorce petition filed by Estelle in 1927 had not yet become effective (and would not be so until the spring of 1931); thus, claimed the suit, none of the subsequent marriages was valid. (Eleanor had filed for annulment because she wanted to marry a Catholic Frenchman, and their Church laws would not countenance divorce.)

Sturges sought distraction in the Paris theater season and then departed, depressed, at the end of June. By the time of his arrival in New York, however, he had summoned his essential optimism and good cheer, as a friendly and confiding letter to Estelle on July 6 indicates.

> Somebody seems to have dug up the fact that your divorce from me was not pronounced final until the spring of 1931. If that is so, you and I were not divorced until that time, I was not married to Eleanor and you were never married to Draper Daugherty. It seems quite a mix-up, but it's really not very important. . . . I think it was a very good thing that Eleanor and I parted. We loved each other very sincerely, but disliked each other so much because of the dissimilarity of tastes, education and ideals that there was no hope for us. I'm quite reconciled to the turn of events, and though my heart is a little sad my head is shouting "Hooray!"

As Sturges told a columnist from the *World-Telegram,* he had spent "a good deal of [his] time in Paris simply knocking about." But he also worked on a new play, *Unfaithfully Yours,* about the entanglements of a judge with women.

On a brutally hot summer afternoon in late July, in the garden of 125 East Fifty-fourth Street, he finished the play — alone this time, without dictating and without distraction. Never produced, it is arguably his best stage work after *Strictly Dishonorable* and marks a major advance in the development of his specific comic talent. *Unfaithfully Yours* (which gave only its name to Sturges's later film, but neither characters nor plot) is a sly and sparkling comedy revealing in every scene its author's influence under the French tradition of farce.

Set in New Jersey on two days in August 1932, the play concerns Judge Michael Costello and his family. While at a legal convention, he had recently been unfaithful to his wife Eugenia, dallying with a woman named Daphne. At the same time, his daughter Naomi learns that her fiancé, Billy, has been unfaithful. But Judge Costello defends men's infidelities. Suddenly Daphne enters, drunk and blowsy, and the judge quickly tries to whisk her out of town.

The second act's comical frenzy creates an entirely different mood from the genteel drawing room comedy dialogue of the first. During the intermission, the judge's quick auto trip with Daphne resulted in an accident, and the two are in the hospital, although not seriously injured. There are fast and wild exchanges of clothing, disguised identities, the introduction of a crazy doctor and nurse, and sudden departures from hospital windows. The judge escapes the hospital room before his family arrives, only to meet with yet another accident.

The third act resolution to the domestic crisis springing from the discovery of infidelity is provided by a suggestion from the judge's mother-in-law. She advises that he tell Eugenia he was helping Daphne: to be proud, be cheerful, be confident — and *lie* most of all — just as the judge advised Billy. But after he lies convincingly to his wife (telling her that Daphne is the illegitimate daughter of his wife's late brother and thus really their niece), Daphne returns alone to apologize to the wife for the infidelity. When Eugenia then learns the whole truth from the judge — that he has been unfaithful all the time of their marriage — she forgives him: "I suppose one can't have *everything*. Something you've done so often can't be so *very* important. But why do you *lie* so?" His reply: "I suppose it's the legal training."

Unfaithfully Yours was not, it seems, offered to producers very energetically by the playwright, and the lack of interest in it may have been caused by a combination of three factors. First, by this time Sturges was associated with an unfortunate trio of failures; second, there were in 1932 sudden cutbacks in production during this worst year of the Depression; third, there had already been a surfeit of marital comedies in 1931 and 1932, some hits but many of them dismal failures (with titles like *As Husbands Go, The Social Register, Springtime for Henry* and *Whistling in the Dark*).

But *Unfaithfully Yours* is a crucial step toward the imminent devel-

opment of Sturges's screwball film style and contains the classic components of farce: extravagant exaggeration and knockabout clowning,
improbable situations logically developed, mistaken identities and
changes of clothing — all of this involving quite ordinary people.

Nowhere was the ancient genre of farce more successfully developed
than in France, and at no time was it more prevalent than during the
heyday of Georges Feydeau (1862–1921), who wrote nearly forty plays
between 1881 and 1916, and whose works were always being performed
before packed audiences during Sturges's years in France. Feydeau syn-
thesized the comic lunacies of *la Belle Époque* and inspired dozens of
imitators: Sacha Guitry's *La Prise de Berg-Op-Zoom*, which set Sturges and
Vely Bey laughing and then fighting in 1912, was nothing so much as a
pale imitation of Feydeau. *La Dame de chez Maxim* (*The Lady from Maxim's*), *La Puce à l'oreille* (*A Flea in Her Ear*), *Occupe-toi d'Amélie* (*Look After
Lulu*) and several of Feydeau's short plays were always offered at one
theater or another in repertory, for they were standard crowd-pleasers.

Feydeau drew on the hilarious tradition of Eugène Labiche (1815–
1888) whose long list of farces raised the genre to a high level of literary
achievement with their precisely drawn characters, raucous slapstick and
engagingly sharp social satire. Where Feydeau excelled, however — and
where he influenced comics and writers as diverse as Charles Chaplin,
Laurel and Hardy, René Clair, Sturges, Jacques Tati, Jerry Lewis, Woody
Allen, Mel Brooks, Neil Simon and Michael Frayne — was in the depic-
tion of a deep disorder, a *madness* amid the complexity of the twentieth
century. The most comic and most absurd situations in his works (and
those in his tradition) involve some kind of marital, sexual or romantic
misadventure and the clear sense that people are at odds with their
environment. In every case, the masterfully contrived plots are stun-
ningly improbable and depend for their success on speed and the presumption that if anything can happen in this increasingly complicated
life, it probably will.

Like the uneasy social world Sturges created in *Strictly Dishonorable*
and *Unfaithfully Yours* — where judges are all too human and men are
good-hearted philanderers needing both compassion and conversion —
Feydeau's atmosphere is tainted but absurdly funny for all that. It is
typified by a scene wherein a man argues with his mistress when she
threatens to kill herself on learning that he is to be married (in *Un Fil à
la Patte*): "Think what you're doing — you can't! You're in someone else's
house! It's not polite — it just isn't done!" It is a world (in the same play)
in which parents hire a deaf-mute as governess for their young daughter

"so that she can't go filling [the child's] head with a lot of nonsense."

On Sturges's part, there was perhaps no conscious borrowing from Feydeau nor from his plots. But the two playwrights had the same preoccupation with honesty, with the tissue of deception and hypocrisy underlying much in relationships. Sturges, after all, had been exposed to so much social subterfuge, so much affectation, so much sexual intrigue in the lives of Mary and of Isadora Duncan — and in the social life of Prohibition-era New York — that he matured with a positive horror of artifice and dissimulation. He always insisted on frankness, and his best film comedies involve the unmasking of sanctimonies. Like Feydeau, he punctured pretense but never condemned the pretender. Perhaps because he felt kin to the weakness of others, he was always kind to them.

Sturges's lack of persistence in marketing *Unfaithfully Yours* had, however, another explanation. After his letter to Universal Pictures' Carl Laemmle, praising the film of *Strictly Dishonorable,* Laemmle tendered an offer. Sturges could join the many playwrights engaged by Hollywood in the early years of all-talking pictures: he was welcome at Universal Studios for three months as a contracted screenwriter. For a salary of a thousand dollars a week, he could work — as he had on *The Big Pond* and *Fast and Loose* — on scripts assigned by the production offices.

The guaranteed income was welcome to Sturges; he could reimburse a number of debts quickly and easily, then return to New York and his writing for the theater. Making no provision to lease 125 East Fifty-fourth Street, he offered it rent-free to his friends Charles Abramson and Jack Gilchrist for the weeks of his absence, stored his Talbot automobile in a local garage and packed only a few items. On September 7, 1932, he and Bianca departed for California.

On September 12, Preston and Bianca arrived in Los Angeles and checked in at the Roosevelt Hotel. He went immediately to work at Universal City, she went to find a house for rental.

At that time, Laemmle's son, Carl, Jr. — called Junior Laemmle by studio employees — had been placed in charge of production on the Universal lot. Universal had not done so well with its first musicals (*Show Boat, Broadway* and *Melody Lane* in 1929); but there was enormous success in 1930 with Lewis Milestone's powerful film of *All Quiet on the Western Front* (based on Erich Maria Remarque's novel), which won for the studio its first Academy Award for best picture of the year.

Junior Laemmle then placed in production a movie version of John

Balderston and Hamilton Deane's play *Dracula* (based on the Bram Stoker novel). Lon Chaney was to have played the part, but he died and the assignment went to the Broadway creator of the role, the Hungarian Bela Lugosi. *Dracula* was such a box-office triumph that Universal effectively began a cycle of horror thrillers: *Frankenstein, Murders in the Rue Morgue* (with Sidney Fox), *The Old Dark House* and *The Mummy* followed in 1932.

Preston's first assignment was a script in that tradition: on September 15, he began work on an adaptation of H. G. Wells's novel *The Invisible Man*. Eager to demonstrate his own imagination and comic style, he virtually ignored Wells's narrative, creating instead an odd tale of revenge and misguided love, with seriocomic characters. In his small, private bungalow at Universal — which existed in its own municipality, Universal City, near North Hollywood at the eastern extremity of the San Fernando Valley — Bianca (also hired by the studio) typed out his scenario, for which at least a half-dozen other writers had already been hired and fired.

From the start, he regarded writing for the movies as essentially the same as writing for the stage, with the added freedom of multiple locations and varied mobility; otherwise, he understood that the theater's traditional "three-act" structure as well as the requirements of character and action development pertain equally to screenwriting.

On the twenty-third, he wrote to Solomon that he could not reimburse his stepfather's eight-hundred-dollar cash loan immediately, since he was still paying rent for 603 Fifth Avenue in addition to Los Angeles expenses for himself and Bianca. "Things are shaping up nicely," he added. "I'm interested in my work and doing the very best I can." But his best, as it happened, did not satisfy Laemmle or the film's director, James Whale. Sturges's version was rejected and the project turned over to yet another writer.

Bianca, meanwhile, had found a furnished house for him at 2070 Ivar Avenue, north of Sunset Boulevard at the foot of the Hollywood Hills. He took a three-month lease for the property, which had two bedrooms, living room, dining room, kitchen with patio and garage; the rent was $110 per month. There was also a smaller separate cottage, and here Sturges installed a houseman named Gordon Ayer and a photographer named Arnold Schroeder, New York acquaintances who needed work and whom he was pleased to assist as they, too, settled and tried to find work in Los Angeles. As for Bianca, she leased a small apartment nearby — a place that was mostly a weak concession to propriety, since she was most often with Preston at Ivar Avenue. She was by this time

Sturges's full-time secretary and companion, permanently separated from her husband. It is difficult to know for certain if the separation was due to Bianca's now well-known liaison with Preston, for all parties concerned were remarkably discreet.

Whatever might have been his mixed motives, Preston continued to send small checks helping his friends Charles Abramson (whose fortunes as theatrical producer had dwindled to virtually nothing) and Jack Gilchrist (also out of work) — both of them still living as Sturges's guests in New York City. (There has never been any record of Jack Gilchrist's reaction to the Preston-Bianca affair. He seems, after several years of a mercurial relationship with her, to have settled for the evaporation of the marriage, and he may have been grateful that he was not being asked to support her.) The checks Sturges sent to Abramson and Gilchrist "are not loans but presents," he wrote to them on November 28. "When your ship comes in and you get rich, you can pay them back or rather make me presents of equal amounts." There was no possible mixed motive regarding photographer Schroeder, however, whose bills for equipment Preston cheerfully paid. Schroeder, for his part, instructed Sturges in the fine points of complicated photographic processes.

The reason for Sturges's fascination for cameras was plain. After a few weeks at Universal, he had learned that the real creative control over a film rested with the director and producer. He began to learn as much as he could about the mechanics of movie-making, therefore, from colleagues on the lot, in production offices, on the soundstages and in the laboratories. In fact by the end of November he had an original idea for a feature film. And if he wanted to insure the survival of his story, he knew he would have not only to sell the script but to direct it as well.

His screenplay for *The Invisible Man* was completed November 1, and while he awaited a new assignment he worked on an original project. The inspiration came from Eleanor's account of her maternal grandfather, C. W. Post (1854–1914), the cereal magnate who rose from humble origins to dominate a major portion of the packaged food industry. Miserable in private life, however, he committed suicide at the height of his achievement.

But Sturges was being paid to work for Universal, not to write free-lance material. Ready to demonstrate good will to Junior Laemmle — especially in light of the announced rejection of his work for *The Invisible Man* — Sturges worked without extra fee (which his contract, strictly speaking, provided for) on a comedy to star ZaSu Pitts and Slim Summerville, *They Just Had to Get Married*. Gladys Lehman, H. M.

Walker and Clarence Marks had variously worked on the script; Sturges tightened a few scenes, polished some dialogue and submitted it within ten days, receiving no credit on the final release print.

As with all Hollywood scripts that passed across the desks of several writers, it is extremely difficult — usually impossible — to know exactly what contributions were made by a particular author. If a screenwriter kept detailed notes and copies of specific pages he submitted, it is possible later to compare these with the contributions of others, with the final shooting script and with the film as it was released. But that can be done in very few cases of multiple authorship, since the stages of script development (especially those of films more than a half century old) are ordinarily not preserved in production files. It is, then, difficult to know what were Sturges's contributions to scripts essentially crafted by committee.

There was, meanwhile, news on the legal front from New York. Eleanor had returned from Paris for her annulment proceedings, with which Preston was trying to be cordially cooperative. On November 4 he wrote to Estelle:

> Eleanor's case against me charging bigamy and asking annulment comes up in New York on November 17. She will be represented by Frederick Bellinger of Coudert Brothers. I am telling you all this because it really affects you more than it does me. If her plea is granted, it means you were never married to Draper Daugherty and cannot possibly inherit the money he left you. It also means you are not married to Myron, although you can step out tomorrow and rectify that easily enough. From my own standpoint, it makes me a criminal in New York State — possibly everywhere — and gives the Hutton family an extra something nice to say about me. I offered to give Eleanor any sort of evidence she wanted. I think this has all been done because the Hutton family is afraid I would sue for damages charging alienation of affection, than which I would rather change my name to Hutton.
>
> Eleanor's lawyers first told her that you had not filed the final paper and that your divorce was not legal. Then they dug a little deeper and told her that some Mexican judge, in looking over the cases of the preceding year, came upon this fact and made the divorce final anyway but that he did not do so until . . . after Eleanor and I married. All I know of my own knowledge is that one day a nervous-looking little man thrust a paper in my hand and then ran like hell. It was in Spanish and I have never been able to read it.

Estelle, too, demonstrated remarkable grace in an awkward situation. Both civil and church officials visited her to discuss the circumstances of her marriage to and divorce from Sturges, as she wrote to Solomon the following February 21; her comments reflect both her good will and her somewhat fey memory.

> It is probably just a formality interviewing me, however, and as this letter [from the Huttons] was perfectly polite and businesslike I didn't see any reason why I should refuse, especially since they have never done anything to [hurt] me. I suppose they will ask me when Preston and I were married and I really don't know. After spending the afternoon looking through some old papers I have finally decided to tell them I think it was during 1923.

Eleanor's annulment was indeed granted, due at least in part to Preston's courteous cooperation, and in several letters she warmly thanked Preston for his gentlemanliness and help, which enabled her to wed a Frenchman in a Catholic ceremony. As for marriage itself, Preston considered it (as he wrote to a friend of Solomon) "a very charming institution but in no sense a necessary adjunct to human happiness. One gets along quite well without it. Being a fool, I shall probably try it again sometime." And as for the entire annulment fiasco, a sensible man like Solomon Sturges regarded the episode as "excruciatingly funny and ridiculous. It all sounds like a tale of bohemians or wild animals, and not of people supposed to be civilized."

By mid-November, aware that Universal was not going to renew his three-month contract at the end of December but also unwilling to abandon the story based on C. W. Post, Sturges wrote to Charles Abramson. After a chance meeting with Hector Turnbull, assistant to Jesse Lasky (an independent producer for Fox), Sturges met privately with Lasky and discussed the draft of the original script he now entitled *The Power and the Glory.* "I am going to do free-lance work," he wrote to Charles Abramson when Lasky expressed interest,

> and I may do [*The Power and the Glory*] with him. There were a great many complications about the 'Invisible Man,' my first continuity. . . . As far as I can make out, Junior Laemmle and the powers that be want something in the picture which they cannot describe but which they insist upon having.

He added that he and Bianca had new Ford automobiles and hoped to learn something about Hollywood nightlife.

But there was not a great deal to learn in that regard at the height of the Great Depression. In Hollywood, people who could afford to patronize chic restaurants and nightclubs — in other words, well-paid employees of the movie studios, mostly — were also those whose alarm clocks rang before first light and who began a long studio day at seven. Crew members had to prepare a set hours before the director and cast arrived; actors were expected in makeup and wardrobe departments at sunup, all so that the day's first shot could begin promptly at eight-thirty or nine. In the 1930s and 1940s, workdays routinely lasted ten to twelve hours, six days weekly.

Nightlife, then, meant for most movie folk either dinner at home or an early supper at a popular place such as the Brown Derby, Musso and Frank Grill or Ciro's on Sunset Boulevard (later the Comedy Store), or the supper clubs like the Trocadero or the Mocambo. Movies themselves — and a selection of still photographs from special events such as premieres — have given the false impression that Hollywood was a wild, raucous community where thousands dined lavishly each night, overindulged at fancy nightclubs, then stumbled home past midnight. Some few fitted this dreary cliché, to be sure; they did not, ordinarily, work very much. In those days before television, when there was little theater, dance, concert music and opera in Los Angeles, those fortunate enough to have employment went out to dinner, then perhaps to a hotel bar or ballroom or private club, or to a sporting event. The city was very quiet before midnight and quite deserted after.

On November 17, days after the office meeting with Lasky, Bianca took a call for Preston at Ivar Avenue. Jesse Lasky, excited by Sturges's "pitch" — his conversational telling of the story — wanted him to submit a treatment (a summary of the story) before proceeding with a full script. Excited about it and full of confidence, Preston nevertheless refused to do a treatment. He would leapfrog that stage of the process, he insisted, and submit only a finished script. "I raised my eyebrows at that," Lasky wrote later.

> He obviously wasn't wise to the ways of Hollywood, [and] . . . he didn't even know enough about screen-writing to know that the first step is to do a *treatment,* or narrative story line.

Instead, in February 1933, Sturges submitted a completed screenplay,

> complete to every word of dialogue [Lasky added], the action of every scene blueprinted for the director, and including specific technical instruc-

tions for the cameraman and all departments. . . . I was astounded. It was the most perfect script I'd ever seen. I dispensed with the usual practice of having other writers go over [it] "with a fresh mind" to make improvements. I wouldn't let anyone touch a word of it.

The detail was certainly there, some of it amusingly diverting. For the long love scene between the leading man and woman, to be seen walking along a country path, Sturges wrote: "We truck [i.e., the camera moves as they do] along after these two, which will enhance the charm of the scene, besides being damned excellent exercise for the director and the cameraman." There are many such technical notes, by which his suggestions were courteously and engagingly offered.

When the press learned of this unprecedented script submission, a furor arose. Sturges was breaking the rules, he was in conflict with the Hollywood tradition of movie writing, according to which a screenplay is first drafted in a detailed prose summary form, then approved for first script draft, written and then submitted, revised in committee, redrafted and resubmitted and usually developed further by other writers working with the producers and/or director.

"This is unusual in the annals of story-telling," declared the *Hollywood Reporter* in a shocked tone, as if Sturges had written an obscene scenario. And he might as well have done just that, for his new approach upset just about everyone in town (not for the last time). "Writers at that time worked in teams, like piano movers," Sturges remarked years later, "and my solo effort was considered a distinct menace to the profession."

"We tried to find something in the script to change," Lasky protested when reporters from the trade papers came to his office, "but [we] could not find a word or situation!"

But there was more, as the shocks from Sturges continued.

The writer had negotiated a contract with Lasky that was also "unusual in the annals of story-telling." He was to receive not a weekly salary of several hundred dollars while under contract to write a script the studio would then own, but rather (as with book authors) an advance against future royalties — $17,500 against three and one-half percent of the film's profits. "Lasky Inaugurates Royalty Plan for Writers," blared the *Hollywood Herald* on February 18, pluralizing an agreement that then applied only to one man. It was the first such deal between a writer and producer, setting a precedent which in time would improve the screenwriter's compensation and bargaining position in Hollywood.

The final revolutionary innovation of Sturges's contract was that he was permitted to sit in on story conferences and to have his opinion heard as to changes in dialogue. Studio executives all over town were outraged, and Preston Sturges was no longer regarded as simply a New York playwright, a nag who had joined a stable of Hollywood writers. He was now considered impossibly audacious, a maverick with new methods and new expectations. None of which fazed him, of course, for his audacity was simply stern self-confidence. He wanted, in other words, not only the glory but also some of the power.

EIGHT

Wildcats

FOR *The Power and the Glory,* Jesse Lasky borrowed from MGM the popular actress Colleen Moore; he then engaged the Broadway actor Spencer Tracy, who was beginning to undertake leading film roles.

Sturges had learned from Eleanor Hutton about her grandfather, C. W. Post, in the same way she had learned about Post from her family — in occasional, half-connected anecdotes, a detail from his professional life in this context, later a fact about his suicide, then some data about his marriages and perhaps at another time some family chatter about his youth and rise from poverty to riches. This is, after all, the way a person's life begins to take shape for another — in conversational shards and fragments, in episodes related over an arc of time. Images are formed and a life gathers coherence without the total picture, lacking the convenient framework of carefully developed chronological construction. ("There is rich material in the brain waves your family has had at various times," Preston wrote to Eleanor on March 8, 1930. "I am going to write [about them] later on.")

This is what intrigued Sturges — the process of learning about another's life and destiny. And that is how he decided to build *The Power and the Glory:* he would reassemble a life in episodic, rambling, unchronological fashion as a friend of the main character recounts it, with no attempt to justify a man's life nor to provide a complete psychological portrait. There would, then, emerge something more modest and yet somehow more apt for film than a compressed, chronological life history: a *feeling* about one particularly complex life and its mysterious, tragic dimension. His method *was* revolutionary — far more so than the terms of his contract.

The Power and the Glory opens at the funeral of Tom Garner (Spencer Tracy), president of the Chicago and Southwest Railroad — "a great man," intones the unseen eulogist, "kindly, far-seeing . . . a man who rose to power rapidly . . . a true leader." During the words of praise, a mourner leaves the funeral chapel: he is Henry (Ralph Morgan), Garner's friend from boyhood who became his assistant. Angry at a Garner employee who denigrates Garner's character, Henry later hears even more negative remarks from his own wife at home: Tom Garner was a mean and wicked man, she says, ". . . and the way he treated his wife . . ." And with that, Henry begins to tell her the Garner *he* knew, and the film becomes a seminarrated flashback, sometimes with and sometimes without voice-over commentary accompanying the visuals.

The Power and the Glory moves backward from the height of Garner's career as powerful industrialist to his simple, rural boyhood and then forward to his young manhood, when his neighbor Sally (Colleen Moore) teaches him to read and write. They marry, and the narrative skips to their son's adulthood, then moves back to an earlier period of their married life, as Sally lovingly but firmly encourages Tom to work for a major career. We see him, in disordered chronology (but with no confusion in our understanding of the life flow) at various stages of his career — foreman for a railroad, supervisor, yard master — and we assemble the disparate parts of a personal and professional life. We also see the effects of a life, *then* its bases or causes.

At the height of financial power, Tom falls in love with a younger woman (Helen Vinson); this he admits to his wife, who regrets that she had forced him toward an obsession for material success and away from human values. She commits suicide by stepping in front of an electric streetcar (thus focusing the ambiguous motif of the train as source of both Tom's power and his misery). He remarries, but his wife is later attracted to a younger man — her stepson, Tom's son by Sally. In a reversal of the earlier situation, it is now Tom who takes his own life. The film (finally bearing little resemblance to the facts of C. W. Post's life) concludes without a whisper of hope or happiness.

The Power and the Glory provided Depression-era audiences with an unblinking account of the potentially destructive capacity of great wealth, and of the deadly effects of power unmoored to moral principle. Whatever may have been Sturges's presumptions concerning the audience's curiosity about lives like Tom Garner's (or C. W. Post's), the script everywhere reveals his own belittlement of wealth for its own sake. For Preston Sturges — and this is the central point the film makes — money was only a means to an end; as a goal in itself it was incomprehensible.

In fact there was throughout his own life a dual attitude toward money. On the one hand, he desired the security that comes from a steady income, the comforts that material success provides and the freedom it allows for creative pursuits. On the other hand, he had a chronic inability to manage money astutely, and he exerted little effort toward staying debt-free (much less toward accumulating wealth). Riches had no special appeal for him, nor did he desire glamorous props. He borrowed freely (from his stepfather especially, from youth to Solomon's death), and he gave to others just as freely — to his mother and to friends.

He could be generous to those who were not close friends, too. In 1935, when director Monta Bell (who had given Preston his first screenwriting job, revising *The Big Pond* in New York) was in need of cash, Sturges promptly wired him a thousand dollars in London and then invited Bell to come to Hollywood and work with him. It was irrelevant that they had never been more than acquaintances.

The first scenes of *The Power and the Glory* were photographed on March 23, the last on May 5. Over those weeks, Sturges kept an unusually rigid schedule, as Bianca Gilchrist noted in a reply (on his behalf) to a letter from Eleanor's father, Harry Close. Sturges rose at 6:45 each morning, was at Fox to see the rushes (scenes photographed the previous day) at 8, then proceeded to the stage for the day's shooting. Lunch followed, then the afternoon's work, then dinner at the studio and usually several hours of work in the evening, polishing next day's dialogue and conferring with director William K. Howard.

Sturges's presence on the scene was unusual, as writers were traditionally denied access to the actual shooting of their own scripts. A reporter from the *New York Times* detailed an "odd sight" during the filming of *The Power and the Glory:* Sturges was

> on the stage constantly, suggesting, working, advising, much as he would with a play in rehearsal. Authors are seldom allowed on sets, sometimes not even in the studio. And they are seldom permitted to make suggestions during the filming of their own [work]. Mr. Sturges, however, sold his screenplay to the Jesse L. Lasky unit on a royalty basis with the proviso that [it not be changed] by the director, a heretofore unheard-of thing, and

the right to be on the set, to advise and be listened to, an equally revolutionary demand.

One day, Tracy introduced him to an actor visiting the set. Joel McCrea had been in films since 1923 and a featured player since 1929. Impressed with what he had heard about the script and shooting of *The Power and the Glory,* McCrea was eager to meet its author. Sturges, flattered, said he hoped they might work together one day; as it happened, Joel McCrea would be the leading man in three Preston Sturges films to come.

That spring, Eleanor remarried, and Preston — still maintaining a cordial correspondence with both of his ex-wives as well as with Harry Close — wrote to Close on April 15, "Please send [Eleanor] my wishes, sincere and heartfelt, for permanent happiness and contentment." On May 1, Close replied, "I hope you will call on me any time if I can be of any help to you here in the East, as I want you to know that I have the fondest feelings toward you." The sentiment was genuine, as Estelle reported to Preston on May 4: "You will probably be pleased to hear that [a friend of the Huttons] said the Closes liked Preston very much indeed and said he had been a 'perfect gentleman' about everything in every way."

There was a second marriage of interest to Preston that season. On April 18 in Chicago, Solomon, who was then suffering the debilitating effects of a variety of illnesses (including heart problems and chronic digestive difficulties), married Marie Agnes Fulton, his nurse — "because it's more convenient traveling [with a nurse]," he told Preston. "Living alone is not pleasant and I advise you to get another wife AND HOLD HER!"

In June, Sturges purchased the hull of an old boat in San Pedro and began to build a fifty-two-foot schooner he christened the *Destiny* (his New York cable address had been DESTI-NY); the *Recapture,* still docked in New York, he eventually sold to a movie studio.

That same month, *The Power and the Glory* — after six weeks of editing and scoring — was ready for a preview at the Fox Wilshire Theater. The early reviews of Preston Sturges's first original screenplay appeared the morning after, in the June 19 edition of the *Hollywood Citizen-News.* "It came very close to being one of the best pictures ever made in America," wrote James Francis Crow, "[this] screenplay by Preston Sturges, an intelligent writer who conceives of the motion picture as something worthy of original stories."

The *Hollywood Reporter,* the same day, began a review:

> Preston Sturges has written, Jesse Lasky has produced and William K. Howard has directed the most daring piece of screen entertainment that has ever been attempted. . . . If [it] does nothing else, it has introduced Tracy as one of the screen's best performers.

Variety agreed: "Preston Sturges has written a yarn that is perfect theatre from start to finish." Because he had fought hard for the primacy of the writer's position on the film, the press had been eager to judge the final picture with particular reference to Sturges. The trade results were, then, both gratifying and influential.

A week later, Sturges informed E. C. Cord, his landlord, that he would soon vacate 2070 Ivar Avenue. In early July, he rented a larger and lovelier house at 6377 Bryn Mawr Drive, just slightly farther north in the Hollywood Hills, with a wide view over the city. For a lower rent ($105 monthly), he had a living room, dining and breakfast room with kitchen, three bedrooms, garage, a workshop, servants' quarters, a study and a den adjacent to a patio — all comfortably furnished in a Spanish style consistent with the architecture. For Bianca he rented a small bungalow nearby, for $17.50 a month, and frequently, by mutual consent, there she stayed when they had a fight and required a little cooling distance.

The house was owned by a local physician, E. Bertrand Woolfan (called Bertie by friends) and his wife, the former silent screen actress Priscilla Bonner. The Woolfans had recently returned from a long European vacation, Priscilla explained many years later.

> My husband had spent quite a lot of money while we were overseas, and so when we came back we moved to a smaller place and rented our place. Through a broker who helped people from the studios find residences, Preston and Bianca came to our house. She found fault with everything and seemed to make no effort to be accommodating, but Preston complained about nothing.

Immediately, a friendship was struck that lasted for the rest of their lives. "My husband's background was like Preston's," according to Priscilla Woolfan.

> Bertie had left home early, too, and went from school to school and floated around just the way Preston had. In their adult lives, both of them wanted

to belong to a family. They longed for a group around them, a *hacienda*. The two men were like brothers. They were both high tempered men and they argued and fought, but they were the best friends.

Among the interests the men shared was billiards — they often played after dinner at 6377 Bryn Mawr — and boxing, which they attended at the Olympic Stadium or the American Legion auditorium, generally twice weekly.

On August 16, *The Power and the Glory* opened at the Gaiety Theater in New York, where reviews were generally favorable but audiences were not large — perhaps because, as the *New York Times* indicated, the picture was "a distinct departure from the ordinary talking picture . . . [a story] not brought forth in a chronological order," but whose episodes nevertheless were "adroitly linked." During that worst year of the Depression, movie patrons preferred easy entertainment and, as critic Andrew Sarris later remarked, the film was "in the never very popular genre of grown-up pessimism about the American dream" and so it had the fate of other important but commercially unsuccessful pictures — von Stroheim's *Greed,* Vidor's *The Crowd,* Welles's *Citizen Kane* (whose style it directly prefigured and almost certainly influenced) and even Sturges's later film *The Great Moment.*

The French director René Clair (always an admirer of Sturges) wrote years later that it was this 1933 film which first

> exploited for dramatic ends the decomposition of time, the mixture of present, past and what might be called the "future perfect tense" of film grammar. This innovation (which film historians of the cinema scarcely noticed) did not change the prevailing orthodoxy of Hollywood screenwriters, and several years had to pass before Sturges's invention was revived, in *Citizen Kane.*

Most copies of *The Power and the Glory* soon disappeared, the negative was destroyed in a fire some time later, and only after many years was a careful restoration possible from variously obtained private prints. It remains, for those fortunate few able to see it, one of the most provocative and intelligent motion pictures ever produced, remarkable for the melding of talents — writer, cinematographer (James Wong Howe), director and cast.

*   *   *

Concurrent with the general release of that film, Sturges completed the first draft of an original screenplay he had begun on July 19, *Biography of a Bum;* the last page bears the legend, "Preston Sturges Spoke, Bianca Gilchrist Wrote." On September 1, it was polished and retyped. The typescript bears the following epigraph:

> Too much has been said of the virtues of honesty. Practically everyone has a kind word for it, although, like exercise, fresh air or parting the hair in the middle, it agrees with certain people only. Meat is not good for cows, whisky is terrible for goldfish, and I propose to show that honesty is as disastrous for a crook as is knavery for the cashier of a bank. A man is what he is. So was he made. So will he be.

The scenario (later bearing various titles, among them *The Vagrant* and *Story of a Man*) went through several revisions until it became, in 1939, *The Great McGinty.* In 1933, however, he could interest no one in this sharply satiric story of a man named O'Hara, a vagrant (and thus like many citizens that year) who is exploited by politicians.

Biography of a Bum, Sturges hoped, would be his to direct. "I believe," Sturges wrote to his stepfather during the shooting of *The Power and the Glory,* "I've learned quite a lot of things which will be useful when (and if) I start directing." In July, he was more confident: "This time I am going to direct it also," he wrote to Solomon. "They [Universal Studios] have offered me $15,000 to write and direct it. . . . I am willing to take less in order to direct, because if I am a success as a writer-director I can almost name my own salary with any company in the business." As always, he very much wanted his stepfather to be proud of him, and the tone of his letter has almost the quality of a schoolboy's happy report to a concerned parent.

But the deal with Universal stalled. There had been no precedent, after all, for a writer to demand that he direct his own screenplay. This was even more absurd to studio executives than the deal he had made with Lasky. But Sturges continued to hope he could soon direct, and several friends agreed this was not unreasonable. "He has a striking physical appearance," Charles Abramson wrote to Bianca on April 13, "a succinct expression and a forceful voice, has executive ability and creative talent, [and] he is fitted to perfection to direct." There would, however, be a delay of several years.

By the middle of August, Preston was asking his stepfather for a few thousand dollars loan "in case I get short" — the shortage due to several thousands he was putting into the refurbishing of the hull for the *Destiny.*

117

"I think you have been exceedingly extravagant," Solomon wrote to him on September 8.

If you want to keep your credit good in Hollywood, take care of it by your own effort and do not always think, "I guess I will spend that. I have father to fall back on." I want you to be careful but I am afraid you will not be.

Preston, meanwhile, was already drafting another (atypically morose) letter to Solomon on September 9: "I am in the depths of depression as I owe several thousand dollars on my boat and have no money left."

"I cannot understand," the elder Sturges replied, "why you have been so low in funds. You certainly made a great deal of money with *Strictly Dishonorable.* What did you do with it all?"

He had spent it, of course. But not all on the boat.

On Sunday morning, August 20, as Arnold Schroeder was negotiating a difficult turn on Bryn Mawr Drive, he somehow lost control of the car. After he was pulled from the wreckage in a ravine an hour later, he was rushed to Los Angeles Receiving Hospital (later Hollywood Hospital) in extremely critical condition, with a nine-inch skull fracture, among other serious injuries. After two months confinement, he began recuperation at Bryn Mawr Drive, but the brain damage proved so serious — with subsequent hallucinations and sometimes violent behavior — that he had to be hospitalized at an institution in South Pasadena. He was only thirty-one years old.

For the rest of his life, Arnold Schroeder's care was paid for by Preston Sturges. Neither Arnold nor his siblings could afford to underwrite his expenses, and Preston would not allow Arnold to become a charity case or ward of the state. Quietly (and without defending himself against his stepfather's occasional charges of extravagance), he paid for his friend's medical care, his eventual return to New York the following year and his rent and expenses for years after.

For eight weeks beginning in mid-September, Sturges was paid one thousand dollars weekly as free-lance writer at MGM. Irving G. Thalberg had hoped to find a suitable project for him, but there was only some preliminary discussion for a film with Katharine Cornell. At the same salary, he then went over to Harry Cohn, the autocratic vulgarian who headed Columbia Pictures, where he was asked to propose film projects for the Austro-Italian beauty Elissa Landi, whom Cohn hoped to engage for a comedy.

Sturges instead offered the outline of a somber script, *Matrix.* The rather grim narrative (whose original title was *So She Married the Jerk*) concerned a woman whose maternal instincts compel her to a marry a worthless cad. The story haunted him for years, and he frequently tried to revive it for possible production, but always unsuccessfully. "I have carried [it] around in my head since landing in Hollywood," he told Darryl F. Zanuck in 1947. "No one has ever seen eye to eye with me on it. . . . I am enormously fond of the story and will surely make it some day." The inability to do so rankled him.

Matrix was, he said toward the end of his life, about "the two different kinds of love that all women have, and that sometimes conflict: the passionate and the maternal . . . and every woman in the world will recognize herself in the heroine." Cohn, however, rejected the idea instantly and dismissed Sturges after less than two weeks employment, adding (and apparently forgetting about *Strictly Dishonorable*) that Sturges obviously could not write comedy. "I am sorry that you and your masterminds decided that I was not a writer of comedy," he wrote in a departure memorandum. "Your joint memories must be failing you."

He then sent *Matrix* to Julian Johnson at Fox, who said that the scenario was just right for European film production, but inappropriate for America, where "people have so many troubles." Johnson evidently thought that Europe in 1933 was awash in good times and good humor.

Three days after leaving Columbia, toward Christmas of 1933, Preston was invited back on salary at Universal Pictures for two weeks, where Junior Laemmle asked him to attempt a rewrite of the forthcoming Claudette Colbert tearjerker *Imitation of Life;* only a few Sturges lines, of no consequence, reached the screen, and William Hurlbut became the screenwriter of record.

The situation was very different on Sturges's next screenplay, however. On January 9, 1934, he was signed by B. P. Schulberg, the former general manager of West Coast operations for Paramount and then independent producer for the same studio. At $1,250 per week, Sturges was to contribute to the screenplay of *Thirty Day Princess,* a trifle of a comedy about a New York girl who has an exact double, the title character. It was written for Schulberg's inamorata, the lovely and gifted Sylvia Sidney, and for Cary Grant. A careful comparison of the finished film with Sturges's original typescript (preserved in the Sturges archives at UCLA) reveals that most of the picture was written by Sturges.

Nevertheless, *Thirty Day Princess* bore the cumbersome final credit for "screenplay by Preston Sturges and Frank Partos, adaptation by Sam

Hellman and Edwin Justus Mayer, from a novel by Clarence Buddington Kelland." Sturges resented sharing credit for something that was mostly his work, and to Schulberg's charge that he was selfish for not wanting his colleagues' names to appear (although they had contributed little to the finished work), Sturges replied in a letter on March 21:

> When and if I care so little about my work that I become unselfish, I will no longer be worth the fancy prices I am receiving at the moment. When and if I am contented to hear another man praised for something I created and, above all, when I am willing to accept praise for the work of somebody else, then I will have gone truly Hollywood, will have accepted the system and will no longer be worth my salt. You have, I believe, always worked from the other side of the fence. By the very nature of your occupation you have accepted praise for pictures as generals accept praise for their soldiers, and it seems therefore logical to you that as you feel, so should your writers feel. . . . Believe me, I have only one desire and that is to see pictures rise to the level of first-class plays and fine books. When those pictures are produced, I don't think they will be written by piece-workers.

This last point was a battle Sturges continued to wage: the insistence that a single vision could best enliven a motion picture, that it is logical for the writer of a film to aspire to direct (and also produce) it, to supervise every aspect and to give it a coherent, single vision. But the union of functions was unheard of in sound films in the 1930s, when Preston Sturges wanted, as he wrote to his stepfather on March 13, "to become a DIRECTOR — something I have been aiming at since my arrival in California."

As soon as his work on *Thirty Day Princess* was complete, he accepted an offer from independent producer Samuel Goldwyn. Director Rouben Mamoulian was having script problems with a fifth movie version of Tolstoy's novel *Resurrection;* the European-schooled Sturges, they reasoned, was the man to shape the sprawling tale, to focus the romance, to sharpen its social context. "Preston Sturges Spoke, Bianca Gilchrist Wrote," was appended again to the last page of the typescript, dated April 27, 1934 at 6:45 P.M. But virtually nothing in the finished film reflects Sturges's draft, and in fact Samuel Goldwyn dismissed Sturges from the project.

*   *   *

Goldwyn soon began a long and important relationship with director William Wyler, who would direct for him (among other films) *Wuthering Heights, The Little Foxes, Mrs. Miniver* and *The Best Years of Our Lives.* But in 1934 Wyler was still at Universal, where since the 1920s he had been gradually building a career. When Goldwyn dismissed Sturges, Junior Laemmle immediately brought him back (at $1,500 weekly salary) to work with Wyler, to whom the Laemmles were distantly related. Under supervising producer Henry Henigson, the project was to be a film version of Marcel Pagnol's Riviera romance, *Fanny.*

The choice of Sturges was logical. Fluent in French, he could read Pagnol's original; he could also draw on his intimate knowledge of European manners, style and humor. And he would be able to converse with Wyler, a French-speaking Alsatian immigrant who had studied in Switzerland and Paris.

The project, however, had a long gestation period. Sturges delivered his script, but its fidelity to Pagnol — and to the central issue of a romance and pregnancy out of wedlock — immediately caused trouble. Universal, in serious financial difficulty, was unwilling to risk the powerful wrath of the Motion Picture Production Code (the Hays Office) and the Catholic Legion of Decency — the two hands of Hollywood censorship that could, from the summer of 1934, strangle an "objectionable" motion picture on release if not during production. Henigson left Universal, Wyler was assigned to another film, the actress Laemmle had hoped to cast in *Fanny* — Jane Wyatt, a popular Broadway player about to begin a long and successful career in movies and television — was shifted to another production and the project was suspended. Retitled *Port of Seven Seas,* it was finally produced by Henigson at MGM in 1938, where it was directed by James Whale and featured Wallace Beery, Maureen O'Sullivan, Frank Morgan and John Beal in leading roles.

Sturges's original script reveals still more phases of his increasingly varied story-telling style. Marius, the young son of César, goes to sea for three years to fulfill a childhood dream; this he does in spite of his stated love for the lovely girl Madelon. At the same time, the gentle and loving older man Panisse, a widower, loves Madelon. Soon she learns that she is pregnant by Marius, and when Panisse offers to marry her, to save her from shame and give the child a name, she agrees. César, a devoted but confused father and a lifelong friend to Panisse, keeps the secret. When Marius returns and tries to claim Madelon and his son, Panisse fears he may be forced to give up his wife and the child, but César points out to his son that this would not be right.

CÉSAR: When that child came into the world it weighed eight
    pounds. It now weighs eighteen. You know what that other ten
    pounds is? It's love. It takes a lot of love to make ten pounds. I
    gave my share, Madelon gave hers, but the one who gave the
    most was Panisse. What did you give it?
MARIUS: Life.
CÉSAR: Life? Certainly — life is cheap. In this world it's love that's
    hard to find.
MADELON: A love like Panisse's.

Marius returns to his life at sea, and Panisse and Madelon to their
baby.

The scene is essentially drawn from Pagnol, but Sturges focused the
emotional conviction as he did the earlier confrontations between César
and Panisse. No one knew better than Sturges the reality of an irrespon-
sible father who later tries to reclaim the privileges of paternity, for this
was precisely his memory of Edmund Biden. Panisse, on the other hand,
is the closest filmic incarnation we have of Solomon Sturges, in every way
but biology the father of the child. This conviction about the locus of real
parenting gives the final moments of *Port of Seven Seas* its impact, aided
greatly by the telling performances of Beery, Morgan and O'Sullivan.
When the film was finally released, the trade reviews of Sturges's script
were cheerfully receptive: "warmly sympathetic transcription by Preston
Sturges . . . the dialog is kept skillfully in the French idiom," wrote the
critic for the *Hollywood Reporter,* while *Variety* called his writing "powerful
and stimulating . . . and beautifully literate."

Sturges's Universal contract was renewed (at $1,500 weekly) in spite of
the deferment of *Fanny,* and he undertook the same project to which the
director William Wyler had been transferred. "He could talk just as well
as he could write and [later] direct," Wyler said years later.

He was a great talker, especially about himself and his work. He was not
a shy man nor a modest man; indeed he had nothing to be modest about.
But he was great fun to be with. He often talked of his colorful childhood. . . . When he and I were alone, we spoke French, which he did
fluently.

The film Wyler and Sturges prepared during the summer of 1934
was to be a starring vehicle for a twenty-three-year-old success story
named Margaret Sullavan, who had made only two previous films. But

her performances in them, as well as her theater training and experience onstage, marked her as one of the most gifted and desirable actresses. She was also widely known to be contemptuous of Hollywood, a difficult and unpredictable eccentric who had wed and unwed Henry Fonda and who was thought to be as intimidating as she was fascinating. With her luminous gray eyes set in a round face that could flash a brilliant smile and suddenly cloud with earnest anxiety, Sullavan had a slightly reedy voice and gave the impression of being somehow guilelessly eager and yet strong and energetic. In 1934 she was about to reach the summit of a remarkably versatile stage and screen career (and a tragic one, too, ending in her suicide in 1960 at the age of forty-nine).

The film was to be based on *The Good Fairy,* a late romantic comedy by the Hungarian writer Ferenc Molnàr that had recently starred Helen Hayes on Broadway; Sturges had seen it at the Henry Miller Theater on December 23, 1931. The story of a young woman whose altruistic instincts cause practical troubles, it was an ideal target for Sturges's offbeat humor, his ability to write scenes of antic mayhem and to create subtle, stylish and racy dialogue. *The Good Fairy* was, on completion, one of his three finest scenarios of the 1930s. It was also his first solo credit in a released picture since *The Power and the Glory*

But it was not easily accomplished. He was very discouraged with his progress, as he wrote to Jack Gilchrist on July 10 — primarily because he felt the year had been such a dither of activity, moving from project to project, studio to studio, that he feared he might be quickly depleted of ideas.

> However, I've been discouraged before without permanent effects and the mood that one is in seems to have very little effect on the final quality of the writing. [But] continuous writing is slightly smothering and very bad for the creative impulse, although I believe very good for the perfection of one's craft.

There was (perhaps not surprisingly) no mention of Bianca in the letter to Jack. She and Preston were, however, working hard on scripts, dining out with a small circle of studio acquaintances and having the usual complement of slightly boozy fistfights.

By August 11 the screenplay was complete and rehearsals began. From the first day, there were difficulties, as Wyler recalled.

> [Sullavan] was a good actress, [but] we were constantly fighting, over the interpretation of her part, over everything. . . . She had a mind of her own

and so did I. The picture was important to me. . . . The story appealed to me, Preston had written a very good script, and the other actors were marvelous.

Sullavan, however, simply refused to read certain lines of dialogue — not because they were risqué, not even because they were awkward, but simply because they seemed to her strained or artificial, or because she was in an ornery temper. Sturges was present on the set daily, rewriting, rearranging, consulting with Wyler, cooperating with the actress. Delays were legion. The start of filming was further held up by weekly memoranda from the Hays Office, for Motion Picture Production Code administrator Joseph I. Breen, with a manic vigilance, saw filth everywhere. He objected, for example, to an exchange in the first draft:

— How much would a girl have to give for a fur coat?

— Her all.

Breen also objected to an insert shot of a book title, "The Least Every Young Girl Should Know, By a Well Known Physician." The implication was sex education, and this Breen's office could not permit. In addition, the line "A young girl must be careful in her relations with men" was unacceptable because "relations" could also mean sex; the line had to be altered to "A young girl cannot be too careful in her dealings with the male gender."

From early October to Christmas, filming of *The Good Fairy* proceeded, but with none of the relaxed good humor of the finished film. According to William Wyler's biographer, the only way the director could win the cooperation of his star was to propose marriage. He did, she accepted, and on Sunday, November 25, they eloped to Yuma, Arizona, in a charter plane. Wyler was thirty-two and this was his first marriage; for his wife, nine years younger, it was the second. Five hours after arriving in Yuma they returned to Los Angeles and next day announced the news to their colleagues on the set at Universal.

"What would you say if I got married to Maggie?" Wyler asked Sturges.

"Well," his writer replied, "she's not marrying you for your money, that's for sure." Sullavan was, in fact, earning considerably more than her contract director. But that was only one thorn in the union, which was dissolved within two years. *The Good Fairy*, however, flickered onscreen with no trace of its production problems, and more than a half century later it retains much of its freshness and humor.

To the Municipal Orphanage for Girls in Budapest comes the man-

ager of a movie palace. "Well," says the directress (Beulah Bondi) to a
teenage girl who announces him, "show him in — there's nothing else we
can do." He is Mr. Schlapkohl, a movie theater manager, and he needs
usherettes. Pretty Luisa Gingelbusher (Sullavan), one of the older or-
phans, is sent out to work for him. (Schlapkohl and Gingelbusher were
typical Sturges additions; daffy names always appealed to him.) Her
parting counsel from the directress is a reminder of her pledge to do a
good deed each day, to "try her wings as a good fairy in society."

In the city, Miss Gingelbusher deflects men's attention by claiming
to be married — the excuse she first gives a handsome stranger waiting at
her stage door (Cesar Romero, in a fleeting role) and then a theater patron
named Detlaf (Reginald Owen) who invites her to the dining room of the
hotel where he is a waiter.

There she meets the wealthy, older man Konrad (Frank Morgan),
just returned from a tour of his South American Meat Packing Company.
He finds her deliciously appealing, "but since I'm just back, almost
anything will do." He invites her to his suite for dinner, where he offers
her any gift she desires:

HE: What would you like to have?
SHE: Well, I like pretty dresses, diamond bracelets, lobsters, fur
    coats, automobiles — almost any old thing.
HE: I see you've given the matter some thought.

Then, when his amorous intentions are pressed, she tells him, too,
that she is married. Konrad decides to shower her with gifts by making
her husband rich. This, she suddenly realizes, is her chance to do a good
deed for an unknown stranger — to be a truly good fairy — and on the
spot she selects a name at random from the telephone directory. The man,
an indigent lawyer named Max Sporum (Herbert Marshall), is approached
by Konrad before Luisa can tell Sporum of her plan; Konrad, thinking
Sporum is her husband, announces his intention to settle a fortune on
him, to appoint him European counsel for Konrad's South American
company, and then to send Sporum off on a tour of the business. But
Max, of course, eventually falls in love with the heroine, and she with
him. The complications of the narrative — involving the love triangle,
the stern protection afforded by Detlaf and the leading lady's attempts to
balance her commitment to good deeds with her flourishing emotional
life — are finally engineered in as amusingly improbable a way as the
story's basic premise.

The Good Fairy is, from first scene to last, a film of great charm and

125

lightning-fast dialogue, and in spite of a certain languor midway, it is remarkable for its vitality and for the engaging credibility Margaret Sullavan brings to an incredible role.

After a hasty conclusion to production, *The Good Fairy* was quickly edited for an early premiere at New York's Radio City Music Hall, whose general manager, W. G. Van Schmus, cabled Junior Laemmle on January 30, 1935:

> FOR THE FIRST TIME IN THE HISTORY OF THE MUSIC
> HALL WE HAVE BOOKED A PICTURE WITHOUT PREVIEW.
> . . . IT IS ONE OF THE GREATEST COMEDIES I HAVE
> EVER SEEN. . . . AN OUTSTANDING SUCCESS.

At the end of its first week at the Music Hall, *The Good Fairy* had blessed Universal with an eighty-thousand-dollar profit, and after the Los Angeles premiere on February 12 that figure doubled weekly. Sturges was lionized at Universal, and he and Bianca were for several weeks seen more frequently at Sunset Boulevard supper clubs. (On February 22, Preston coolly received the news of his natural father's sudden death. Edmund C. Biden was buried in Elmira, New York, without any public acknowledgment from the son with whom he never had any positive relationship.)

About this time, Bianca Gilchrist began to pressure Preston into marriage, but to this idea he was wholly indifferent. "Bianca was a wonderful secretary," according to Priscilla Woolfan,

> she was multilingual and very smart and she made Preston work. He had to have someone get him started at work, and she did. But never did he entertain the idea of marrying her. That was her idea — she thought she was going to get him.

The fact is, however, that Sturges was never more than the calm, occasionally distant lover of a high-tempered, gifted but demanding mistress. The relationship was apparently a torrid one, but it was also squally and unpredictable, and they fought bitterly, sometimes violently. Theirs was nothing like a sadomasochistic symbiosis, nor did it have the pathological character of abusive lovers. "She was just awfully hard to live with," according to Priscilla Woolfan. "She was a real wildcat and very possessive." Bianca and Preston could not remain together forever; so much was clear even to them by 1935.

*   *   *

Junior Laemmle, meanwhile, was eager to put Preston to work again; by February, Sturges was revising a script originally prepared by Doris Malloy and Harry Clork, based on the life of James Buchanan Brady, better known as "Diamond Jim." Sturges's salary was now $2,500 per week, "which puts me in the top bracket of Hollywood writers," as he wrote to Solomon. (His income for 1935 was just over $65,000.)

Brady (who lived from 1856 to 1917) was a man who fired Sturges's imagination very much the way C. W. Post had inspired *The Power and the Glory,* for although the good-humored and much-loved financier was nothing like Post or Tom Garner, there were similar themes rustling beneath the surface of their stories. And of course Sturges had very clear memories of seeing Diamond Jim and Lillian Russell in New York years before.

Brady rose from humble origins, through jobs as hotel bellboy and salesman of railroad equipment to directorships of vast railcar companies. Philanthropist and bon vivant, he provided all the elements for a zesty period piece, on which Sturges worked until mid-April for executive producer Edmund Grainger and director A. Edward Sutherland.

But *Diamond Jim* is a curiously unamusing film, remarkable only for its fascination with trains, train sequences and new train parts. (Sturges enjoyed toy trains, and trains figure prominently in *The Power and the Glory, The Palm Beach Story* and *Hail the Conquering Hero.*) The romantic subplots, which fill most of the narrative, are neither finely tuned nor carefully explored, and Brady is never presented as anything but vaguely childish, mildly querulous and occasionally vulgar; he is not, in other words, a fully developed character, no matter the extent of actor Edward Arnold's padding or blustering as Brady.

Perhaps because his research on the gourmand Brady had prompted caution about caloric indiscretion, Sturges began a strict regime that spring, and by autumn 1935 he had reduced from 204 to a healthier 170 pounds. That summer, he revised the lyrics for a song by his old friend Ted Snyder, who had moved from New York to Los Angeles and was attempting a career as composer for motion pictures. The song, "Paris in the Evening," was eventually (but only partially) inserted into the Jesse Lasky–William Wyler comedy *The Gay Deception,* which was released in October. (In May 1936, his unexceptional love lyrics for Ralph Irwin's melody "Secret Rendezvous" were heard in a movie-within-the-movie, in the Francis Lederer–Ida Lupino comedy *One Rainy Afternoon.* Like "Paris in the Evening," it was never published.)

The most psychologically rewarding projects of that year, however, had no monetary compensation for Sturges. Always fascinated by gadgets and the advances of modern science with particular reference to engines and electronic devices, Sturges was also quick to grasp complicated principles of physics, mechanics and engineering. In 1932, he returned from Paris with a small, primitive mimeograph machine that produced multiple copies of pages in various colors, and occasionally since that time he had tried to perfect it for differentiating the various drafts of typescripts.

Also in 1932, he had worked in New York on an invention related to diesel engines, completing drawings for an energy-saving device he called the Silent Sturges Constant Pressure Engine. He had also collaborated with a man named Amos Addison, an engineer and inventor, on an opposed piston diesel engine with an independent scavenging plunger; and with another technician, Howard Cheshire, a machinist, he built a one-cylinder, four-cycle, four-horsepower gasoline motor.

With those developments behind him, in 1935 he agreed to finance the manufacture of diesel engines, and he purchased a license to make, use and sell an improved design of internal combustion machine at the Sturges Engineering Company, which he set up in a leased warehouse south of Los Angeles. The first device was ready for assembly by April 1936, and from that time he occasionally visited the factory, discussing plans with the foreman and maintaining a keen interest in technical developments.

By 1938, the Sturges Engineering Company had changed its name to the Owen Engineering Company (after the building's owner, Owen D. McDougall). Located at 527 West B Street in Wilmington, the company specialized, as the letterhead announced, in "Precision Machine Work: Tools and Dies." Sturges took special interest in the details of producing jigs, fixtures, diesel engines and special machines. He loved to consider himself an inventor, and in fact he saw writing as a form of invention. To all these activities and interests, his hobbies and his writing he brought unremitting energy and unflagging optimism. (The engineering company was liquidated after World War II.)

Preston Sturges seemed, indeed, often to derive more satisfaction from occupations than from relationships, and throughout his thirties and forties he seems not to have formed strong emotional ties or relationships. Bertie Woolfan was a genial buddy, Bianca Gilchrist a fiery mistress, and there were good colleagues (like William Wyler) at the studios. But his early peripatetic years, after all, had not encouraged him to entrust himself deeply to anyone or any place, and his work had been (until

128

Strictly Dishonorable) unpredictable and unfulfilling. Then two marriages had gone awry.

Now, in 1935, he was renting another man's house, living with someone else's wife and bouncing from studio to studio as work was offered. His personality was engaging, and people loved to be with him. In fact Hollywood was the perfect place for him to be: the craft of movies needed his talent, his alacrity and his wit, and the business of movies required (indeed desired) nothing from a writer in the way of permanent commitment.

Sturges and the movies, in other words, seemed made for each other precisely because they survived from season to season, dependent on momentary profits and whatever satisfaction could be derived from successful completion of the project at hand — and with no primary, personal commitments or constraints. From 1933 to 1943, there were few professional unions as successful as that between Preston Sturges and Hollywood. Each was at a peak of energy and creativity. An uninterrupted decade of such mutually profitable collaboration between a writer and a system is, by later standards, an astonishing record.

NINE

Easy Living

U NCLE CARL LAEMMLE has a big faemmle," observed the irrepressible humorist Ogden Nash about the founding head of Universal Pictures in 1929. Nash had been inspired by the announcement that Laemmle — after installing his son Carl as production chief on Junior's twenty-first birthday — counted more than seventy of his relatives on the Universal payroll.

But by the end of 1935, Junior Laemmle had dashed any dynastic hopes, greatly disappointing his family and pitching the studio into enormous debt. Earnest and assertive, the bantam (five-foot) executive had labored to rival MGM's Irving Thalberg, who had once been successful at Universal himself. Junior Laemmle was called a boy wonder, like Thalberg, and like Thalberg he aimed to produce stylish and intelligent entertainment; but the comparison seemed simply a contrast benefiting Thalberg. Only *All Quiet on the Western Front, King of Jazz, Imitation of Life* and four horror features were very lucrative for Universal during Junior Laemmle's tenure.

Nevertheless, the young heir continued to overbudget almost every production at the studio, and after one too many extravagances — culminating with the elaborately overproduced, two-million-dollar failure *Sutter's Gold* in 1935 — the company was compelled to borrow cash from a private partnership and the Laemmles put up their controlling interest in Universal as security. Further huge expenses connected with the remake of *Show Boat* that year hastened the inevitable, and in March 1936 the lending company exercised its option, bought the studio and escorted the Laemmles to the studio's front gate.

No one was secure that spring, as Preston wrote to Solomon on March 5, and he himself was "in the dumps" — a condition that must have been at least partly cushioned by his weekly paycheck of $2,500. He would spend more wisely than Junior Laemmle that year, he assured his stepfather. He would also try to be a better correspondent to Solomon, who was sometimes hurt when Preston failed to reply to affectionate and proud requests for more news of his increasingly famous son. "You may hear from me oftener than you deserve," Solomon wrote in an undated letter (probably in 1937), "not, mind you, that my letters can benefit you particularly, though they might show you that I think of you and love you."

Preston had good reason to be solicitous for his stepfather in May 1936, for the news from Solomon was not so cheerful: then seventy, he fractured his leg after a fall and was confined to the hospital for several weeks. That may have encouraged Solomon to draft a new will, which he did after several months; seventy-five percent of his assets were assigned to his nurse-wife Marie, the balance to Preston. ("You may not get much, Preston," he wrote on January 13, 1937, "but I love you sincerely and want to do the best thing for you both [i.e., Preston and Marie].")

There was word from Estelle early in 1936, too. Rather like her former mother-in-law, she was still on her restless search for the perfect mate. She had visited Solomon (their friendship still flourished) and asked him to share the news in a letter to Preston: she had divorced the engineer Myron Davy and married a businessman named Joe Shine, about whom very little was known. Seven months later, however, she divorced Shine and remarried Davy. Solomon wrote to Preston about Estelle (on October 24) with his usual uncritical compassion: "She has experienced a lot in a short life and I think she is a good kid at that."

Solomon's favorable estimation of Estelle was certainly reinforced when they all learned the following July that she had resolved to deal frankly and judiciously with an alcohol problem. The Sturgeses, it seemed, had not known that she had been drinking excessively over the last several years, but everyone admired her decision. "Liquor certainly made a nut out of me," she wrote to Solomon July 20, 1937, "and I would just as soon start taking morphine as think of ever touching it again" — a substitution that she wisely never made.

Eleanor, too, maintained a friendly correspondence with Preston during the 1930s. In 1937, for example, she offered to shop for those on his Christmas list and to bring any requested items from Paris. For a number of them she refused to accept Preston's reimbursement: "The customs official was very positive about my getting them in on a lower rate of duty [than if they were to be resold]," she wrote on December 24. "So you see, unless you want me to be liable to a fine, we better not hear any more about it. Merry Christmas and my best regards."

By March 1936, Sturges had been recontracted as a screenwriter by Paramount, at $2,500 weekly. It was his first job there since *Thirty Day Princess,* and much had changed on the lot at Marathon Street.

The studio had just been reorganized after a troublesome half-dozen years, the last three in bankruptcy. The vast combine known (since 1930) as Paramount Publix had owned hundreds of movie houses throughout the country, but like Universal it suffered from financial mismanagement. "The chief villain," according to Paramount historian John Douglas Eames, in fact

> was the Publix theatre chain. Many deals during its frantic growth had been swung by paying the theatres' sellers partly in stock, redeemable at a fixed date and price. After all, who had ever heard of Paramount shares going down? But too many redemption dates arrived after the stock market crash, thereby causing the guaranteed repurchase prices to appear astronomical.

From a profit of over eighteen million dollars in 1930, the studio wrote a deficit of almost sixteen million dollars by 1932. The following year a New York Federal District Court declared Paramount-Publix bankrupt. By 1935, however, the company had recovered its strength — as Paramount Pictures, Inc. — with the indomitable former furrier Adolph Zukor as chairman of its board.

Financial crisis or no, Paramount had retained an extraordinary number of major stars during the early 1930s: the studio was professional home base, for example, to Claudette Colbert, Jeanette MacDonald, Carole Lombard, the Marx Brothers, Gary Cooper, Harold Lloyd, Clara Bow, W. C. Fields, Cary Grant and Mae West. The studio's brilliant director Josef von Sternberg had also been one of their successes. He had gone to Germany in 1930 as part of a collaboration with the Berlin-based UFA studio; there he directed *The Blue Angel* and returned with a gift for Paramount — Marlene Dietrich, who made six more films with him in Hollywood and was one of Paramount's biggest stars.

In addition to Sternberg, there were other notable Paramount directors. William Wellman had directed Paramount's *Wings*, which received the first Academy Award for best picture in 1928 — the same year actor Emil Jannings, also at Paramount, won best actor for his performances in *The Last Command* (directed by Sternberg) and for *The Way of All Flesh* (directed by Paramount's Victor Fleming). Cecil B. De Mille returned to the studio in 1932 after an absence of six years and had a hit with *The Sign of the Cross*. Leo McCarey's comic sensibility sharpened the Marx Brothers' lunacy in *Duck Soup*. And Ernst Lubitsch's ironic and sophisticated tales brought him and Paramount enormous success with *The Patriot, The Love Parade, Trouble in Paradise, Design for Living* and *The Merry Widow*. (When Sturges arrived at Paramount in February 1936, Lubitsch just finished a term as production manager for the studio.)

Because the studio's directors collaborated from the outset with writers, designers and cinematographers, Paramount's films were remarkable for a unity of style and content. This careful attention to production values resulted in the accurate atmosphere of Paramount's exotic and painstakingly realized sets for foreign locales: North Africa (*Morocco*), Paris (*Trouble in Paradise*), China (*Shanghai Express*), Russia (*The Scarlet Empress*), ancient Rome (*Cleopatra*) and Spain (*The Devil Is a Woman*) were, for example, all manufactured by studio artists, just north of Melrose Avenue — and so perfectly that Lubitsch noted his preference for Paris, Paramount over Paris, France.

Of greatest interest to Sturges, however, was the fact that writers were welcome at conferences with directors at Paramount. That had been true of Ben Hecht with Sternberg on *Underworld* and Hans Kräly with Lubitsch on *The Patriot*, both of which won Oscars for best screenplays of 1927/28 and 1928/29. And there was an extraordinarily fecund collaboration between Lubitsch and writer Samson Raphaelson, which resulted in (among others) *The Smiling Lieutenant, One Hour with You, The Man I Killed, Trouble in Paradise* and *The Merry Widow*.

Into this intense but strongly collegial atmosphere Sturges arrived in March 1936. He had submitted an original idea for a comedy to star George Burns and Gracie Allen, who had been popular in vaudeville for over a decade and were broadening their success in Hollywood. Sturges worked on his script — to be called *Hotel Haywire* — throughout March and April, but after his first story conference he was told that Burns and Allen had withdrawn from the picture. The unfortunate, talky scenario was about a feuding couple and their wacky daughter (the title remains a mystery, since there is no hotel).

Sturges then decided to take his first trip away from Los Angeles in four years. After a nomadic youth, he seems to have firmly planted his roots in southern California, and except for this one journey and a single trip to Nevada in 1938, he never left the area between 1932 and 1947.

The July 1936 departure was occasioned by a Honolulu yacht race, for which Sturges's *Destiny* was ready. By July 15, he had arrived in Hawaii with his small crew, having finished twentieth in the race, almost the last to arrive. He cabled Bianca, who had remained in Los Angeles for cosmetic surgery, that he was bringing her a grass skirt.

He did not, however, sail the *Destiny* back to California. That he left to his employees, while he booked passage aboard a liner. Paramount had wired him to hurry back, for there were two projects awaiting him: a comedy based on a Vera Caspary story, to be directed by Mitchell Leisen (a former designer and art director), and another starring Bob Hope, George Burns and Gracie Allen.

When he read the story department's outline for the first, *Easy Living,* he wasted no time beginning a draft. By this time, however, Bianca found his erratic work hours harder and harder to accept, for Sturges in fact worked less than ever at his Paramount office and more at home in the small hours. At the studio he took telephone calls, answered mail, had long luncheons with colleagues, visited sets and generally absorbed the new atmosphere. The writing — invariably dictation to Bianca — he did by night at home, after dinner and several drinks, pacing, acting out the roles, pausing while a scene flashed across the screen of his mind, assuming the characters' voices.

This he did until four, five, six in the morning; then he dozed for three or four hours, brewed a pot of coffee and drove to Paramount — where, after lunch, an hour's nap was all he needed to supplement earlier sleep. Although he was approaching forty and smoked heavily, ate foolishly, drank copiously and rarely exercised, he was enjoying good health and had a level of energy astonishing even for men half his age.

Easy Living seems to have been everything *Hotel Haywire* was not — and a lark for Sturges to create. More than a half century later, it remains a superb example of screwball comedy.

Wealthy banker J. B. Ball (Edward Arnold) argues at breakfast one morning with his son John (Ray Milland) about the young man's future career. The younger Ball departs, insisting he will prove himself capable independently of his father's fortune. Moments later, J.B. is furious with his wife (Mary Nash) over her purchase of a $58,000 sable coat. He throws the fur off the roof of their penthouse, and it lands on Mary Smith

(Jean Arthur), who is seated on the open upper level of a Manhattan bus.

"What's the big idea?" she asks a turban-swathed exotic behind her.

"Kismet," he replies placidly.

Mary tries to return the coat to Ball, but he gives it to her, buys her a suitable matching hat and offers her a ride to her job at a magazine, *The Boy's Constant Companion.* Soon unfounded rumor circulates that she is his mistress.

At the same time, hotel owner Louis Louis (Luis Alberni) risks losing his property to Ball, who holds a mortgage Louis cannot pay. The hotelier decides to win Ball's favor by favoring Mary: Give her a suite to live in, he figures, and Ball cannot foreclose. The suite is palatial, but its kitchen refrigerator is empty, and Mary goes to an Automat for supper. Johnny Ball is working there (to prove he does not need his father's support), he meets Mary, likes her and literally opens doors for her — the little Automat food doors — in a sequence notable for its wild slapstick, food riots and pratfalls.

The complications continue, Ball's financial empire is threatened (but saved), the young people fall in love and seem to lose each other (but do not), Ball's wife is estranged because of the rumors (but returns) and the financially unstable hotel justifies the title of Sturges's previous film. En route to the happy ending, several characters seem to be modeled on Sturges's own acquaintances: there is a humorless broker named E. F. Hulgar — a "vulgar E. F. Hutton," to be sure — and the situation of Ball *père et fils* recalls the relationship between the older and younger Sturges.

Easy Living is a classic screwball comedy — a happy accident of the Great Depression, when audiences relished escapist entertainment. This subgenre of comedy began in 1934 with Frank Capra's multi-Oscar-winning *It Happened One Night* and continued throughout the decade and into the early 1940s with films like Gregory La Cava's *My Man Godfrey,* Capra's *Mr. Deeds Goes to Town,* Howard Hawks's *Twentieth Century* and *Bringing Up Baby,* Leo McCarey's *The Awful Truth* and *Nothing Sacred* and George Cukor's *Holiday* and *The Philadelphia Story.* The targets of screwball comedy were the complacent wealthy, and their stuffiness and self-importance were contrasted with the eager romantic love of young people whose actions always seemed to say, "You keep the money, we'll have all the fun." It was exactly what worried audiences wanted to hear.

The pleasures of screwball comedy were carefully calculated, as in each a couple violates a number of social proprieties while falling in love — Claudette Colbert and Clark Gable, for example, forced to share a room (but not a bed) in *It Happened One Night,* or Katharine Hepburn trying to exit an elegant restaurant as Cary Grant covers the torn seat of her gown with his hat in *Bringing Up Baby.* Often a wedding is halted, parties are disrupted, rules of etiquette are broken. But screwball comedy is quintessentially American: the smugness of the rich is deflated, and young love — needing no wealth — triumphs.

Offbeat, crazy yet amiable stories of reconciliation, these film comedies exaggerate the physically comic aspects of their theatrical bases (as, for example, in *You Can't Take It with You* and *Holiday*). But without exception they also endorse honor, decency and love. If a ritzy wedding is abandoned, it is only for a more comfortable alternative wedding.

Although Sturges's script for *The Good Fairy* and William Wyler's direction of it had screwball elements, *Easy Living* is a better example, and with it — by collaborating with its American director Mitchell Leisen — Preston Sturges came closer to fulfilling his best gifts as a kind of American Georges Feydeau.

The script has all the components of the comedy of incident that had originated with Mack Sennett, his Keystone Kops and his custard pies: the juxtaposition of social incongruities, violence without injuries, the speed of slapstick, the mockery of pompous images. But there is also another level of comedy here — the comedy of romantic situation, of love found, tested and proven. Apparently improvisational and spontaneous, its speed was in fact a pleasant diversion as the story raced through absurdity to a happy ending. In *Easy Living* as later, Sturges always fulfilled the first requirement of farce: he created characters operating under false premises (Mary Smith as Ball's mistress, Mary Smith as an heiress, Johnny Ball as a penniless cafeteria worker) and proceeded from there — *à la* Feydeau — with inexorable logic. The social worlds they raced through and overturned were seen to be largely irrelevant when they were not downright absurd.

This motif of absurdity in the universe and in its social underpinning was always implied in the comedy of Sennett, Charlie Chaplin, Buster Keaton, Harold Lloyd and Harry Langdon. But it was central in a darker, more ominous and yet equally enjoyable way in the French theater farces of Georges Feydeau. It was he who exploited all the staples of broad comedy (rich but cuckolded husbands, selfish wives, misunderstood foreigners, physical pratfalls) and influenced every succeeding generation of European humor (down to the present, with Monty Python and

Benny Hill); and this was what Preston Sturges had first known. "My work has a French humor, filtered through an American vocabulary," Sturges wrote to Marcel Pagnol on March 25, 1947.

In *Easy Living* — as in all Sturges's later work — there are visuals inspired by classic American silent, situational comedy. The European wit had already been brilliantly brought to American film comedy by Lubitsch, in *Trouble in Paradise* (1932). Now it would flourish, becoming both quintessentially American and defiantly Continental in spirit, in Lubitsch's creative heirs, Preston Sturges and Billy Wilder.

Sturges's approach to his material was always rigorously non-intellectual — almost anti-intellectual, in fact. He outlined several times in his career his ingredients for a winning film comedy and what to show the audience in it:

1. A pretty girl is better than an ugly one.
2. A leg is better than an arm.
3. A bedroom is better than a living room.
4. An arrival is better than a departure.
5. A birth is better than a death.
6. A chase is better than a chat.
7. A dog is better than a landscape.
8. A kitten is better than a dog.
9. A baby is better than a kitten.
10. A kiss is better than a baby.
11. A pratt fall [*sic*] is better than anything.

Much of his time in 1936 was devoted to helping his former colleague, composer Ted Snyder, settle in Los Angeles, and helping to finance Snyder's dream of owning a casually chic Hollywood nightspot. When Snyder's Café finally opened (at 8789 Sunset Boulevard, the later site of Spago), business partner Sturges led the first-nighters.

He was usually there five or six evenings a week as a *propriétaire,* the genial, welcoming co-host, hailing guests by name, ordering drinks — too often at his own expense, or worse, at no one's expense, which is not the best way to operate a restaurant.

Preston and Bianca joined Snyder in this atmosphere of boisterous conviviality, singing around the piano as Preston hammered out a few tunes. He enjoyed the good times and paid scant attention to the café's financial situation. When the balance sheets for 1936 were examined, they showed a loss of $3,248. The following year, the loss leaped to

$12,371, and by the time the place closed in February 1939 there was an enormous debt. That did not, however, deflect Sturges — never one to take indebtedness seriously — from his stated intention of soon owning his own restaurant.

Late nights at Snyder's left everyone ready for bed — except Sturges, who was ready to dictate on arriving home at Bryn Mawr Drive. For her part, Bianca found this schedule untenable, and she urged him to advertise for a paid secretary — a man, she added.

By January 1937, Sturges had engaged the ideal assistant: Edwin Gillette, a tall, handsome, university-educated technician in his twenties, with an earnest respect for writing talent. Gillette had a keen sense of humor and a liveliness to match Sturges's. For five years (until he went into military service in World War II), Sturges's young assistant was secretary, organizer, chauffeur, referee in battles at home and office, and general factotum. "He was very easy to take dictation from," Gillette recalled many years later.

> I wasn't such a great typist, and he dictated slowly for my sake. He was very easy-going — in fact he liked to have fun more than anything, much to the consternation of assistant directors who were like studio foremen, charged with keeping things going, getting pages of scripts and so forth.

Gillette was as much a companion as an employee. He soon learned that Sturges's life with Bianca had narrowed his friendships. "People didn't just drop in at his house," according to Gillette, "and he was becoming something of a loner. He didn't have people around, and he *liked* to have people around. He needed warmth."

According to Gillette, Paramount was the ideal place for Sturges,

> a very friendly place to work, and there wasn't the kind of pressure that existed at some other studios. Bill Le Baron [in charge of production] and Y. Frank Freeman [Paramount's vice-president] were very friendly people, and by and large everyone — right down to the guard at the gate — was very good to work with. It helped quite a bit in that business.

But by mid-1937, the assignments at Paramount were becoming routine — script doctoring and revisions, mostly — and Sturges's repeated requests to direct a script were heard patiently but with no positive reply. A certain monotony had crept into his life, and although Sturges offered a genial, smiling exterior, it was clear that he needed a wider field for his talent and energy. The life of a slightly rumpled bon vivant, often a little hung over, had its easy charm, but his work was not challenging. He maintained a sharp sense of humor, however, and an almost transcendent optimism that, as they always had in his teens and twenties, things would somehow improve. Quite rightly, however, he also needed affirmation — professionally and personally — from those he respected.

> He asked for support [Gillette remembered] and appreciation, and he liked to try out lines of dialogue on me and on people at the studio. He seemed to need input to keep himself going in the late 1930s — like a shot in the arm.

One way to harness his energies that year was in the responsibilities of a new home. After five years of being a lessee, he finally bought property south of Bryn Mawr — a cheerful, modest house at 1917 Ivar Avenue, at the base of the Hollywood Hills. He immediately drafted plans to upgrade the second-floor bedrooms, to add a bathroom, to expand the living-dining area, and eventually to add a pool, badminton court and a small barbecue — all for about six thousand dollars.

Preston's *hacienda* gradually expanded in 1937 and 1938, and eventually the image was complete, even to the sparkle of a two-hundred-piece sterling silver dinner service and the barking of his dachshunds Adam and Eve (and their puppy, Haile Selassie, named for the emperor of Ethiopia; eighteen other offspring of Adam and Eve were given away over the next few years).

Home improvements did not, however, improve life at home: Preston and Bianca were, by the late spring of 1937, locked in more and more frequent disputes which were, as Edwin Gillette recalled, "sometimes linked to too much drinking."

In June, one of their major battles landed him in surgery. He tried to diminish the importance of the event in a letter to Solomon dated June 22:

> While indulging in some horseplay I jammed my left arm through a plate-glass window and severed three arteries. I am writing this from Hollywood Hospital. One of the muscles was sliced, but fortunately none of the motor nerves nor tendons were injured.

To Solomon's friend and business associate Sidney C. Love, however, Preston was more candid (in a letter dated July 27):

> I was running after Bianca to return a friendly slap. She closed a door to stop me [but] the door was ripple glass and my arm went through it. . . .

I was in the surgeon's chair without any anesthetic whatsoever for an hour or more. They put fourteen stitches in me, and then I spent two weeks in the hospital.

Remarkably, his letter concludes, "Bianca joins me in sending you our best love."

That autumn, Paramount renewed his contract, and his next assignment may have seemed oddly appropriate after his sojourn in the hospital. He was to work on a draft of *Never Say Die* in November 1937 (Don Hartman and Frank Butler also shared the final credit), a negligible comedy starring Bob Hope and Martha Raye that shows little of the Sturges touch.

By the beginning of 1938, Preston was earning $2,750 per week at Paramount; few Hollywood writers earned more, while very many lived more luxuriously. He was put to work on a screen version of Justin Huntly McCarthy's 1902 play *If I Were King,* a relaxed and unchallenging fictionalization of the life of perhaps France's greatest lyric poet and one of its most fascinating rogues, François Villon.

From February through early May, Sturges dictated and Gillette typed; a 164-page script was submitted May 7, with new scenes and additions following conferences with Le Baron and director Frank Lloyd that summer. To enliven the project that he said "leaves me cold," Sturges translated Villon's French lyrics and ballads, claiming the Rossetti and Swinburne translations were boring and flawed. And the portrait that Sturges limned at director Lloyd's (and Paramount's) preference was a gallant and dashing, highly civilized romantic very much at variance with the complex Villon of history.

As played by Ronald Colman, Villon is full of dignity, good humor, altruism and general virtue — too much virtue to be quite credible, in fact. When he admits that he has been "consorting with cutthroats, thieves and wantons," the effect is slightly silly: he is the sort of man who always dresses for dinner.

The script, however, is remarkably free of the solemn clichés that afflicted Hollywood's historical films of the late 1930s; instead, Sturges laced it with a dashing, slightly sarcastic wit. When the nasty king enters a torture chamber, he sniffs the air: "Smells like the cook burnt the roast."

Later, a girl asks Villon, "What's an epitaph?"

His reply: "Oh, usually something good about somebody bad — after they're dead."

And later still:

CATHERINE: What a glorious death — to die for France!
VILLON: Well, it's better than some I could think of, but death in any form should be avoided.

Sturges guaranteed the audience's enjoyment by first seeing to his own: the dialogue, sharp and colloquial, reveals a writer relishing the chance to break the clichés of movie genres.

While he worked, Bianca was supervising carpenters in the new kitchen. "Is Bianca living at 1917 [Ivar Avenue] with you?" Solomon inquired on March 3, 1938.

> This is the only address I saw on the letter she wrote me. I think if this is so it is bad for both of you. It is too non-conventional for the United States. It might be okay for Paris or some of the European cities, but many of your California friends might hesitate to mingle very much, under such conditions. With her husband living with your friends in New York and you living with her in California, the situation is rather complicated. I am not a saint nor a prude but I think this is a bit too crude. If you cannot get along without Bianca, marry her and clear the situation.

The situation would indeed soon be cleared, but without marrying Bianca, for in March Preston met a neighbor whose telephone had failed after a heavy rainstorm. She had some flooding in her basement and asked if she might telephone a local plumber.

Louise Sargent, ten years younger than Preston, was born in Fort Dodge, Iowa, on January 29, 1909, and after living several years in California had married (in 1931) a San Francisco sportsman and entrepreneur named Gordon Tevis. She was a tall, dark-haired beauty with magnificent skin, damson eyes, an expressive voice and a highly refined and intelligent manner. Preston was mightily impressed. Their meeting, however, was brief and neither one thought it would be repeated. Louise made her call, thanked him and departed down the hill.

But another coincidence soon occurred. A friend of Louise's heard that Snyder's Café was a popular place on Sunset Boulevard, and she invited Louise and Gordon Tevis for dinner there one evening. Bianca and Preston were present, and Priscilla and Bertie Woolfan. "Bianca was a volcano," according to Priscilla,

> but Louise was just the opposite — very beautiful and very cool and very much apart from anything hysterical. She had a pure, natural, Grecian beauty and in every way she was the complete opposite of Bianca.

141

Edwin Gillette remembered the next meetings between Sturges and Louise. "Her marriage to Tevis was breaking up, and there were no fireworks over that, no fighting about it. She was a very calm, very sweet and very beautiful woman. He couldn't have done better." As for Louise:

> I have no idea what it was that drew me to him, but whatever it was, it was very intense. He had never had a chance to know himself in his younger years, I felt, since he had moved all around, never living in any single place as his mother parked him with one family and then another. That may have been one reason why I had such great sympathy for him at first. And he had great humor, and of course I loved that. Bianca, it was clear, felt threatened. She tried distressingly hard to please.

Very soon, they were meeting quietly and often, and before summer, Preston was most passionately in love with Louise. Bianca, furious, fled to Mexico City, apparently to worry him into begging for her return. Her absence, however, only facilitated more rendezvous with Louise.

"She is tall, beautiful and of angelic disposition," he wrote in a letter about Louise, and to Eleanor he admitted that "she is much too young for me, and much too nice also, but in the meantime what a lovely world this is." The world must have seemed lovelier still when he learned that summer of Louise's uncontested divorce from her husband.

Also that summer, Preston finally negotiated the purchase of his own restaurant, and over the next fifteen years it would be his refuge, his pleasure and his greatest anxiety. At 8225 Sunset Boulevard there was a three-tiered club for sale in probate. For $22,500 he bought it from the Security-First National Bank of Los Angeles, and from the first day he had a name — The Players. He also had a plan: to make it *the* Hollywood meeting place for hearty food, generous drinks, boisterous camaraderie and, eventually, dancing and entertainment. He was, in this regard, his mother's son, and The Players would be his version of the Desti Club of London.

"The Players," as Louise recalled, "was a place where he could be Grand Pasha after hours — that was the main attraction for him." Edwin Gillette agreed: "He liked being the ultimate innkeeper, sort of a Hollywood boniface at The Players." Forever after, it was important for him to have a place he could welcome an extended family, where he could be a cheery host.

But The Players would not be an arty spot, like the Desti Club. As its guarantor and master supreme, he would make it a place for unwinding after work — for himself, most of all. Eventually, Sturges imported from New York his old friend Alexis Pillet, late of Pirolle's, to be chef and manager.

In early September, Solomon and his wife Marie visited Los Angeles. "I admire you very much and have a deep devotion for you," his father wrote just before their arrival. Preston, delighted at the visit, settled them into a rented house at 1227 Ninth Street, near the beach in Santa Monica. The elder Sturges was so taken with the area, in fact, that in October — with his stepson's encouragement — he bought (for $6,500) a three-bedroom house at 363 Twentieth Street, planning to move there permanently after a winter return to close his home and business in Chicago. He was at last ready for retirement, and it pleased both father and son to anticipate living nearby one another. Solomon was also delighted, one evening at Snyder's, to meet Louise, who he thought was a treasure.

Bianca returned from Mexico determined to win back her lover. But this was a vain endeavor, and early that autumn Preston convinced her to move to the nearby apartment he had always rented in her name. This she did with great reluctance, taking along — with Preston's equally reluctant permission — some antique dinner plates and framed English prints. Within days, afraid to break the news that he planned to marry Louise, he enlisted his friends the Woolfans for the task.

"Preston was scared to death of her, and he wouldn't tell her himself," Priscilla recalled.

> He asked Bertie to go tell Bianca that she was going to receive $350 a month for the rest of her life from Preston. That night Bertie and I were to go to a play staged by Max Reinhardt. Now Bertie, you see, was as much afraid of Bianca's temper as Preston was, and so he asked *me* to go along with him to see her.

Then, however, a medical call came for Dr. Woolfan, and to Priscilla fell the burden. A violent scene followed, as Bianca screamed and cursed Preston in four languages and then proceeded to circle the apartment, smashing every plate and framed print that had belonged to her lover.

> I was scared to death [Priscilla remembered], and when Bertie came back he shouted, "Christ, what happened?" There was overturned furniture, glass all over the floor, everything was broken. Bianca was sitting in a chair with her arms drooping. She was spent — even a wildcat eventually runs out of energy, after all. But the place was wrecked! And there I was,

sitting on the floor behind a sofa, shivering and shaking. "Come on," Bertie said simply to me, "I have to get up early in the morning." We left, and that was the end of that.

After Solomon and Marie left Santa Monica in late October, Preston and Louise quietly departed for the Belmont Apartments in Reno, Nevada; he registered in a separate suite as "Gene Eddy," a name perhaps inspired by Louise's best friend, a Hollywood secretary named June Eddy. "He was officially working on a screenplay at the time," Gillette recalled,

> so I accompanied them. Theoretically we worked, but I don't think I touched the typewriter more than once while I was there. They were billing and cooing, and I was somewhat in the way. Then I came down with the mumps and returned early to Hollywood.

On November 7, 1938, in the Federated Church of Reno, Preston Sturges married Louise Sargent Tevis. When they returned to Ivar Avenue, he refused to confront Bianca directly. Instead, he sent Bertie Woolfan to tell her of the marriage and to convey again Preston's offer of financial support for several years. According to Priscilla, Bianca wept bitterly, but without any display of violent temper. Perhaps fearful and perhaps feeling guilty, Preston still rejected his friends' advice to offer Bianca the courtesy of a personal visit, and on November 21 she wrote to him:

> Had I known you were going to get married, I would have gone away. It is too awful and stupid for me to be here now — all tangled up with money troubles and big heart troubles. . . . I want to see my mother and have a good cry. I've been mostly too stunned to cry here. . . . Now that you don't want to be friends, to talk to me kindly, to advise me sanely, I'm lost. If you only knew, I really am your friend. I can rejoice in your happiness and pray with you for the son you've always wanted.

Preston kept his father informed of the details in Chicago.

> Louise and I are extraordinarily happy and life is very sweet. Bianca has gone to New York to see her mother. I am giving her enough for comfort and a few extravagances also.

This news, however, reached an ailing Solomon Sturges. Diagnosed at first with heart failure, he had been admitted to the hospital in November for a week and required nurses at his apartment thereafter. "I am back home," he wrote Preston late in November,

> and getting along very nicely. The doctor thinks I will have to be very quiet for a month. I will not write very much as it is rather an effort. We both send much love to you both.

A few days later, Marie wrote to Preston that there was a dramatic decline in Solomon's condition: he no longer wrote, typed or dictated his usual letters to friends. He was acutely depressed, he refused food and he had a distracted, withdrawn attitude; in fact, he seemed to have lost a will to live. By December, the daily air-mail letters from Marie were more alarming still. Solomon was having grotesque, frightening hallucinations — in one, he shouted that Marie was standing by his bedside badly wounded and bloody. He rarely slept, and his conversation was mostly irrational. For two days, Preston himself was sick with anxiety over this unexpected development. He insisted his father travel west as soon as he was able.

On January 15, 1939, Solomon and Marie arrived in Los Angeles and Preston saw for himself how rapidly his father was failing. He insisted that they stay with him and Louise at Ivar Avenue and asked the Woolfans to dinner to welcome the beloved old man. "He was just a darling, dear man," according to Priscilla,

> and Preston obviously loved him enormously. He was so proud of him, and when Solomon felt better, Preston took him to the studio, showing him off devotedly to everyone. He spoke of his biological father as just that, his "biological father," but when he said "my father" he meant Solomon Sturges, whom he adored. He said over and over that he was proud to bear his name and would never do anything to shame him. This was the love he had always relied on and knew he always could.

Louise offered a warm welcome to Solomon, too. "He was put to bed in Preston's room," she recalled, "and there he remained until he was well enough to move to his new house. But he was not entirely well mentally. Preston adored him because this was the first person who had ever shown genuine concern for him." Solomon improved in this attentive atmosphere, and by the end of January his high blood pressure had dropped significantly.

When he and Marie finally moved to Santa Monica in early March, Solomon wrote to his son and daughter-in-law. Whatever mental confusion he endured had not dimmed his ability to articulate warm affections:

My dear children, I will never be able to thank you enough for your many kindnesses to me during the past six weeks. I do appreciate, however, your thoughtfulness for my every comfort and your gentle way of doing things. I thank you for letting me be a guest at your home during my illness and for your many kind gifts. Really I haven't the words to express my feelings.

Your devoted father

Over the next several months, Solomon's health improved dramatically, and by autumn he was entertaining friends at a lawn party. His confusion subsided, his appetite returned and two or three times a month he was Preston's guest at the Paramount commissary, where he was thrilled to see Hollywood celebrities.

At first, it was clear to their friends, Preston and Louise were a blissfully happy married couple. He relied on her sensitive and intelligent reactions to scenes he composed and which he read to her at any hour of the day or night, whenever he needed comments. "He wanted me there for him," she reflected years later. "He wanted some kind of peaceful stability in his life." This was exactly what Louise provided, with her calm, elegant manner, her poise and her support of his work. There was no unpredictable ill humor as with Bianca, no jealous bursts of angry possessiveness.

Secure in Louise's love, Preston during the first months of 1939 worked on an original screenplay for Mitchell Leisen at Paramount: a tender, uncharacteristically sentimental love story at first titled *Beyond These Tears* and then *The Amazing Marriage* before Sturges finally settled on *Remember the Night*. Throughout the spring, he worked — sometimes literally around the clock — to complete a script that bore resemblances to the kind of wholesome redemption story more typical of Frank Capra. "His work habits during those months," according to Louise,

> were brutal. He worked so hard at night that it was time to stop only when Gillette turned a gentle shade of green from hunger and exhaustion and started to fall off the chair. Preston could do this for days at a time, for although he was extremely lazy, he was also extremely ambitious and he knew that eventually he'd have to turn something out.

The tension in Preston between indolence and initiative was a delicate one, and Louise was on the mark in regarding its dynamics. His prime pleasure was joining cronies at Snyder's and, as it took shape, at The Players, and his first order of business was never business but rather a social circle of laughing, joking friends, sharing a round of Manhattans and a platter of steaks. Instead of working on scripts, he preferred attending boxing matches twice weekly, or tinkering with designs for a badminton court and for a kidney-shaped pool at home.

But these activities required funds. Those funds came from screenwriting, which was in turn nourished by the colorful episodes of his own past, by his gift for improbably comic exaggerations and amusingly offbeat stories. From his earliest years, he had observed some of the most picturesque real-life characters any child could meet, and he never forgot them. Later, he loved spinning tales and spicing characters with fanciful names and antic escapades. He also had a lively imagination, and with his natural ability to command attention and his affinity for a good story, he found he could turn this to a profit.

His writing, then, was simply a congenial occupation, a means to earn a comfortable living and sustain his outside interests. To command respect and (this was an important component in his motivation) to earn his father's approval and pride, he continued to do what paid him well. But he never had the sense that for growth the writer's life requires a strategy of some discipline and reflection. He never developed a self-consciousness or snobbery about his work, but at the same time there was no indication that he aspired to other forms of writing, that the money from movie work could free him to write novels, for example, or return to the theater. He was simply a genial entertainer who was the first to enjoy his own stories.

"Paramount put up with a lot from Sturges," according to Gillette.

> He was always late with material, and always giving excuses. They had to squeeze the work out of him. He hated to work, in fact. What he wanted really was to play around, to entertain freeloaders at The Players, to go out on his boat. He loved to hang around and be the great raconteur, but he had to work to get the money to enjoy himself. [But] he stretched things out until the studio screamed.

When necessity intervened and when a lover, a wife, a secretary or a studio executive reminded him that he had responsibilities, he would be forced, as Louise said, "to turn something out." Getting started was the problem. When he did, the effort generated surprisingly fertile results, for Sturges the inventor would formulate a plot, tinker with it, create a mechanism and make it work. Ordinarily, a first draft contained most of what finally reached the screen. Revisions were made within days of the original dictation, and then again on the set during a rehearsal or camera setup. Sturges's creative speed matched the pace of his films.

*   *   *

Remember the Night has the benevolence and security that came from this happy early period of his marriage to Louise Sargent, and as tribute "John Sargent" is the name of the hero and "Lucy Sargent" is his warm, loving, wise and protective mother. The film has a prevalent romantic glow and its dialogue expresses a directness about love that could come only from a man close to that experience. The story unfolded easily for Sturges.

During the Christmas shopping rush, troubled Lee Leander (Barbara Stanwyck) steals a jeweled bracelet. When she tries to pawn it she is arrested — it is her third offense — and assistant district attorney John Sargent (Fred MacMurray) is called to prosecute just as he is about to visit his family in Indiana for Christmas. The case is continued until after the new year so that a psychiatrist can be summoned. Lee, however, has no money to post a bond. When John learns that she, too, is from Indiana but from a deprived and miserable background, he offers to take her to her mother for Christmas and to return to New York with her afterward.

At her home, Lee's widowed mother (Georgia Caine) has remarried and is not at all pleased to see her daughter: " 'Good riddance to bad rubbish,' I said the day she left." John will not leave her at such a woman's mercy, and so Lee is invited for a family Christmas with his mother and aunt (Beulah Bondi and Elizabeth Patterson), during which time he falls in love with her. When they finally return to New York, she insists on taking the penalty for her crime, and John promises that he will await her return and they will marry. There is no doubt that decency, love and honor have triumphed.

During its first week of release in January 1940, *Remember the Night* grossed the record amount of forty-five thousand dollars at New York's Paramount Theater. "It's an exceptionally good story and screenplay," wrote the *Hollywood Reporter* that month. The New York critics agreed, praising Sturges's breezy repartee and his warm-hearted story. Even the Hollywood censors liked it, ignoring a line that irked their Canadian colleagues and had to be excised from prints shipped across the border: "He may have a little fever for me," Stanwyck says to Bondi, "but it isn't going any further and it hasn't been anyplace, either."

That spring, Sturges was intrigued by the story of a man he considered one of the greatest fellow inventors of modern history, William T. G. Morton (1819–1868), the Boston dentist and pioneer anesthetist. He had read a biography of Morton and was intrigued with its possibilities as a seriocomic biographical film. William Le Baron was doubtful but wanted to keep Sturges content, and so in June 1939 he approved Sturges's first draft of a script called *Triumph Over Pain* (after the book) and permitted him to continue revisions as part of his work under contract.

An even more engaging story was brewing, however — the project Sturges had begun in 1933 and which he had variously titled *The Vagrant* and *Biography of a Bum*. The inspiration for the story — a satire on corrupt politics, bosses and favors — came from the time of Sturges's marriage to Estelle, when he met a Brooklyn lawyer named Andrew J. McCreery who had risen in the political system to become a New York City judge.

> It was he who told me about politics and how [the political machine] got the vote out in bad weather, and [how they got] repeaters to vote under the names of many people who were deceased and others [who were] sick.

Sturges's satiric script went through a number of drafts and revisions before it was ready to show Le Baron at Paramount in 1939. When he did so, he repeated his request to direct it. But in addition to the lack of precedent for a screenwriter to direct his own work, Le Baron was wary of Sturges's erratic work habits and his general lack of discipline.

"When a picture gets good notices," Preston said the following year, "everyone but the writer is the prince. So I decided, by God, I was going to be one of the princes." In 1939, Sturges felt confident that only he could realize the picture, and he made a startling offer: if Le Baron would permit him to direct *Down Went McGinty* (as it was then called), he would sell the script for a mere ten dollars.

> I thought [Sturges said the following year] that the background of politics would be timely in an election year. I also liked the idea of handling comedy scenes instead of heavy drama for my first directing assignment. Another thing is, I'm a little stubborn. Once I get an idea I've got to see it through.

This part of the deal had, typically, a mealtime setting, as he later told a reporter:

> I had been bothering everybody at Paramount to let me direct a picture, but I was known as a writer . . . and I hadn't the ghost of a chance to get out of that category.
>
> Then one day I asked Bill Le Baron . . . to come to my house for dinner. You will remember that I always had a flair for cooking, and the

meal I dished out was an absolute gem of perfection. . . . I talked casually about directing and my wife watched Mr. Le Baron anxiously. He seemed undecided, [but] he said, "I don't see how a man who can produce a dinner like that could possibly fail to make an excellent picture."

As producer, Le Baron wisely appointed Paramount's Paul Jones, a gregarious man who liked Sturges and appreciated his contributions to the studio's comedies. On August 19, Paramount Pictures paid a check in the amount of ten dollars to Preston Sturges, "for full payment for the story and screenplay *Down Went McGinty*." Work on the script continued throughout the autumn, and shooting was scheduled to begin in December. On his way to the studio commissary for lunch one day, Sturges was asked by Le Baron about progress on the script revisions. "I wish I hadn't written it so I could tell you how marvelous it is!" Preston replied.

Just before the first day of principal photography in December, Sturges added a subtle but important tribute in his production notes on *Down Went McGinty*. For the opening sequence in a café, he wanted the band to play the popular song "Louise."

TEN

Precedents

SINCE THE DAYS of silent movies, there had always been a number of directors who provided scenarios or collaborated on their own film stories. But Preston Sturges was the first screenwriter to assume direction of his own original scripts. After this precedent, his Paramount colleague Billy Wilder made a similar transition — as did John Huston, Joseph L. Mankiewicz and Richard Brooks, among many others.

As one of America's most gifted filmmakers, Wilder as director and co-writer created a score of important and popular films such as *Double Indemnity, The Lost Weekend, Sunset Boulevard, Witness for the Prosecution, Some Like It Hot* and *The Apartment.* In 1988 he recalled:

> When I came to Hollywood [from Europe] in 1934, I had my heroes. They were Lubitsch, Sternberg, Stroheim and Murnau. . . . And there were writers I very much admired, whose work was so outstanding, so alive, so modern, so forward-looking. At Paramount I met one of them, Preston Sturges, but I had known his name even before I arrived. I had seen *The Power and the Glory* in Paris six or eight times after I left Germany. Being a writer, I was fascinated by it and was later vividly reminded of it when I saw *Citizen Kane.*
>
> Even before he started to direct, you had the feeling that the films he wrote were basically his. But I guess he felt the directors of his scripts in the 1930s didn't do him much justice, and he wanted to finish the writing process by showing it to the audience the way he intended it.
>
> So Sturges became the first writer who branched out into directing.

We became directors only because we realized that the script could often be diluted and not be paid the proper respect by directors or actors.

Down Went McGinty began production in December 1939, two months after the release of Frank Capra's uplifting, affirmative political-romantic comedy *Mr. Smith Goes to Washington,* with James Stewart as the eponymous hero who treats the government to a dose of remedial idealism. Sturges's bitterly satiric film about political corruption is virtually a counterstatement to Capra's sunny optimism.

The film opens with an epigraph:

This is the story of two men who met in a banana republic. One of them was honest all his life except one crazy minute. The other was dishonest all his life except one crazy minute. They both had to get out of the country.

The action begins in a seedy café in an anonymous Latin American country. We are first introduced to a former American bank cashier (played by Louis Jean Heydt, the original Henry Greene in *Strictly Dishonorable*), who after one indiscretion had to leave the country and his family. He is saved from suicide by the bartender, Dan McGinty (Brian Donlevy), who tells his own story: he was more than a bank cashier, he was a state governor.

His account is told in flashback. In an unnamed American city, an incumbent mayor running for reelection provides free meals to the indigent, who are invited to collect two dollars by voting illegally for the mayor. The cagey, out-of-work drifter Dan McGinty votes not just once but all over the city — thirty-seven times, collecting seventy-four dollars.

The corrupt mayor's political machine is managed by The Boss (Akim Tamiroff) and an assistant named Skeeters (William Demarest), who invite McGinty to join them. "I can use some guts in my business," The Boss says. "There's been too much rod-play in this city. It introduces a very bad element."

McGinty is hired to collect protection money from tenants (a fortune-teller and a bar owner, for example) — "Good protection, too. If it wasn't for me, everybody'd pick on 'em. They'd be at the mercy." He will also be paid a twenty percent commission ("I pay hospital bills, too," adds The Boss, indicating this may be dangerous work). But McGinty does his job well, and soon there are even bigger plans for him: he will become the tool of a corrupt machine. "This is the land of opportunity," claims The Boss. "Everybody lives by chiseling everybody else!" Skeeters expresses the odd principle that "If it wasn't for graft, you'd get a very low type of people in politics — men without ambition."

McGinty is made alderman and is then put forward as candidate for reform mayor. He is then advised to get married, since women now have the vote "and they don't like bachelor candidates." McGinty's secretary is the ideal partner; she is Catherine (Muriel Angelus), a lovely young woman with two children by a husband who deserted her. They marry but agree it will be merely a paper union, unconsummated: they will remain employee and employer. (To celebrate the political venture, they share a drink in his office. "Where's the bourbon?" he asks her. She points to the file cabinet, replying: "Under 'E.' " That would be apt, since Sturges's favorite brand of bourbon was Early Times. It is one of the film's several private jokes.)

But in Catherine's company, Dan McGinty becomes a devoted husband and father and finds himself falling in love with her. Then he is elected mayor and begins a program of municipal improvements for the purpose of providing kickbacks for the political machine.

Soon he runs for governor, but in that office McGinty changes. Awed by his responsibilities, influenced by his wife's goodness and eager to make her happy, he aims to eradicate child labor, tenements and sweatshops — a moral and political conversion for which The Boss rightly blames Catherine: "Aha! Your wife! That cheesecake you married! Don't you know a rib started all the trouble? Didn't you never hear of Samson and Delilah, or Sodom and Gomorrah?"

The Boss is arrested for attempting to shoot McGinty, but McGinty himself is jailed for "something about a bridge I built when I was mayor." With the help of Skeeters, the two men escape prison and flee south of the border. McGinty stops to telephone Catherine that she and the children will be happier and safer if he leaves forever; he also tells her that he has provided for their material welfare. At the finale in the Latin American café where the film began, we see that McGinty, The Boss and Skeeters are reunited, still fighting and still accomplices.

To assure that the on-screen credits would proclaim, "Written and Directed by Preston Sturges," he wrote to John Lee Mahin, president of the Screen Playwrights, Inc. (ancestor to the Writers Guild of America), who in turn wrote to Jack Karp at Paramount: "Since there is no provision in the Basic Agreement for such a condition wherein the director is also his own screen playwright, it seems only fair that [Sturges] should have the credit worded as he wishes." And so it would be.

153

Sturges was immediately relaxed as director. He traded jokes and accepted suggestions from forty-year-old Brian Donlevy, whom he cast as the tough Irish-American, gentle at the core. Since his starring debut in *What Price Glory?* in 1924, Donlevy had enjoyed a successful Broadway career and acted in many films, most recently *Destry Rides Again* and *Jesse James*.

In the role of Catherine, Paramount's casting department sent Sturges a luminous, thirty-year-old beauty named Muriel Angelus. In her native London, she had been a successful actress on stage and in films. She then came to America, where she was enormously appealing in the Richard Rodgers–Lorenz Hart–George Abbott hit musical *The Boys from Syracuse.* Paramount brought her to Hollywood and put her in a trio of costume dramas, but she was wearying of them and of Hollywood life in general when she received a call from Sturges.

"He was so charming and Old World in his manner," Angelus recalled many years later in an interview.

> He was not a quasi-intellectual but a truly expanded man, not cut from the same cloth as the rest of Hollywood. He was cultured and courtly, but never pretentious. And he was so advanced in his understanding of actors and in his way of handling the camera. On *McGinty* everything fell into place with the greatest ease. He had a natural genius for making things right on that film.

The picture was released August 14, 1940, as *The Great McGinty,* after Sturges and the studio agreed in June on the change of title. They may well have intended a reference to F. Scott Fitzgerald's satiric novel of American success, *The Great Gatsby* (1925), which shares the central concern of honesty versus dishonesty and the motif of the spurious value of ill-gotten gains and bogus reputation.

Critics and the public were delighted, and that year the film appeared on every "ten best films" list of American newspapers. Fifty years later it was still a standard for measuring the success of political parody.

At home, Louise suggested that Preston invite the cast and crew of *The Great McGinty* for Sunday-evening buffet supper several times during production, and thus the Sturgeses began a tradition continued over the next several years.

"These suppers were legendary in Hollywood," according to Muriel Angelus. "He had everything just right there, too. I remember seeing an icebox outside his bedroom door on the landing, quite convenient for him. And there was a piano, a billiard table, model trains — all the hobbies of a successful gentleman." The lavish suppers had a corollary on the set, too, where Sturges often brought treats for his cast — a gesture begun on *McGinty* that continued on his next picture. ("Our director," reported an extra, "has just brought candy to everyone on the set. He is a dear.")

But Sturges's generosity with his players sometimes failed with Louise. "He was a very contradictory man," she recalled,

> and there wasn't a day in his life that he knew how to handle cash. He kept wanting me to put aside money so that when the inevitable happened — when he was out of work or bankrupt — he'd be sure to have enough. So he told me to stash away sums he was giving me as household allowance. I replied this just wouldn't do, that he'd have to give me more for those lavish Sunday suppers and for our increasingly complicated household. But he kept me on a very short rein, and it was difficult.

Preston also could not understand that for Louise all of life did not center around his production schedule or his nighttime writing sessions. Just after their first anniversary, troublesome signs occasionally appeared, as she remembered.

> As a birthday entertainment for me, we went to see *Gone With the Wind* on January 29, 1940. Preston was not very admiring of Scarlett O'Hara, Vivien Leigh's character. He said she had no appreciation or gratitude. And then he said to me, "You haven't, either." I laughed for a moment, until I realized he was very serious indeed.

Even before *The Great McGinty* was completed or in the editing room, Sturges had an eye toward his next project — a film version of his play *A Cup of Coffee*, which in January he quickly revised for the Pasadena Playhouse. Then, while *McGinty* went through the post-production process and musical scoring, he dictated a script of *Coffee* to Edwin Gillette; a first draft of one hundred nine pages is signed and dated April 30, 1940 at 4:36 A.M., with revisions through May 9.

A Cup of Coffee had been a favorite project over the years. Universal had purchased rights to the play and first-draft script in 1933, and several times it had been announced as a sure production — with Spencer Tracy as the star, for example, after *The Power and the Glory*. For the next three years, it was always somehow close to filming, but not close enough to be a reality; Universal in fact announced in its weekly studio bulletin on June 16, 1934, that it would be a feature next season. "When you serve *A Cup of Coffee*," Solomon wrote his stepson June 22, 1935, "it will be so strong that at least the audience will be kept awake to see the performance. It has been steeping an awful long time." Finally, Paramount bought film rights from Universal for Sturges to direct it in 1940.

On April 3, Solomon Sturges died of heart failure at home in Santa Monica, at the age of seventy-four. "We never stopped loving each other," Preston wrote shortly before his own death, "and he died in my arms in Hollywood, where he had come to be near me at the end." On his father's bookshelf he found the first published copy of *Strictly Dishonorable*, which Preston had inscribed to the man who had given him the unfailing devotion of his life:

> In sickness and in health
> In poverty or wealth
> Your strength was there for me to lean upon.
> I wonder where I'd be
> If in adversity
> I had not had your strength to lean upon.

Only a week before his own death years later, Preston confided in a letter to Louise:

> Father had very much more to do with the shaping of my character than Mother ever had. I had always a tremendous desire to be admired by him, whereas my Mother's admiration meant very little to me and, having always had it, I took it for granted. But I wanted to be tall because Father was tall, and honorable because Father was honorable, and looked up to because Father was looked up to and admired, and popular with other men because Father was one of the most popular men in Chicago. . . . When he taught me, at the age of four, not to tell a lie, I decided never to lie, and I never have.

Solomon had changed his will. Except for a token legal bequest of five dollars to Preston, he left everything to his wife Marie. "I desire," he wrote, "to make mention of my deep affection for my said adopted son and my full appreciation of him, but because of his ample financial circumstances," no other provision was made.

Preston had, however, a legacy of undiluted love, and that he treasured ever after. It was his only comfort, since he felt, as he wrote to an old army buddy, that "this life is it. Enjoy it, because it is very doubtful that you will have another one."

Estelle wrote her condolences and a lengthy letter of reminiscence. "So much water has gone over the dam, Preston. . . . I think we should make a practice of seeing each other once every ten years so we won't be too shocked by the changes time makes."

With the screenplay for *A Cup of Coffee* complete and accepted (and with a new title, *The New Yorkers*), casting began for a May production. Dick Powell and Ellen Drew were signed, and principal photography began on June 2 on Stage Four at Paramount. Also in the cast were William Demarest, Franklin Pangborn, Torben Meyer, Julius Tannen, Alan Bridge, Byron Foulger, Robert Warwick, Jimmy Conlin and Dewey Robinson — all of whom comprised Sturges's list of stock players, and most of whom reappeared with increasing frequency in his films. In addition, he engaged Alexander Carr (who had played Sam Small in *The Guinea Pig*), and his old friend, actor Georges Renavent, both of whom were finding film work hard to obtain. He also gave the role of a police officer to another friend, the retired and impecunious boxer Frank Moran.

The story concerns Jimmy MacDonald and his girl, Betty Casey, both of whom work at Maxford House Coffee. Jimmy has entered the company's jingle contest, and mischievous colleagues send him a bogus telegram of congratulations that he has won the twenty-five-thousand-dollar first prize. Jimmy and Betty plan not only their future marriage but also embark on a generous spending spree, shopping for gifts for everyone in their families and neighborhood. When the ruse is revealed, Jimmy's job is jeopardized — but only briefly, for the contest judges then determine that yes, indeed, Jimmy MacDonald's slogan is the best, and the prize will be his.

During production, which lasted until July, the title was changed almost daily. By the time editing began it was called *Something to Shout About,* and Paramount finally decided to release the picture that autumn as *Christmas in July.*

Censors at the Hays office, meanwhile, demanded the omission or revision of several lines from the final submitted script, and the objections registered are a fair indication of the absurdities Sturges and film studios had to face in those days of firm pressure from the guardians of public morality. "God rest his soul," uttered by a sweet Irish mother, must not be said, Code administrator Joseph I. Breen demanded ("May his dear soul rest in peace" was the substitution); the word "schlemiel" must not be used, "as it makes the character sound very Jewish" (Sturges substituted "schnook," which somehow pacified the objectors); and the words "stinks" and "punk" were found offensive. On these last two Sturges held firm, pointing to the much more controversial line recently uttered by Clark Gable in *Gone With the Wind* — "Frankly, my dear, I don't give a damn," which, some censors still maintained, would probably cause the fall of Western civilization.

Sturges managed also to retain an amusing shot in the early part of the film, an intercut from Powell and Drew on the rooftop to two snuggling rabbits in a corner cage. This particular visual allusion had been attempted by filmmakers and rejected by censors so often that virtually no director bothered to try to include it any longer. At the preview screening, however, someone nodded and it remained, to the censors' later chagrin.

Sturges on the set was, according to Edwin Gillette,

> very imposing — tall and stocky, with his deep, loud voice and his authoritarian tone. He commanded respect with both his voice and his presence, for he had a great ego.

Perhaps in imitation of the renowned and highly publicized cameo appearances of Alfred Hitchcock (whose first American film, *Rebecca,* had been released that spring), Sturges appeared in a wordless bit in his own film — at a shoeshine parlor, wearing a straw boater and listening intently to the radio. Like the film's character Jimmy MacDonald with his neighbors, Sturges also enjoyed lavishing gifts on his cast and ordered cocktails or beer for the leading players at the end of each day, and he was impervious even to a child actor's prank. When a bit player, a boy named Pinkie Corrigan, hit him in the eye with a suction-tipped arrow, Sturges presented the offender with an Indian costume.

Christmas in July was previewed for the Hollywood press in September and received very favorable notices. When it was released on November 5, reviewers nationwide agreed, praising it as ingratiating entertainment and an indulgent satire on big business. In advertisements for the film, Sturges appeared peeling potatoes ("Genius at work!"), playing billiards ("The man's on cue!"), riding a stationary bicycle and typing furiously. When *Christmas in July* reached foreign audiences, the reactions were just as enthusiastic, as critics from London to Rio found it immediately acceptable to their own cultures.

Even before this good news, however, Sturges had started production on his third film of 1940. On October 7, he completed a draft (and ten days later a revision) of a comedy to be titled *The Lady Eve,* which began shooting two weeks later. Vaguely based on a nineteen-page story owned by Paramount called *Two Bad Hats* by the Irish writer Monckton Hoffe, the script was a complete reworking by Sturges of one he had first dictated in the autumn of 1938. He quickly negotiated for Barbara Stanwyck, Charles Coburn and Henry Fonda in leading roles.

The narrative line of the completed *Lady Eve* was the wildest Sturges had created so far, with slick repartee and a whirlwind action.

In the Amazon, Charles Pike (Fonda) — the heir to a fortune earned from "the ale that won for Yale" — has spent a year pursuing his real love, the study of snakes. He now returns with a rare specimen he names Emma. Aboard a luxury liner on his way home, he meets cardsharp Jean Harrington (Stanwyck) and her accomplice father Harry (Coburn), who plan to exploit Charles's innocence and cheat him of a fortune. The Harringtons are a lovable, classy pair, however, and given to pithy aphorisms ("Let us be crooked but never common," advises Coburn), and Jean discovers after a staged seduction scene that she really likes the naïve Charles. (Inviting her to his stateroom, he asks, "Would you care to come in and see Emma?" She smiles wisely — "That's a new one, isn't it?")

Charles learns from the ship's staff that Jean and her father are crooks and, disbelieving her protest of love, he separates from her. Back in America, Jean plans revenge for the rejection. She arranges to be invited to a suburban houseparty at the Pike residence, as "Lady Eve Sidwich," the phony niece of a former card partner (Eric Blore). Charles's bodyguard (William Demarest) insists she is the same woman they met on the ship, but the rich, lovestruck young man is unsure of her real identity.

Charles finally proposes marriage, but on their honeymoon "Lady Eve" confesses a long, fabricated list of premarital indiscretions designed to humiliate him. He separates from her again, but on the ship returning to the Amazon he meets her as Jean. Still unsure which woman is who, he yields to her embrace at the final fade-out.

"There's nothing difficult about it except standing around all day," Sturges said of his new job directing films. To provide himself and others with pleasant diversion against the tedium of waiting for new camera setups, he assured that there would be guests and even the general public

159

around him at work. His set — chaotic, rowdy, full of last-minute script decisions and sudden insertions of business — was open to all journalists and passersby.

Visitors to this set at Paramount found a very different kind of Sturges movie in progress. Where *The Great McGinty* and *Christmas in July* had been about ordinary folk in common settings, this new project was Sturges's first with an elegant, upper-class atmosphere. There was to be only glamorous gaiety in *Eve* — luxurious first-class staterooms, men and women in formal attire and lavish Connecticut mansions with extravagant house parties. Paramount was giving him his biggest budget thus far for *The Lady Eve* — and his biggest stars — and Edith Head was told to create twenty-five gowns for Stanwyck and fourteen changes of costume for Fonda. (Sturges loaned his own antique sterling silver for the dining sequence of *Eve,* for the sake of authenticity.)

Ever his own best publicist, Sturges realized that favorable reports and advantageous publicity begin with the first day of production. He eagerly cultivated, therefore, an eccentric appearance that itself invited photographers and reporters, and the atmosphere during production was as zany as the pratfall-punctuated, heavily slapstick action. Sturges, who had directed *Christmas in July* wearing a straw boater and carrying a bamboo cane, invariably paraded on this set with a colorful beret or a felt cap with a feather protruding, a white cashmere scarf blowing gaily round his neck and a print shirt in loud hues. (At home and to the studio he wore whatever tumbled from his closet, however rumpled or ill-matched. "One day Louise took a look at me as I was going to work in my corduroy trousers and asked, 'Why can't you be satisfied with just being *one* of the ten worst dressed men in the world instead of the *worst?* Why must you be the leader in everything?' There had just been such a list published in Hollywood, and Bing Crosby put my name at the top.")

The reason for the peculiar outfits, he told visitors, was that they facilitated crew members' finding him amid the crowds of actors, technicians and the public.

The second half of *The Lady Eve* is something of a patchwork jumble. Characters are introduced and abandoned, motivations are hazy and improbable, and there is, finally, too much talk: the action is restricted to an annoyingly cumulative series of slapdash physical pranks, falls and food fights.

In the best parts of the picture, however — the first third — his direction was cannily on target. There is also considerable lovemaking amid the humor of *The Lady Eve* — eight long love scenes with hugging and kissing that Sturges knew would challenge the censor. The first shows Fonda and Stanwyck in tight closeup for almost five uninterrupted minutes, head to head, while she caresses his ear lobes, cheeks, neck, shoulder and he fairly shivers with yearning and fright.

The Lady Eve, with its interlocking, cyclic episodes of deception leading to discovery and honesty leading to love — and back again, with love leading to dishonesty, discovery and the final benevolent deception — is as close to the structure of a Feydeau farce as Sturges came. The comedy of situation, involving an intelligent but bumbling victim (Fonda) and a canny huckster (Stanwyck) is a tableaux of manners with multiple social commentaries. Slapstick, the chase and disguises provide for Sturges, as they did for Feydeau, the classic devices of meaningful lunacy.

Sturges's characters, like Feydeau's, never do or say anything inconsistent with their natures. Both writers directed their own scripts, often telling an actor to omit a line because they discovered the play did not require it and it simply stalled the action. And the aim of both was to entertain, with no goal beyond that. "I try only to please the public, not the intelligentsia," Sturges said in December 1940.

> I've no patience with those who find solace in "artistic success." After all, the theater's idea is to get people inside. If you can't do that, the effort isn't worthwhile. Remember, Shakespeare and Molière weren't above inserting popular hokum in plays to attract cash at the entrance.

By year's end, he had renewed his contract with Paramount — this time for two years, beginning at $2,750 per week for his services as writer, with timely increments; for directing, he would also henceforth receive a bonus of $30,000 per picture. In addition, no more scripts were sold to Paramount for the token ten dollars, so there was also a fee for the rights to his scripts as well as for his services as writer. He had completed three films in 1940, and the bulk of his salary (almost $200,000) went toward the completion of The Players. (In 1941, he earned over $225,000.)

Nevertheless, in 1940 he borrowed $20,000 from Paramount, to be repaid at $1,000 a week beginning June 16, 1941; the sum was needed for the ongoing redesign, reconstruction and redecoration of his restaurant-nightclub. Sturges planned the dinner menus, designed the staff uniforms, chose the paint and supervised the carpenters. His club was opened, reported one town magazine, "so he'd have a kitchen to kibitz in when the mood struck him." He brought Alexis Pillet (late of Pirolle's and Snyder's) to manage The Players, at a salary of seventy-five dollars per week; within five years, Sturges was borrowing pocket money from him. By April 1941, The Players was, according to *Photoplay,* "one of the smartest places in town."

As everyone close to Preston knew, he longed for a son. At Christmastime 1940, there was great celebrating at Ivar Avenue when Louise's pregnancy was announced.

ELEVEN

Prodigal Son

IN THE EARLY 1940s, Preston Sturges was in the international press as frequently as any celebrity. "[He] is the sensation of Hollywood," began a typical article in a South American journal.

> He is the man who is revolutionizing the art of picture-making. Preston Sturges writes his own pictures, produces them and directs them . . . and [he] is acclaimed by the critics as the outstanding director of the moment. He combines the deft touches of Lubitsch with a remarkable flair for comedy, and especially for rhythm of movement.

By February 27, 1941, war was raging in Europe and there was widespread anxiety in America about global conflagration. At the Biltmore Hotel in downtown Los Angeles, the thirteenth annual Academy Awards, for the year 1940, were distributed as usual. A fifteen-foot neon replica of Oscar glowed over the entryway and reporters and photographers jostled for the best positions while movie fans and aspiring starlets overran restraining ropes in their rush for autographs. Descending the grand staircase in the main foyer, the blond, twenty-two-year-old actress Carole Landis stopped to greet an admirer, and to have her poise tested as her underskirt suddenly and naughtily slipped to the floor.

The proceedings had another element of surprise. Beginning with that evening, sealed envelopes contained the names of honorees, known only to two or three board members until after dinner. The previous year, an early edition of the *Los Angeles Times* had prematurely revealed the voting results. This must never reoccur, vowed Academy president Walter Wanger, a producer who appreciated a good thriller.

Inside the vast dining room, movie folks gathered to congratulate themselves on the previous year's achievements: among the notable releases had been *Rebecca, The Great Dictator, The Letter, The Grapes of Wrath, Our Town* and *The Philadelphia Story.* Many of the leading players and executives responsible for these films were present. James Stewart made his way through a crowd of cheering fans; he was later photographed with fellow nominees Bette Davis, Ginger Rogers and Joan Fontaine. Director Frank Capra chatted with colleagues William Wyler, Alfred Hitchcock and George Cukor, while actress Rosalind Russell and producer Darryl F. Zanuck rehearsed their presentation remarks and tested the buzzing microphones.

Promptly at 8:45, there was a call for silence, and from the nation's capital President Franklin D. Roosevelt's voice was heard over crackling loudspeakers by telephone link. For six minutes, he praised Hollywood for its generosity to defense fund-raising efforts and singled out newsreel producers for their service to the country and the world. "In these days of anxiety and world peril," the president said, "our hearts and minds and all of our energies are directed toward the preservation of democracy — especially where it is imperiled by force or terror."

At the podium, Bette Davis then thanked the president and introduced eighteen-year-old Judy Garland, who sang "America." Red-coated waiters then served dinner and finally, at ten-thirty, the awards were presented — first to the winning film editor, sound recordist, special effects supervisor and art director, then to the cinematographer and composer.

Then came the citations for writing. Up to that year, the Academy voted for two aspects of this craft — best original story, and best screenplay; henceforth, there would be an award for best *original* screenplay as well. (Eventually the matter was simplified, with Oscars for "best screenplay written directly for the screen" and "best screenplay based on material from another medium.")

There was considerable tension over that first-time award. The nominees were Ben Hecht, for his theatrical saga *Angels over Broadway;* Norman Burnside, Heinz Herald and John Huston, for *Dr. Ehrlich's Magic Bullet,* about the first treatment for syphilis; Charles Bennett and Joan Harrison, for the seriocomic thriller *Foreign Correspondent;* Charles Chaplin, for his comedy of conscience *The Great Dictator;* and Preston Sturges, for his political satire *The Great McGinty.* A half hour into the ceremony, Sturges's name was heard over the loudspeakers. He had won.

He stepped quickly to the podium but suddenly discovered that he had lost the paper with remarks he had prepared in case of this honor. Ever the unpredictable entertainer, he waited for silence after the applause. "Mr. Sturges isn't here this evening," he said with an expression of mock solemnity, "but I will be happy to accept the award for him." Then he bowed deeply, stood for a moment with his gleaming statuette, broke into a wide grin, winked and returned to his table. But the joke backfired, for most people did not recognize him; the applause was tepid and perfunctory.

Three days earlier, *The Lady Eve* had been screened in a press preview at Paramount, and the advance word — like the public's subsequent reaction — was a director's dream. The film won the *Hollywood Reporter*'s monthly award in four categories (best picture, direction, screenplay and actress) and the Box Office Blue Ribbon Award for March 1941, when it was the highest grossing picture in America. By year's end, *The Lady Eve* had become a major international hit.

Fame did not, however, make most filmmakers recognizable celebrities. "We were leaving the Brown Derby restaurant one night," Louise remembered,

> and our car stalled directly in front of the place. A collection of onlookers gathered, since this spot was an autograph-hound's delight. But when they looked into our car and saw us, one of them uttered the classic line, "Wouldn't you know it — the car stalls right here and there's nobody in it!"

At Paramount, meanwhile, William Le Baron was replaced early in 1941 as production chief by songwriter George Gard (B.G.) De Sylva, always called "Buddy." By this time, Paramount's two most colorful and newsworthy directors were Sturges and Cecil B. De Mille, and in fact a subtle rivalry was encouraged by the studio's publicity department. De Mille was both producer and director (but not writer) of vastly entertaining and financially successful epics (*The King of Kings, The Sign of the Cross, Cleopatra, The Crusades* and *Union Pacific,* and later *Samson and Delilah, The Greatest Show on Earth* and a remake of his *Ten Commandments*).

His films were lavish, the production requirements expensive, his manner notoriously formal and autocratic and his shooting schedules protracted. Sturges, on the contrary, worked much more economically (to the studio's great relief), and De Mille, then sixty, learned that several actors preferred the younger director's casual, noisy, friendly work atmosphere. De Mille socialized at the studio with a substantial retinue of workers, lackeys and admirers; he also had his own commissary table, where Paramount paid for a score of his luncheon companions each day. By spring of 1941, Sturges had set up a table in the studio dining room, too, but with one crucial difference: he paid for whomever he invited. This sprang not from budgetary concern but from Preston's insistence on his guests knowing that *he,* not the company, was host. De Mille and Sturges nodded greetings to one another; there were few extended pleasantries.

The differences between the two directors were everywhere evident. De Mille, who had directed over sixty films in twenty-eight years, wore riding trousers and puttees and issued sharp reprimands to everyone who failed to heed an instruction. The novice Sturges wore loud colors, often substituted a pajama top for a shirt, sometimes sported a bathrobe for comfort, and had an array of mad caps. He often reclined on the floor of the set to direct a closeup, constantly drinking coffee, puffing cigarettes, and instructing his actors as warmly as he welcomed strangers to the set, eliciting their comments and scanning their faces for reactions. (To anyone who suggested a line of dialogue worth using, Sturges tossed a fifty-cent coin.)

But in 1941 the war and the increasing likelihood of American involvement made Paramount's intramural life very petty indeed. President Roosevelt had reminded Hollywood, in his Oscar night address, that films could tell "the unfortunate people under totalitarian governments [about] the truths of our democracy." A number of producers and directors became immediately outspoken and committed to more serious products. None of the filmmakers was more grave about the responsibility than Frank Capra, whose entertaining pictures *Mr. Deeds Goes to Town, Mr. Smith Goes to Washington* and *Meet John Doe* were departures from screwball comedy and which (sometimes sentimentally) celebrated common human decency as the antidote to venality, cynicism and materialism.

Sturges, however, was offering the world comedy. They were, to be sure, satires attacking political corruption (*The Great McGinty*), the madness of get-rich-quick schemes (*Christmas in July*) and the frequent silliness of life among the idle rich (*The Lady Eve*). But the films were insistently *funny* and lacked both cozy sentimentality and a strong message — elements which at the time won Capra very great public and professional support.

Fresh with the laurels for *McGinty* and *Eve,* Sturges immediately began work on a kind of *apologia* for his kind of movie-making; it would be entertaining but unmistakably serious, and whereas *The Lady Eve* had several long love scenes, the couple in his new film would never even embrace. In February 1941 he began to dictate a screenplay called *Sullivan's Travels;* the first draft was submitted to De Sylva on April 22, hours after the last word was typed by Edwin Gillette.

Sullivan's Travels tells of a director of light entertainments who sets out to make a message film, a picture with a strong social commentary, but he learns that this would be denying his own best talent and cheating his audiences.

"JUST FINISHED SCREENPLAY," De Sylva wired Sturges from New York on April 27,

AND THINK IT'S A HONEY. WILL YOU PLEASE TRY TO MAKE TWELVE PICTURES A YEAR SO EVERYONE WILL BE SAYING THAT DE SYLVA IS A GREAT EXECUTIVE PRODUCER?

Sturges's eventual output — eight films at Paramount between December 1939 and September 1943 — was astonishingly prodigious. (Even the prolific, punctiliously organized Alfred Hitchcock, with seven productions completed in the same period, could not match Sturges.) But in addition to the demands imposed by the flourishing of his creative powers, there was a compelling material motivation. The Players needed his salary and invariably received it; the place became an enterprise into which he continually poured good money after bad, and this explains why Preston Sturges — throughout the 1940s one of the highest paid men in America — was also consistently short on funds and in debt for taxes.

At Paramount were the perfect couple for *Sullivan's Travels:* tall, smoothly handsome Joel McCrea, then thirty-five, had long been a leading man with an appealing combination of strength and innocence; and twenty-one-year-old Veronica Lake (who had recently appeared briefly in two Mitchell Leisen films, *I Wanted Wings* and *Hold Back the Dawn*), petite, girlish but sultry, with her long blond hair strategically falling over one side of her face in a calculated "peekaboo" style. Lake very much wanted a leading role, and she seemed just right for the unnamed "Girl." There was only one problem, of which Sturges was unaware. When filming began May 12, she was six months pregnant, although not obviously so.

"Preston Sturges suggested me for the part to Paramount's brass," the actress recalled years later. "He kept hammering away . . . until they gave in. How could I tell him I was pregnant?" She finally did so, at the insistence of Louise, who was on the set almost daily even though she, too, was close to delivery. Preston was livid with resentment, for he feared the more physically demanding moments would be beyond her, and that the finished film would show a pregnant woman. From mid-June until the conclusion of filming on July 21, Lake's condition was indeed noticeable on the set. Costume designer Edith Head was called back, new costumes were designed, bulky coats were used wherever possible, and new camera setups were devised for Veronica Lake — all so skillfully, however, that no one in the audience was aware of the actress's condition. (Her child was born exactly one month after the film's last take.)

Sullivan's Travels take the title character on a curious odyssey. Before the action we read an epigraph that reveals the director's intention:

> To the memory of those who made us laugh: the motley mountebanks, the clowns, the buffoons, in all times and in all nations, whose efforts have lightened our burden a little, this picture is affectionately dedicated.

The action then begins — at night, with two men fighting to the death atop a rushing train. Both plunge into a river, from which emerge the words "The End." We are in a studio screening room, and John L. Sullivan (McCrea) jumps up:

SULLIVAN: You see? You see the symbolism of it? Capital and labor destroy each other. It teaches a lesson — a moral lesson. It has social significance.

PRODUCER: Who wants to see that kind of stuff? It gives me the creeps.

SULLIVAN [to executive named Le Bran, in tribute to William Le Baron]: Tell him how long it played at the Music Hall.

EXECUTIVE: It was held over a fifth week.

PRODUCER: Who goes to the Music Hall? Communists!

SULLIVAN: Communists? This picture's an answer to Communism. It means we're awake and not dunking our heads in the sand like a bunch of ostriches. I want this picture to be a commentary on modern conditions — stark realism — the problems that confront the average man.

LE BRAN: But with a little sex.

SULLIVAN: A little, but I don't want to stress it. I want this pic-

168

ture to be a document. I want to hold a mirror up to life — a
true canvas of the suffering of humanity.
LE BRAN: But with a little sex.
PRODUCER: Something like Capra.
SULLIVAN: What's the matter with Capra?

The executives try to convince Sullivan that his forte is comedy, that
he knows nothing about poverty and suffering, but the successful director
is adamant about changing his style of film. He wants to make a drama
called *O Brother, Where Art Thou?* and he decides to go out and live like
a hobo, the better to learn the hard life firsthand.

At home, however, his butler tries to dissuade him:

> I have never been sympathetic to the caricaturing of the poor and the
> needy, sir. . . . If you'll permit me to say so, sir, the subject is not an
> interesting one. The poor know all about poverty and only the morbid rich
> would find the topic glamorous. . . . Rich people, and theorists — who
> are usually rich people — think of poverty in the negative, as the lack of
> riches — as disease might be called the lack of health. But it isn't, sir.
> Poverty is not the lack of anything, but a positive plague, virulent in
> itself, contagious as cholera, with filth, criminality, vice and despair as
> only a few of its symptoms. It is to be stayed away from, even for purposes
> of study. It is to be shunned.

But Sullivan insists, and the studio capitalizes on his plans by
sending a publicity team along as he begins his travels. A slapstick chase
ensues as Sullivan hitchhikes with a racer and the studio van follows in
wild, unsuccessful pursuit.

Free of the studio accompaniment, Sullivan at first works for two
sex-starved spinster sisters who take him to a triple-bill of movies: *Beyond
These Tears* (Sturges's original title for *Remember the Night*) and two other
melodramas, *The Valley of the Shadow* and *The Buzzard of Berlin*.

Escaping the weird sisters, he again hitchhikes and is back in Hollywood. At a café he meets a girl (Lake) who has been trying to work as
a film actress. "Give me an introduction to Lubitsch," she asks in return
for buying him coffee and a doughnut. "Who's Lubitsch?" asks Sullivan,
in unlikely ignorance. "Drink your coffee," she says with a sigh.

Soon he tells her his identity and offers to buy her rail ticket home;
but first she accompanies him to his mansion for lunch, so that he can
obtain cash for her. She begs to be included in his travels, and he finally

agrees, disguising her as a young boy. They ride a freight train with other homeless indigents, one of whom refers to them as "amateurs."

The tone of *Sullivan's Travels* now changes markedly. The pair live briefly at a shantytown with desperately poor folk, and then they move on to a mission. Life is so harsh for them that Sullivan advises the girl to return to find work in Hollywood, which she does.

Later, as Sullivan is alone distributing money to the hobos, one of them trails him. Sullivan is beaten on the head and dragged aboard a passing train, and when the thief is found dead (hit by another train as he tries to retrieve cash on the tracks), he has Sullivan's identification card (which had been hidden in his shoe). Thus the news is broadcast that the director has met a bizarre death.

Suffering amnesia from the assault blow to his head, Sullivan lashes out at a railroad guard who mistreats him. Taken to court, he is found guilty of battery and sentenced to six years' hard labor, where he is cruelly interned, placed in solitary confinement for minor infractions and dreadfully abused. One night the prisoners are taken to a local church, where they are allowed to watch a Disney cartoon. When he joins in the laughter, Sullivan realizes that this merriment is the mercy that falls on all the poor and the disenfranchised: their moment of happiness provides the grace of endurance.

To be freed, Sullivan then devises a scheme. He confesses to the murder of John L. Sullivan, famous director, and of course his picture appears across the nation's newspapers. This has the desired effect, he is released, and when the studio executives agree at last to allow him to make *O Brother, Where Art Thou?* he insists on making a comedy:

> There's a lot to be said for making people laugh. Did you know that's all some people have? It isn't much but it's better than nothing in this cockeyed caravan.

And with the clear, honest, wiser gaze of the hero and a brief montage of people laughing — people everywhere, from every social background — *Sullivan's Travels* concludes.

The film was clearly a deeply personal one for Sturges, who again appears in a signature cameo — as the director of a Hollywood costume drama Lake is filming when she learns that Sullivan is not dead. Earnest, grave and sometimes heartbreakingly poignant (the sequences on the chain gang, for example), *Sullivan's Travels* is a defense of humane comedy against those preaching "more serious" entertainment.

Sullivan's Travels is an act of faith in the director's own gifts and in his audience's capacity to best respond *through* entertainment in fulfillment of their needs. In this regard, it is perhaps significant that the film chosen for the moment of epiphany is not an obviously human comedy that makes some kind of social statement (an excerpt from Chaplin, for example), but a "silly symphony," a mindlessly engaging cartoon. Laughter per se is both remedy and reward; the rest is up to those who laugh.

"He was," according to Veronica Lake, "sure, confident, and had the critical ability to express just what he expected from his talent in any given scene." And Joel McCrea, who quickly established a fast friendship with Sturges, presented Sturges with a watch engraved with gratitude "for the finest direction I've ever had."

In addition, Anthony Mann, who was assistant director on the film and later directed his own films, recalled that Sturges was a helpful and encouraging technical mentor.

> I directed a little [of the film]. I'd stage a scene and he'd tell me how lousy it was. Then I watched the editing and I was able gradually to build up knowledge. Preston insisted I make a film as soon as possible. He said it's better to have done something bad than to have done nothing.

During the filming, an important person entered Sturges's life. Jean La Vell, a twenty-one-year-old who lived near the studio, had worked in the secretarial pool at Paramount. Bright, brown-haired and petite, with a warm smile and quick humor, she seemed to Evelyn Winters (head of the music department at the studio) better suited to acting than a stenographic career. Winters accordingly took her to soundstages to meet Cecil B. De Mille (who was not available for an introduction) and Preston Sturges (who was).

La Vell had no interest in acting, and when Sturges asked her goal in life, she replied simply that she wanted to earn enough for herself and her mother. "That touched something in him," she recalled years later. Sturges invited Jean to dinner, and then to watch some nighttime location shooting for *Sullivan's Travels* at the railroad yards. Next day, La Vell's superior in the secretarial pool dismissed her for socializing with a company director.

Within hours, she received a telephone call at home. Sturges engaged her as alternate secretary with Gillette, doubling her salary to thirty-five dollars a week. Very soon the relationship was not simply professional but passionate, and the director and his secretary were spending much time together. "He was so bright," she said,

> so full of energy and charm — and it was real, not phony charm. He looked into your eyes and that was it. He just took over my life, and he was terribly jealous. I couldn't buy my own clothes — he bought them for me — and he was terribly generous about that, in fact about everything.

About their relationship, Sturges was not particularly discreet, and soon it was simply accepted that on Tuesday evenings, for example, Preston and Jean were in fourth-row-center seats to watch boxing bouts at the Olympic auditorium, and at the American Legion matches on Friday evenings. "From morning to night," La Vell recalled, "he never let me out of his sight." That year, Preston was less and less at Ivar Avenue.

On June 24, during some particularly tricky location photography on the film, Preston was told that Louise had been rushed to Good Samaritan Hospital. The next morning at five o'clock, a son was born, two months premature and weighing four pounds, three ounces. The infant was so frail that his survival was doubtful, and a week later a transfusion was needed. A month passed before mother and baby were released, and their arrival at Ivar Avenue was marked with a lavish reception. The proud father had arranged for a brass band on the lawn, and dozens of guests raised their glasses in toast. There was never any doubt about the name of a male child: he was to be called after his paternal grandfather.

"I was the child born with the platinum spoon in my mouth," recalled Solomon Sturges IV, who was always called Mon.

> My father hired the head nurse [Mary Morrow] of obstetrics at the hospital to be my private nurse at home, and a suite of rooms was built for me at 1917 Ivar. I don't think there was ever a more pampered Hollywood infant.

Preston was at first a keenly attentive father. "There was a change in him after the fame of his Oscar," according to Louise. "I think he started to know himself for a time. There was a settling in his character, and that may have been connected to his ability to direct as well as to his proud fatherhood."

*   *   *

Editing *Sullivan's Travels* proceeded that summer.

"How is it?" Ernst Lubitsch asked Sturges at Paramount one afternoon.

"Different. It's a combination of smart comedy, slapstick and serious drama with a message. If it doesn't jell correctly, it's likely to be a big flop."

"It's about time!" Lubitsch replied.

Also that summer, Sturges went with Brian Donlevy to see a preview of Donlevy's new film *Skylark,* based on Samson Raphaelson's 1939 Broadway play. The co-star was Claudette Colbert, and Sturges was immediately struck by her charm and her flair for comedy. Next day, he invited her to view a rough cut of *Sullivan's Travels,* and this convinced her: yes, she told Sturges, she would certainly be pleased to appear in a forthcoming film by him; and yes, she agreed that Joel McCrea would be a fine leading man for her.

The script was in progress even as they spoke — a screwball comedy that might be called John L. Sullivan's next film, the replacement for *O Brother, Where Art Thou?* and the recommitment to laughter. His working title was *Is Marriage Necessary?* (perhaps an allusion to the famous comic essay by James Thurber, "Is Sex Necessary?").

Editing one film and beginning to write another, Sturges was working at full tilt. His "idea book," a place for occasional jottings, reflects more entries for the summer and autumn of 1941 than for any other time of his life. "Idea for a De Maupassant type story," one item is titled, with a date of September 7:

> A slightly drunken young man hits somebody with his car. In a panic he realizes that with alcohol on his breath he has not a chance of escaping prison and flees. Tormented by his conscience, he gets up at dawn, buys the newspaper and in the list of fatalities of the previous day reads the name of a man killed by a motorist. Later that day he finds the man's widow, tells her that he witnessed the accident and befriends her. His friendship effects his total reform. He becomes a success, marries the lady and during his honeymoon discovers that her husband was run over by a truck, that he was a useless bum and that the lady herself is four months pregnant.

On September 30, there is another typical entry:

> A very kind-hearted young woman, who no longer loves her husband and wishes to leave him, cannot bear to make him as intensely unhappy as she

knows he will be. She decides therefore to kill his love for her before she leaves him, and the body of the picture concerns itself with her efforts to do this. Unfortunately, by the time she succeeds she has made so much sacrifice for him that she now loves him deeply.

As for Sturges's private life, the months following his son's birth were tricky, as he tried — not very successfully — to attend to his infant son and his wife even while his affair with Jean La Vell flourished.

"He loved the Sturges Engineering Company," Louise recalled,

and he loved to walk around the place, literally petting the engines. He supported the company financially and psychologically, but that was about the extent of it. Later, after Pearl Harbor, there were engineers from the War Department doing something very top secret there.

"He fancied himself an inventor," according to Edwin Gillette,

and although he was simply the financial backer for the work [at the factory], he loved the place. The device that was called the Sturges Engine — a diesel engine with opposed pistons on rocker arms — was really developed by someone else, but because he provided initial funding it bore his name.

He did, however, supervise the supervisor of the place, and he knew who was working there and how the physical plant was operating. As for inventing, Sturges continued to putter, and some of his idle hour fancies reached his films: the electric davenport in *Christmas in July*, with its mobile dressing tables, clock, radio and various gadgets, for example, and the suspended airstrip for planes to land, in his next picture, *The Palm Beach Story*.

Jean La Vell got most of his attention, however. "He was always so amusing," she said years later, "and so very generous. But with me as with his actors, there was only one way to do things — his way, on his time, at his convenience."

On October 3, Buddy De Sylva had an additional task for him: the job of supervising producer for a film called *The Passionate Witch* to be filmed by someone Sturges much admired (and to whom he had already been compared) — the French director René Clair, who had just completed the new Marlene Dietrich picture *The Flame of New Orleans*, his first American film.

Since he was neither to write nor direct *The Passionate Witch*, Sturges proceeded with his own new comedy, by then renamed *Is That Bad?* But he realized that this title was an invitation to wisecracking critics' reply, so the project was finally called *The Palm Beach Story* before it began photography in Paramount's Stage Seven on November 24. This would be his most expensive film so far; Colbert's salary of $150,000, McCrea's of $60,000 and almost as much for supporting players Rudy Vallee and Mary Astor (as well as the cost of several lavish sets) inched the budget to almost a million dollars.

"I'm not trying to imitate C. B. De Mille," Sturges said at the time of the enormous sets for the Palm Beach mansion; it was simply a matter of authenticity.

> As a matter of fact, I am more than slightly imitating my former mother-in-law, Mrs. E. F. Hutton. . . . I assure you it is not an exaggeration. . . . [She] had a place like it. Why, she used to receive guests in the bathroom!

A hilarious pre-credit sequence opens *The Palm Beach Story* — a sequence that (deliberately) makes absolutely no sense at all. A uniformed maid in an elegant apartment is seen speaking on the telephone. Suddenly terrified by something we cannot see, she faints. The action cuts to a vested minister waiting at an altar before invited guests. Outside, Joel McCrea arrives in morning coat; the scene is obviously Manhattan, for the Romanesque façade of St. Bartholomew's Church, at Park Avenue and Fiftieth Street, is clearly visible in a background projection plate. Again there is a cut: to Claudette Colbert in silk lingerie, bound, gagged and locked in a wardrobe closet. Another cut: the maid has recovered and staggers along a corridor, sees Claudette Colbert in a wedding dress and promptly faints again. Cut to the waiting preacher. Cut to Colbert still behind a locked closet door, undressed, kicking to be released. Cut to Claudette Colbert in full wedding gown exiting her apartment and hailing a taxi. Cut back to the maid, recovering again — only to find Colbert crawling through a hole she has knocked out of the closet door. The maid faints a third time! Cut to Joel McCrea trying to dress in a taxicab . . . cut to the preacher . . . to the arrival of McCrea and Colbert at the church . . . back to the swooning maid . . . and back to the marriage service and the on-screen legend: "And they lived happily ever after — or did they?" The years dissolve across the screen: "1937 — 1938 — 1939 . . ." — to 1942.

As the story then begins, Colbert and McCrea are forced to give up their elegant Park Avenue duplex apartment because they cannot pay the rent. (Their names are Tom and Gerry, an obvious reference to the famous cat and mouse of animated cartoons.) A rich, elderly and practically deaf man, who has come with his wife to consider taking over the lease, generously offers Gerry seven hundred dollars to cover her debt and pay household bills. She calls Tom at work: he is an inventor, describing to a potential lender a midcity landing port for airplanes, to be suspended on steel mesh and cables directly over the city streets, with vast slats to admit light and air. Tom needs ninety-nine thousand dollars to proceed. (Sturges had himself suggested such a device to Paris Singer a dozen years earlier, and as late as 1948 he was still petitioning the Regional Planning Commission of Los Angeles for permission to establish something like it for helicopters so he could have deliveries of fresh Atlantic seafood to The Players. The issue died, rejected by residents, the Civil Aeronautics Board and the sheriff's aerial squad.)

Later, Tom returns to Park Avenue to learn, with the predictable suspicions, that an old man has paid the bills: "Sex didn't even enter into it?" he asks his wife. Although he is jealous, we now learn that this couple is on the verge of divorce, and after dinner he offers to sleep on the living room sofa: "You know we don't love each other anymore," Gerry says (with words directly recalling the dialogue between Preston and Estelle in 1927). "We're just habits — bad habits." But the scene concludes as he carries her upstairs. The end of the marriage, it seems, is not planned with much conviction.

Next morning, however, Gerry leaves to pursue a Florida divorce (a taxi driver tells her the procedure is easier in Palm Beach). At Pennsylvania Station she meets the tippling members of the Ale and Quail Club, a team of eccentrics committed to drinking and hunting; they pool contributions for her train ticket. The train departs with her and without the pursuing Tom, but the elderly deaf man reappears at the Park Avenue apartment to give him the cash to fly to Palm Beach to retrieve her.

En route to Florida, Gerry meets the wealthy oil heir John D. Hackensacker III (Rudy Vallee). When they arrive in Florida, he replaces the wardrobe she has lost in a wild mishap on the train, and he invites her on his yacht, *The Erl King* — a typically Sturges pun, playing on the legendary German poem of the *Erlkönig* or Earl-King, and also on the "oil king" Rockefeller, for whom Hackensacker is a clear surrogate. He also introduces her to his wacky, talkative sister, the thrice-divorced and twice-annulled Princess Centimillia (Mary Astor, who somewhat recalls Eleanor Hutton, wooed by Prince Jerome Rospigliosi-Gioeni after her divorce from Sturges). The princess is currently pursued by a bumbling admirer who can utter only one English word — "Greetings!" — and whose name is Toto, "short for Alexander."

Tom arrives and meets the yacht at Jacksonville, thinks Gerry is in love with Hackensacker, and is instantly set upon by the ever-eager princess ("She goes out with anything," says John blithely). Gerry tries to tell Tom that, although they are soon to be divorced, she is trying to convince Hackensacker to provide funds for Tom's airport invention. She introduces him as her brother, and Hackensacker agrees to give her money to leave her husband who, he thinks, is back in New York. The princess, meanwhile, is clearly besotted with Tom. ("You never think of anything but Topic A, do you?" he asks her. "Is there anything else?" she replies seductively.)

The Hackensackers learn that Tom and Gerry are a couple, and Gerry then announces that she and her husband (in a sudden twist ending borrowed from Plautus, Shakespeare and Feydeau) have identical twins. Now Sturges cuts to the conclusion of the manically mad wedding sequence from the film's beginning, and we see the doubles of Colbert and McCrea marrying the Hackensackers, as their twins remarry one another.

In tone and style, *The Palm Beach Story* is squarely in the tradition of Feydeau farce (and at times Sturges shares an unfortunate weakness for Feydeau's garrulity). There are also the doublings and pretenses and the presence of an incoherent buffoon. Sturges's film most clearly, in fact, recalls Feydeau's *Le Mariage de Barillon,* a farce about the confusion of marriages and mates. It is impossible to know if he saw or read the play, but he views relationships with the same keenly cynical Gallic eye.

When *The Palm Beach Story* had its world premiere in war-torn London in the summer of 1942, reviewers, grateful for laughter amid life's bleakness there, were uniformly favorable. That December, the picture finally opened in America, to considerable (if not undiluted) praise. In the *New York Times,* Bosley Crowther spoke for a common complaint about the film: "it is generally slow and garrulous [and] short on action."

Critics as well as a number of viewers began to notice, upon its release, that a number of players turned up repeatedly in Sturges films. By this time, more than thirty actors had appeared in the previous quartet of pictures, and not only the Paramount casting department counted the important regulars: since *The Great McGinty,* for example, William Demarest, Vic Potel, Frank Moran, Jimmy Conlin, Dewey Robinson, Robert Warwick and Harry Rosenthal had appeared in each film. Alan

Bridge, Torben Meyer and Julius Tannen were added in *Christmas in July* and every production since, as was Robert Greig (since *The Lady Eve*) and Chester Conklin and Roscoe Ates (since *Sullivan's Travels*). Esther Howard, Georgia Caine, Elizabeth Patterson and a number of other women skilled in character and comic roles were also signed several times over the years at Paramount. "If Preston writes a role that fits you," reflected Georges Renavent, "he'll move the earth to sign you for it; if you don't fit a Sturges role, he won't risk miscasting just to give you the part."

The stock company not only provided Sturges with familiar, reliable character players who knew precisely what he wanted and therefore facilitated rehearsals and production. In fact, just when his family life began to fail, Sturges acted to reinforce his social support with men and women from his familiar, genial roster.

For *The Passionate Witch,* Paramount's story editor recommended screenwriter Robert Pirosh, who had written the original story and co-authored the script for, among other recent films, the Marx Brothers' *A Day at the Races* (1937).

"This was a dream come true," according to Pirosh,

> since I admired both Sturges and Clair. I was sent down to the set where Preston was shooting *The Palm Beach Story*. Rather shyly I introduced myself to the great man and said I'd love to work with him and Clair. I also told him I spoke French, which could be obviously helpful, and he invited me to lunch to meet Clair next day, and we all spoke French.

Sturges was, according to Pirosh, greatly admired at Paramount. "He was eccentric and dictatorial, but greatly appreciated. The release of a Sturges film was a major studio event, a festive occasion." He also recalled Sturges's "grandiloquent manner, wearing a dramatic scarf or a velvet cloak, and holding court at lunch with celebrities and a retinue of attendants."

Sturges's office at the studio expressed the difference from other contract directors. He had a larger suite of rooms than everyone except De Mille, with a comfortable sofa, sufficient electric fans for comfort, a soft-drink cooler and homey additions — as well as an eclectic library that complemented an already vast collection at home. "There he wittily presided," recalled Nel King, who was an assistant film editor at Paramount,

> surrounded by things for us all to enjoy: old books, new books, works of art, food, drink, gadgets . . . amusing toys, musical instruments, and

always, people. A steady stream of odd, delightful characters enlivened his premises — and how he loved to talk!

Clair and Pirosh worked well and swiftly, and in less than four days a complete outline and treatment were prepared. Sturges liked the treatment, approved it, and encouraged the writer and director to proceed with a full script.

> We had very little contact with Sturges while we worked [Pirosh continued], and then one day he arrived while we were busy. "Well," he said, "I worked last night and I've rewritten everything you've done so far!" That was about fifty pages we had submitted. He simply discarded our script and rewrote it. Instead of keeping to the story of *The Passionate Witch,* he completely changed it. Now it was mostly a comic feud between the leading characters. After we read it with him, he asked Clair what he thought, and Clair replied that he hated it, that it was entirely different from what he had been hired to do, and that if this were orders, he would leave the project at once.

To save the picture, an emergency meeting was called in Buddy De Sylva's office. "Sturges," according to Pirosh, "then gracefully bowed off the film, and we went forward. When it was released [as *I Married a Witch,* in the autumn of 1942] Sturges took no credit, since he had nothing to do with the final product."

Two years later, René Clair reflected on his experience with Sturges. His comments to a reporter from *Time* magazine were pointed and perceptive.

> Preston is like a man from the Italian Renaissance: he wants to do everything at once. If he could slow down, he would be great; he has an enormous gift and he should be one of our leading creators. I wish he would be a little more selfish and worry about his reputation.

With his compensations for writing and directing, Sturges was high among major American wage-earners. The Treasury Department had issued a list of the biggest Hollywood salaries for the year 1940 and Preston Sturges — with an income the previous year of $143,000 — was the seventh highest paid person in film. For 1941, he claimed an income of $155,255 — and listed his occupation as film director, sole owner of an engineering company employing ninety, and owner of a restaurant valued at over one hundred thousand dollars.

Within two years, Sturges would double his income, but he also posted an enormous loss at The Players — of a quarter million dollars for 1941 alone. "He lost everything through sheer negligence," according to Gillette.

> Employees were helping themselves to things, and there were just too many doors. Alex Pillet insisted there ought to be only one door, supervised by himself and with his wife as cashier, the old French family way. But there were so many light-fingered people and so many freeloaders, and Sturges just wanted to throw parties and have friends over and charge it off to the restaurant. He liked being the host.

"The Players seemed just a way to lose money," Robert Pirosh reflected years later, "but that didn't seem to matter to Sturges." Louise elaborated:

> He had several different opinions about why The Players was so important to him, depending on whom he was speaking to at the time. If he was speaking to tax men, he needed a possible brace against the problems of staying in the movie business. If he was talking to someone else, he wanted it as a shelter against enormous taxes. But if he were talking honestly, what he really wanted was a place he could stay after hours — as late as he wanted, since he owned the place.

Everyone's life was sobered by the news of Pearl Harbor in December 1941. That autumn, Sturges had (without fee) assisted on an Army Signal Corps training film ("Safeguarding Military Information"), acting in an advisory capacity to Brigadier General Dawson Olmstead, then chief signal officer of the army. He suggested a few camera setups and offered some memories of his own World War I experience; the only industry record is an acknowledgment letter from Darryl F. Zanuck, chairman of the Research Council of the Academy of Motion Pictures Arts and Sciences, dated October 18. In dispatching a quick task like this, Sturges was not alone, whereas other directors who went into battle — Frank Capra (who was more than a year older than Sturges and directed eleven war documentaries), John Huston (who directed three) and William Wyler (who made two) — worked longer and more immediately in the war effort.

"I have absolutely no desire to get in [to the service]," Sturges wrote in 1942 to S. J. (Jay) Milligan, a co-cadet from his days at Park Field.

Either this war has not been as well advertised as the last one or else there is a great difference between 18 and 44, or else you don't fall for the same guff twice or something. . . . Maybe if people got to be old enough there wouldn't be any war, maybe it is just youthful exuberance, a form of exercises in the spring.

In the spring of 1942, Sturges claimed, as a reason for exemption from war duty, permanent injury to his left arm (because of the smashed window accident during the fight with Bianca). He also cited an "athletic heart, diagnosed 1915," and in addition to family responsibilities he stated he was the sole support of Arnold Schroeder of New York, "a forty-year-old friend who suffered a fractured skull and has been mentally deranged." Sturges was given a deferment until May 1943 and then a medical exemption.

America's entrance into the war in fact sealed Sturges's displeasure with President Roosevelt, whose fiscal policies he already much resented. "Preston was certainly not conservative in money matters," according to Priscilla Woolfan,

> but he was a conservative Republican. Everyone should care for his own money, he felt — except him. It was one of the most complex aspects of his character. He felt F.D.R. did so much damage to the country it would take a century to correct it. "If you don't have it, don't spend it," he used to say, but in his own life he was just the opposite — he was as prodigal with money as one could be.

By this time, a good portion of his household money had gone toward completing the living room at 1917 Ivar Avenue — a parlor-dining expanse that had been extended to thirty by sixty feet, with walls of books stacked on built-in shelves, handsome billiard furniture, a card table, a new fireplace and room enough for twenty seated at dinner. In spite of his high salary and his favorable tax situation, however (with deductions from his two business interests), he could not afford these luxuries. But as Robert Pirosh reflected, "that didn't seem to matter to Sturges."

TWELVE

Madness and Miracles

IN SPITE OF a quarter-million-dollar loss during the previous year, Preston Sturges opened an additional, third-floor dining room at The Players on January 14, 1942. Called The Playroom, it was built over the lower, less formal restaurant and cocktail bar. On an outdoor terrace adjacent and between the floors, Sturges organized another area for drinks and sandwiches, and a casual meeting spot popular with actors, writers and directors was soon opened, too. (By June 1944 there were three floors with three distinct atmospheres.)

"The prices are high at The Players," wrote columnist and professional hostess Elsa Maxwell, "but the food is excellent and the clientele select. Invitations to the parties Preston gives at The Players are much sought after."

The gala first night at "The Playroom of The Players" attracted a capacity crowd of two hundred, including Joel McCrea and his wife Frances Dee, Adolph Zukor, Rudy Vallee and a number of the owner's acquaintances. But rarely did such enthusiastic attendance follow that event, and soon no one was quite sure how the owner could expand his establishment so grandly when there had been, as *Variety* commented on January 15, "a history of barren patronage" and continuous losses. But such objections did not fully consider Sturges's tenacious optimism, his love of the host's role and his habitual, cavalier disregard for balanced books.

That same month, *Sullivan's Travels* opened in London, Los Angeles and New York; ever since, it has divided critics and audiences. "If allowed

182

only one picture, I would be willing to hang my hat on this one," Sturges wrote to the critic Bosley Crowther of the *New York Times* several years later; Crowther had been one of the few to offer the film unalloyed praise.

The world premier, January 2 in London, evoked cautious laurels: "a perverse piece . . . disconcerting but brilliant and disturbing. His films have the rich disorder of a fertile mind," wrote C. A. Lejeune in the *Observer*. Four weeks later, the New York run at the Paramount Theater set an all-time house record: moviegoers paid $75,650 the first week, although it is hard to know whether they were compelled by critical controversy or the appearance onstage of the Glenn Miller band. The basic split in reactions was synthesized by *Time* magazine, which found *Sullivan's Travels* "a confusing mixture of satire, slapstick, drama, melo-drama and comedy."

Before the first month's receipts on *Sullivan's Travels* had been entered, De Sylva advised Sturges that the planned film about Dr. Morton's first public demonstration of anesthesia must emphasize only the biographical facts and avoid both art and comedy. *Triumph Over Pain* (the title of René Fülöp-Miller's book) had been a favorite project for Sturges for almost four years. He was intrigued by (and perhaps identified with) the story of an idiosyncratic inventor who pursued his own way, tinkered with chemicals, defied the establishment, longed for success and yet boldly risked failure with his flair for publicity and his maverick style. "But it just wasn't his type of picture," according to Jean La Vell, who remembered the many difficulties in the realization of the movie.

Hoping to avoid the movie clichés of resolutely pious biographies (*The Story of Louis Pasteur* and *Dr. Ehrlich's Magic Bullet,* for example), Sturges planned to introduce in a prologue the unhappy aspects of Morton's life, the arguments and controversy about his methods and intentions — and then flash back to the sources and stages of the controversy (as he had done so successfully in *The Power and the Glory*).

He felt, however (from working on *Diamond Jim* and *If I Were King*), that an engaging film biography required the kind of humor that was his particular strength, and his outline included bumbling, amusing accidents and slapstick interludes. Sturges saw Dr. Morton not as a plaster saint nor as a hoary, bewhiskered wisdom figure audiences could worship from afar. Instead, he wanted something different — to open the film, for example, with a full black screen and a voice heard saying, "Open your mouth." Then, after a slow fade-in, the camera would have the viewpoint from within an open mouth, with teeth drawn apart, and we gaze between them (as if from inside the mouth) at a dentist.

Sturges's insistence on casting the role with Joel McCrea indicated his intentions about Dr. Morton, for McCrea could well portray the earnest but average man — one who could be by turns sincere, eager, drunk, idealistic, vulnerable and in love. McCrea's angular good looks were part of his open, accessible screen personality, and he knew immediately what nuances the camera exaggerated. Moreover, he never overplayed, and he combined a natural appeal and romantic charm with a slight poignancy of adult confusion.

That winter, the trade press announced that Joel McCrea (then thirty-six) would appear again in a Preston Sturges film, this time with Betty Field (twenty-four), who had been so impressive in the film *Of Mice and Men*. At the same time, Paramount sent Sturges one hundred sixty-three pages of single-spaced research from their library. Throughout March, he dictated and revised his increasingly lengthy and cumbersome script, finding it extremely difficult to counterpoise his complex serio-comic version with De Sylva's respectful reminders that in a medical biography the tone must be predominantly serious. In wartime especially, it was implied, a triumph over pain was no laughing matter. Instead of confronting De Sylva, however — and thus perhaps either successfully arguing his own viewpoint or suggesting the project be abandoned — Sturges simply marched ahead with *Triumph Over Pain* according to his own lights. He did not even propose alternate titles.

Production of the costume drama set in the nineteenth century proceeded from early April to mid-June 1942 at the studio's Hollywood lot, enduring the War Production Board's restrictions of a five-thousand-dollar maximum for the cost of any new sets for a motion picture (excluding labor). Like other studios, Paramount was thus forced to use both existing and standing scenery, and to rely heavily on painted backdrops. (In this regard it is important to point out that audiences' bemused reactions decades later to the obvious artificiality of many background materials for this film, as for others in the early 1940s, owed to government impositions and not to studio sloth.)

By July, a prolonged and contentious editing period had begun, as the studio and the director exchanged memoranda elaborating their varying opinions as to what the final story should be.

The first dispute was over the title: Sturges submitted *The Great Day, Out of the Darkness* and *The Magic Moment* — always preferring, however, *Triumph Over Pain,* which Paramount rejected because it contained one of Hollywood's taboo title words. De Sylva's first choice was *Great Without Glory.*

184

But disagreement over title was the least problem. For more than two years, *The Great Moment* (as it was finally called) was held up from release, edited and reedited under the supervision of De Sylva and his executive production associate Henry Ginsberg.

Sturges's fundamental idea had been to tell of an ambitious dreamer and inventor who is briefly successful but is betrayed by others' jealousy. His screenplay and his arrangement of sequences deftly interwove tragedy and comedy, the better to establish Morton as a recognizably human, frail but determined trailblazer. Unwilling to risk disobeying the established canons for film biography, Paramount heartily disagreed. *The Great Moment,* they insisted, must be a serious tale about an earnest dentist and his philanthropic endeavors, and editors at the studio were ordered to arrange this kind of story from the available materials turned over to them by the director.

The more they tried, however, the more awkward the result became, precisely because of what Sturges had shot. And the more they rearranged and omitted sequences, the more complicated, confusing and emotionally pallid the picture became.

Only after *The Miracle of Morgan's Creek* and *Hail the Conquering Hero* were released in 1944 — Sturges's next (and final) two films at the studio — was *The Great Moment* at last sent out to theaters. By then Sturges had left Paramount, and the studio's version — released in late 1944 and virtually unrecognizable from the intent of the film he delivered — was just what he predicted in a letter to Y. Frank Freeman, dated June 22, 1944: "a mediocre and shameful [film] . . . a guaranteed, gilt-edged disaster." It was the only Paramount picture credited to Preston Sturges that failed to earn a profit. (By the time of the trade showing in August 1944, however, the brouhaha over *The Great Moment* had become a news item, and it was clear to critics who was at fault: "Sturges shouldn't bear the full responsibility for the picture," wrote Harrison Carroll in the *Los Angeles Herald and Express.* "Paramount cut it after he quit the studio, and the cutting is jumpy and confusing.")

All during 1942, family life at 1917 Ivar became quietly, dignifiedly strained. Even before the birth of their son — and concurrent with Preston's continuing affair with Jean — sexual relations between him and Louise had ceased. Since early 1941, they not only maintained separate bedroom suites; they were also leaving notes for one another in the upstairs hallway. In fact, they had virtually no life together. She had one circle of friends, he another.

Louise Sargent was indeed exactly the opposite of Bianca Fernandez Gilchrist, and her calming, serene character had certainly appealed to him in 1938. But in Preston's attraction to so different a woman he may not have realized that it was precisely in her difference from Bianca that Louise was also different from him. Louise valued manners and propriety, fidelity and pleasantly traditional socializing with friends — just what may, to her husband, have seemed unimportant if not deadeningly unimaginative. In any case such a life could not satisfy his need for constant stimulation and diversion — to which he had been accustomed since earliest childhood. (In this regard, he resembled his mother.)

Louise had very often, at Preston's insistence, attended the day's studio shooting at Paramount. She was (like Eleanor and Bianca before her) expected to consider his work as her prime interest, and to consider nothing more significant than his scripts and the progress of his films. He could not understand that she might find motion picture production irrelevant to her own life, and that she was unwilling to cede all parental responsibilities for their child to a professional nanny. When Preston had a problem with De Sylva (with whom he was actually quite friendly, according to Jean La Vell and others) or when Preston had untied a knot in a scenario, Louise was expected to react as if nothing else could be so important.

Most critically at issue, however, was the fact that although he wanted a solid and dependable family life and a constant wife, he also had an incorrigible need to fall in love with women around him. In a song from the musical *Finian's Rainbow,* a character admits: "When I'm not near the girl I love, I love the girl I'm near." The sentiment could have been uttered by Preston Sturges.

"Sturges was always looking for the ideal woman," Jean La Vell reflected,

> but when he *got* the ideal woman — or whom he *thought* was the ideal woman, he was bored, lost interest and it was over. I don't think he ever went that far in the way he thought of me. We were a couple, I was "the boss's girl," but I don't think I was ever a kind of ideal for him.

La Vell was also an efficient and intelligent secretary, and he needed her skills as much as anything else. Sturges still had the custom of rewarding with a fifty-cent piece anyone who invented a sharp line for a script, or a neat bit of business for an actor: "It was another of the things he did with a flourish, for show," she recalled. And during the production of the next film, more of those silver coins were tossed at Jean La Vell than anyone.

In midautumn 1942, Louise took her infant son and his nurse, Mary Merrow, with her for a holiday at the Soboba Mineral Hot Springs in San Jacinto, California. Jean and Preston at once moved temporarily to Ivar Avenue. "And that," she remembered,

> was when I learned what had happened to his mother's ashes. They were kept next to his bed. The first time I was in that bed, he pointed and said, "There are mother's ashes," and I headed for the bathroom — it wasn't something I wanted to discuss!

That September, Sturges sent De Sylva a revealing two-page concept for a film to be called *Love in the Afternoon*. It could, perhaps, only have derived from this period in his life.

The outline described a husband and father, attracted to a multitude of women and blithely, romantically involved with several of them over a span of time. Finally his grown children privately reform him, but his new life of enforced fidelity turns him miserable. His wife, unaware of his prior adventures, tells the children that perhaps their father should stray occasionally: if he will be discreet and quiet about it, she suggests, it may do wonders for his mysteriously depressed spirits. The story ends as it began. It was never developed by the writer or the studio.

Preston pitched himself during the summer and early autumn of 1942 into the dictation of a new comedy whose basis was a personal incident in his New York life twenty years earlier. Among his friends had been a girl named Adelaide Kip Rhinelander.

> She was about my age and invited me over to her house once in a while, although she had no romantic interest in me, nor I in her. She had a different kind of interest in me, though. . . . She was in love with a very handsome young man she had met called Jack Schackno . . . but for some reason she was not allowed to go out with him. She was, however, allowed to go out with me.
>
> It was only a question of time, therefore, until she evolved a little plot which I used with much success in a motion picture called *The Miracle of Morgan's Creek*. In the picture, Betty Hutton, forbidden to go out with soldiers, gets Eddie Bracken to pretend to take her to the movies, then ditches him for the evening and rejoins him only when she is ready to go

home. This was the noble role I played in the life of Miss Rhinelander and her handsome young man. The first time she asked me to take her out, I was faintly flattered, but not for long.

By June, Sturges had welcomed Paramount's suggestion of the vibrant and brassy, blond singer-actress Betty Hutton, then twenty-one and a former jitterbugger who had been with the Vincent Lopez band and was being groomed for stardom. She had met Sturges earlier that year when they appeared in a Paramount wartime musical comedy cavalcade, *Star-Spangled Rhythm;* he had played himself in a brief cameo, screening a film and welcoming visitors to the studio.

Also in that filmed variety show was twenty-two-year-old Eddie Bracken, once a child actor and then also under contract, whose charm derived mainly from his shy manner and an appearance rather like a startled guppy. Hutton and Bracken had starred together in a pair of films, *The Fleet's In* and *Happy Go Lucky,* and Sturges was pleased when casting sent him Bracken for his leading man. For the role of Hutton's wisecracking teenage sister, Sturges happily accepted a contract player, fifteen-year-old Diana Lynn, who had just played opposite Ginger Rogers in Billy Wilder's first American film as director, *The Major and the Minor.*

Sturges then added his stock company of supporting and bit players where possible: "They adored him," according to Jean La Vell, "because of course he kept them working."

The Miracle of Morgan's Creek was outlined by Sturges for De Sylva and his staff in September 1942, and the additional ten thousand dollars was paid for story rights (and one dollar each for two songs he had written: "Sleepy Summer Days," for which Ted Snyder had composed the melody, and "The Bell in the Bay," for which Sturges had hummed the tune an orchestrator then elaborated). But by the time filming began in October, Sturges had discarded virtually everything he had written and was writing bolder dialogue than had ever been submitted to the Motion Picture Production Code for approval.

Only ten pages of script were ready on the first day of shooting; the remainder was dictated at night over the next ten weeks. He was so dependent on momentary creative impulses during the production, in fact, that he was not quite sure just what the title signified until he reached the end of his own story.

In its final form, the picture remains one of Sturges's most engaging and inventive comedies. Under the opening credits, men rush to stop the presses of a small town newspaper. One of them demands to speak by phone with the state's governor, who turns out to be none other than Dan McGinty (Brian Donlevy, as he had appeared in *The Great McGinty*) during his pre-exile term of office.

"Morgan's Creek?" he replies testily to an announcement of some startling news we cannot hear. "Is that in my state? Never heard of it! . . . *What* happened?"

Enter The Boss (Akim Tamiroff), still directing political traffic as he did in his *Great McGinty* heyday. "A little creek should have a big dam," he mutters slyly.

And then we have the (by now almost inevitable) Sturges flashback, his favorite device by which we can follow an earlier story from the viewpoint of its final results or effects. In the town of Morgan's Creek, stern Constable Kockenlocker (William Demarest) forbids his daughter Trudy (Hutton) to attend a dance with local soldiers off to war duty next day. To get her way, she asks the shy young Norval Jones (Bracken) — exempt from service because of a nervous stutter — to take her out to a movie: she plans to abandon him, borrow his car and drive off for a night of revelry with the men in uniform.

Next morning when she returns with Norval's now-ruined car, she is still boozy and cannot recall all the details of the previous night. But there is a ring from a curtain rod on her finger, and then she vaguely remembers dancing with — no, there were so *many* young fellows. And could it be that — yes, she seems to remember going off and marrying one of them.

In the next scene, we see Trudy at a doctor's office, receiving sobering news. Clearly she not only married someone she cannot clearly recall, but the someone is also going to be the father of a baby. ("Some kind of fun lasts longer than others," as Norval soon observes.)

Her sister Emmy (Lynn) is her ally, and she expresses the script's pointed and satiric matter in wartime: "You're not the first dumb cluck who couldn't find her husband. What with the war and all, there'll probably be millions of them. They say they have much the prettiest babies, too." Then Emmy gives Trudy an idea: perhaps they can convince Norval to marry her. Trudy, however, believes this would be bigamy, and she will not exploit poor Norval *that* far.

As it happens, Trudy falls genuinely in love with Norval when he offers to marry her (a situation perhaps borrowed from *Port of Seven Seas*). Norval then has the idea to don an army uniform and marry Trudy under the name of the soldier she at last remembers — Ratzkiwatzki. But at the ceremony before a local justice of the peace, Norval accidentally reveals his own name, and he is taken off to jail as a fraud and attempter of bigamy.

Trudy's father then arranges to spring Norval from prison so they can locate the real husband, and finally they learn that they are free to marry. The "miracle" then occurs: to the consternation of the entire world, Trudy has sextuplets.

As with all Sturges's films, speed itself is parodied: everyone moves quickly but usually ends fallen or unkempt, and success itself is problematic. The action in the town of Morgan's Creek becomes more and more crazy until the finale itself and its triumphantly mad improbability.

For the first six weeks of production that autumn, the company traveled daily for location shooting at the Paramount ranch, where the exteriors of *Morgan's Creek* were built. Sturges rode with his leading players in a station wagon, discussing the day's scenes and rehearsing dialogue. Over several days in December, he perfected three extravagantly complicated long takes in which Hutton and Lynn (twice) and Hutton and Bracken have extended conversation while walking several blocks of town streets. Without a cut, the actors had three pages of dialogue lasting five minutes, as they proceeded along a sidewalk, crossed a residential street, walked another block, turned a corner and continued down a business street for another block.

The shots were enormously complex for these scenes, with the camera on tracks and pulled back by six crew members as sound technicians also walked backward, holding microphones suspended over the heads of the players, and with other assistants (grips) maneuvering three hundred yards of cable and still others engineering lights and reflectors for the proper shading. Over eleven thousand feet of film were used before Sturges had the correct footage for a final four hundred feet. The shots were impressively fluid, and in spite of arguments all during production about the time and cost necessary for their achievement, even Buddy De Sylva had to admit that the sequences as Sturges had designed them were superb. The film was finished by mid-December 1942.

By spring 1943, Sturges was still working without respite (and still cautioning De Sylva and Ginsberg about *The Great Moment*). He was, in fact, ready to present an outline of his eighth film in less than four years. After he and De Sylva had abandoned plans to remake a film version of Mark Twain's *A Connecticut Yankee in King Arthur's Court* with Bing Crosby (they could not obtain movie rights), Sturges conceived an idea for a picture to star Eddie Bracken in a role that was in fact a sequel to his Norval in *Miracle*. In that comedy, he had worn a World War I dough-boy's uniform to masquerade as a modern soldier. Now, at the height of World War II, Sturges wanted to tell the tale of a man wrongly hailed as a hero, a man whose deception is innocent, a man who pretends heroism so as not to disappoint his mother.

On May 30, 1943, Sturges told the story to Jean La Vell, and then together they told De Sylva's secretary. During lunch at Lucy's, a popular bistro near Paramount, Preston and Jean then told it to Betty Hutton, who agreed that it was just right for Eddie Bracken. Next day, Sturges began dictating dialogue, working almost round the clock. In one June afternoon, he prepared a thirteen-page synopsis of the film for art direc-tors and designers, and by July 12 the script was complete and ready for the cameras two days later.

Paramount paid Sturges ten thousand dollars for story rights to this next film, at first called *The Little Marine* and finally *Hail the Conquering Hero*. Subsequently, the studio also paid him the nominal one dollar for all rights to the words and melody he wrote for "Home to the Arms of Mother," a song (with an ironic subtext in the story) in the tradition of sentimental "home fires" songs from World War I.

One problem emerged in the early days of production. Ella Raines, a twenty-one-year-old newcomer, had been sent to Sturges by the casting department for the role of the hero's fiancée. Once Paramount executives saw the first week's rushes, however, they were unimpressed and told Sturges to dismiss Raines from the film. This he adamantly refused to do — not because he was so impressed with her talent, but because by then the Hollywood trade papers had announced her, and he would not fire someone who had been so elated at winning the role and who was working cooperatively with him and the other players. If Paramount had no concern for Raines's feelings, he added, they should at least consider that a change of leading lady after a week of filming — which would also be major news in the trade papers — would give the false impression that the picture was in trouble and that the actress was irredeemably inade-quate. He would not subject her — nor his picture — to this unfair publicity. Sturges won the battle, but the argument caused considerable tension between him and Paramount executives.

Completed by September 1943, *Hail the Conquering Hero* satirizes false military heroism the way *Miracle* had parodied a wartime idolatry of soldiers and innocent, faithful girls at home.

On leave in San Francisco, a group of Marines (one of them is named

Gillette, for Sturges's former secretary then in military service) goes to a bar. There they meet Woodrow Lafayette Pershing Truesmith (Bracken), rejected after a month in the Marines because of chronic hay fever. His shame is compounded by the fact that his father was killed at Belleau Wood during the First World War, and on the very day Woodrow was born. Now, sent off as a hero in the making, he is afraid to return home to Oak Ridge with a medical discharge.

But the senior of the group of Marines (William Demarest) knew Woodrow's father, and he has the idea to send the boy home in uniform and with a borrowed medal — for the sake of Woodrow's mother, and in tribute to his late father.

The entire town turns out to welcome (as they think) a returning war hero. His mother (Georgia Caine) is ecstatically proud, and even his former girlfriend (Raines) is there, reexamining her feelings although she has become engaged to a handsomer man who also has chronic hay fever.

Oak Ridge's estimation of Woodrow is so high that in no time he is put up to run for mayor against the incumbent windbag (Raymond Walburn), whose campaign manager discovers the truth about the "hero." Before they can publicly unmask him, however, Woodrow reveals the truth — and is promptly hailed as an even greater hero for so doing. His former girlfriend becomes his fiancée again, he is acclaimed next mayor, and virtue, apparently, is more than its own reward. The six Marines who had devised the benevolent deception scheme — like surrogate brothers to the hero *manqué* — leave Oak Ridge, accepting the thanks of the Truesmiths and the entire population.

"He's a wonderful director," Eddie Bracken asserted of Sturges at the time.

> He gets everyone relaxed and acting naturally. In four months, I got peeved at him only once, about a long speech [in which he admits the hoax]. You know, his pictures go snap, snap, snap, as fast as you can follow them. That's the way he thought a particular speech should go, too. But I thought it was too good a speech for that. It should be slow and tender with enough time to get it over. So we shot it both ways, his and mine. It's mine that's in the picture.

It was indeed a generally held opinion that, as Jean La Vell said, "Sturges was a fine writer who could visualize everything, but he also needed good actors, dependable actors who could bring their own imaginations and bits of business to the roles." (And that, of course, was another reason he preferred the members of his stock company.)

By Christmastime, *Hail the Conquering Hero* joined *The Great Moment* and *The Miracle of Morgan's Creek* as a trio of Sturges films complete but unreleased. He spoke at the time of making his next picture a musical with Betty Hutton — *The Incendiary Blonde,* based on the life of Texas Guinan, the colorful actress and bordello madam. Paramount, however, was lukewarm to this idea.

But there were more problems in his relationship with the studio executives. That autumn, D. W. Griffith (who had not directed a film since 1931) hoped to direct for the screen a play about Lizzie Borden called *9 Pine Street,* to star his former leading lady Lillian Gish. Negotiations for Sturges to produce and for Dudley Nichols to write, however, were stalled during a tense series of meetings at which Sturges was reminded by Paramount that his 1940 contract called for him to direct two pictures annually, each for a bonus of thirty thousand dollars, dated from the twentieth of December (in addition to his writer's salary, by then $3,250 weekly). He had, however, directed only one film (*Hero*) since December 20, 1942. Paramount suddenly used this point (disingenuously, since the studio was quite satisfied not to have to pay the bonus) to stymie Sturges's production of the Griffith picture.

Most serious, however, were the continuing problems over *The Great Moment,* which, Sturges felt, Paramount executives had by then entirely ruined with their editorial meddling and on which they had not sought his contributions.

Moreover, Sturges had been pressing Paramount to provide him (as they provided C. B. De Mille) with his own production unit within the studio. That request, too, had been stonewalled at the executive level. He was, in fact, feeling as if his successful output at Paramount since 1940 bore no weight in his favor when he justifiably sought to expand his autonomy, and that the problems the executives themselves had caused over *The Great Moment* were being used as a weapon against him.

The tensions and disagreements between Sturges and the studio had, then, been accumulating. Two days before Christmas 1943, the *Hollywood Reporter* announced that he and Paramount Pictures had mutually agreed to sever their relationship at the end of the year, when his contract expired. Two weeks later, at home, he wrote notes for a letter to Y. Frank Freeman. (The letter was never sent, but the notes survive in the Sturges archives.) He outlined his keenest memories:

the dreadful hours with Buddy [De Sylva] after the break, urged by his sycophants, had occurred. The reasonable and depressing talks we had later, both fond of each other, when it was too late to mend the break. My leaving Paramount, which was my home, and sitting as near its gates as possible, the fans and the men, the good-byes at the commissary, the piano — all those things come back to me, far from cheerfully. . . . I grew up at Paramount and I was happy there.

Later, writing to a friend about the arguments with De Sylva and other studio bosses (arguments he referred to as "experiences," and which he found childish and unprofessional), Sturges recalled

my disagreements with Buddy De Sylva, which culminated in my being forced — very reluctantly, believe me — to leave Paramount. I don't know whether you remember the actual issue but it had simply to do with my right to leave the company services if I was unhappy about the cutting of the picture. In other words, I didn't want to be exposed to a long and humiliating series of experiences such as the one I had just been through with Buddy. No man of value could stand it very long. If he could stand it, he would no longer be a man of value. I remember very well the final meeting with Buddy and with Henry Ginsberg. I said I was very happy there [in prior years] without any contract at all. . . . My loyalty and affection for [them] was my contract.

Undaunted and optimistic, by year's end Sturges began collecting autobiographical material for what would eventually be the longest project of his life — his memoirs, which he planned to entitle *The Events Leading Up to My Death.*

For his files, he had written to Estelle, asking the names and ages of her husbands after himself. Her reply demonstrated her humor and her courage, and evoked his admiration and his concern:

It is difficult to remember the exact ages of so *many* husbands, so you must forgive me. . . . My operation last week was for the removal of a tumor from my breast. I spent a bad week beforehand, but thank God it was not malignant. Best of luck and happiness to you.

> Affectionately,
>
> Estelle

Over the next six years, Estelle suffered the debilitating effects of a slow death from cancer, which she endured with a graceful and valiant spirit. Her friendship with her former husband never meant so much to her as in these coming years, even though they seem to have met only two or three times. "Hello, Preston," she wrote at year's end, and then listed some of the places they had been together:

> Sometimes my mind goes back to the Hotel Gotham, to Lexington Avenue . . . to New Jersey . . . to Walton Street, Sheridan Drive, Hotel LeGrand, the Mill Pond, 132 East 39th Street. . . . My mind in fact just did, hence this letter.

When he telephoned Estelle, she was, as usual, cheerful and funny and proud of his fame. Preston had to learn the gravity of her illness from mutual friends.

THIRTEEN

Lovers

A T SIX o'clock on the frigid morning of January 19, 1944, two thousand people were huddled in the pre-dawn darkness, a long, serpentine crowd stretching round two New York City blocks. Occasionally a place in line was held as a man bolted for containers of steaming coffee for himself and friends. By eight o'clock, mounted police estimated over four thousand people on that line and barricades were hastily installed.

When the box office at the Paramount Theater finally opened at ten o'clock, there were eighty-five hundred waiting customers. The day's tickets were gone by noon, and within a week 147,333 seats had been bought and more than one hundred thousand dollars had been earned. The second week, those figures were exceeded, after management had been authorized to sell standing room places. A half million dollars was received within a month. (At admission prices fifty years later, the revenue would be almost ten times that amount.)

Preston Sturges's new comedy *The Miracle of Morgan's Creek* was on its way to historic success as "the funniest film of 1943–1944" — thus the *Wall Street Journal*, not remarkable in those war years for an appreciation of satire or iconoclastic humor. Audiences all over the country agreed. But executives at Paramount, reaping enormous profits, may have worn rueful smiles, for since the previous December, Preston Sturges was no longer one of their profitable director-writers. The regret may have seemed even more bitter in February, when Sturges announced a new cooperative venture in movie-making, a partnership with the millionaire Howard Hughes. Sturges was to be executive producer and Hughes would

196

provide financing. Space was to be rented at the Goldwyn Studios on Formosa Avenue at Santa Monica Boulevard.

"I can't devote any time whatsoever to the motion picture business until the war is over," Hughes told the press.

> Preston Sturges, whose work I have always admired for many years . . . is one man in whom I have complete confidence. I am happy to turn over to him the full control and direction of all my motion picture activities.

As for Sturges: "I am merely going to keep on making movies, just the way I've always done." If the Hollywood cynics said that sounded too simple to be true, they were on the mark.

Seven years younger than Sturges, the Texas-born Hughes was orphaned at age eighteen, when he inherited the Hughes Tool Company and its vast profits from the manufacture of oil-drilling equipment. By the time he was twenty-one, Hughes Tool had made him one of the world's richest men. He settled in Los Angeles, where he invested in films and became a producer (of, among others, *Two Arabian Knights* [1927], *The Front Page* [1931] and the classic *Scarface* [1932]). He also directed *Hell's Angels* (1930), notable for establishing Jean Harlow as a major star. She was only one of many women Hughes placed under personal contract, attempting to control her personal life and becoming her jealous, generous and financially manipulative lover.

Over six feet tall, lanky, handsome, chronically unkempt and almost totally deaf (and a bachelor until the age of fifty-two), Hughes was a lifelong aviation zealot. In the 1930s he worked pseudonymously for American Airlines in order to learn piloting, and subsequently he became a designer, builder and flyer of experimental and ultimately progressive planes. After founding Hughes Aircraft in Los Angeles, he broke the world's landplane speed record (in September 1935) by flying 352 miles per hour before crashing. Two years later, in a Lockheed plane, he circled the earth in a record-breaking ninety-one hours.

During World War II, he continued working on a wooden seaplane intended to transport 750 passengers. The "Spruce Goose," as it was called, was the largest aircraft ever designed; flown once in 1947, it has since then remained a tourist curiosity.

In 1943, still pursuing his movie-star obsession, he introduced the twenty-one-year-old apprentice actress Jane Russell in a film he produced and directed. *The Outlaw*, fancifully based on the legend of Billy the Kid, was remarkable only for its exploitive publicity campaign focusing on Russell's figure. Once the actress's cleavage was revealed, however, the bareness of the film was also obvious, and *The Outlaw* quickly became (in *Newsweek*'s phrase) "a bust in more ways than one." The film was distributed only briefly, withdrawn, recut and rereleased in 1947 and again in 1950, each version more tedious than the last.

Sturges and Hughes shared a keen interest in tinkering with inventions, and each had a reputation for eccentricity and a unique brand of persuasive charm. Physically, they resembled one another, too, each having a large, imposing build and a clipped mustache.

Hughes believed that Preston was the man to supervise his film interests while he attended to his wartime aeronautic projects. The written contracts for their joint corporation (first known as Sturges-Hughes Pictures, then as California Pictures) took most of 1944 to be settled; Hughes Tool owned fifty-one percent of the common stock, Sturges the remainder. No pictures were to be produced nor any loanouts of his services were permitted without Sturges's consent, and on his part Hughes would never be compelled to back a project he rejected. After the pressures he felt to please Paramount, Sturges thought he now would have the opportunity to develop stories and to manage his own studio; and he would draw his salary ($115,000 that year) as his own boss.

"Sturges-Hughes is the beginning of something big," Preston told a reporter in March.

> I turned down offers from several companies . . . to go in with Howard. He has wanted me to work with him since he saw *Strictly Dishonorable*. He tried to borrow or buy me from Paramount, and when Paramount said no he waited till my contract expired last December.
>
> We are starting out fresh but not on a shoestring, [with] as much money as any major company but none of a major company's releasing obligations. . . . I can only make two pictures a year myself. The rest will be made by people whom we shall finance and guarantee freedom of expression.

Among early projects, Sturges planned to make a film based on Joseph Hergesheimer's story *Three Black Pennies,* about three generations of an American industrial family. By May, however, he was telling the press that the premiere production would be an original project to be called *The Sin of Hilda Diddlebock,* starring Charles Boyer. No one at the California Pictures offices, however, and neither the press nor any of Sturges's friends, had a very clear idea of how the Sturges-Hughes collaboration would work for their first production.

Hughes was notoriously unpredictable; he liked, for example, to call his stars and workers in the middle of the night to talk, but after a long pause he barked, "I'll call you back — I have a new idea!" and then he would vanish for days. And in spite of his earlier work in film, Hughes did not have a very clear sense of the complex craft of movie-making, much less of how to structure a coherent narrative. Sturges, on the other hand, had no gift for financial intendance and prized only creative freedom, and both men lacked discipline. All his friends and colleagues (from Priscilla Woolfan to Billy Wilder and others) were nervous about the partnership.

In July, Sturges began negotiations to bring out of retirement Harold Lloyd, the great silent screen comic. There was still no script, just a title (*The Sin of Hilda Diddlebock*): Sturges had no idea of who Hilda was, much less the nature of her sin, just as he had earlier known nothing about Morgan's Creek nor what miracle occurred there.

Harold Lloyd had in the 1920s been the highest paid comic actor in America, a silent clown with extraordinary athletic ability who performed his own wild stunts. He was perhaps best known for *Safety Last* (1923), in which he played a small-town lad who goes to the big city and, to impress his fiancée, pretends to manage a large department store. The humor and the excitement of the film derive from the bespectacled Lloyd's unwitting involvement in all sorts of dangerous physical situations: the image of him hanging from a huge clock on the side of a skyscraper, dangling high over Los Angeles, is pure Lloyd and has entered American film iconography forever. Sturges greatly admired him — not only for his physical courage, but for the attractive alchemy of love, wit, pain and boldness that informed his pictures. Like Sturges, Lloyd had appreciated the comic potential of the chase, with manic cross-cutting and the kind of kinetic energy that gave audiences no time for logic. On November 9, a deal between Lloyd and California Pictures was settled. He would make his first screen appearance since 1938 for Sturges.

That year, Louise continued to host occasional weekend buffets for friends and to receive the unpredictable Howard Hughes for meetings with Preston at odd hours.

"I deliberately continued the custom of the large Sunday evening gatherings," she recalled years later, "as a means of keeping myself so exhausted that I didn't really have time to think, so that his other {romantic} life might blow over if I just ignored it." When she confronted his infidelity and asked why he was allowing the marriage to deteriorate by repeatedly breaking promises, he shrugged and asked,

"Haven't you ever heard of a campaign promise?" ("Life wasn't easy for my mother," their son Mon Sturges said years later, "because Pop was an absentee husband. His attitude was, 'It's nice to have a woman around, and sometimes there's the family, but dammit let me get back to work.' ")

As for Hughes, he arrived unheralded at Ivar Avenue at midnight, two in the morning, ten in the evening — whenever he was taken by a fancy for a meeting. Louise made sandwiches, a batch of oatmeal cookies and a pot of coffee, and Hughes departed — usually without any business conversation, and ordinarily after saying very little to anyone. His deafness, as only a few knew, created the impression that he was aloof and antisocial.

Nevertheless, plans for the Lloyd movie proceeded, and by the end of 1944 Sturges had dictated to Jean La Vell a second draft of *The Sin of Hilda Diddlebock*. By February 1945 it was *The Saga of Harold Diddlebock*, and he told a Los Angeles reporter that the film would open with the final scenes of Harold Lloyd's classic silent comedy *The Freshman* (1925): "It's sort of a satire on football heroes," he said without elaboration.

But there was another project Sturges put into development at the same time — a screenplay to be based on Prosper Mérimée's 1840 novel *Colomba*. Two assistants submitted a synopsis to Sturges in the spring, and he began dictating a story under the title *Vendetta*, about a young Corsican girl who forces her brother to commit murder for revenge. Sturges seems, at this time, to have wanted to adapt a French costume drama, perhaps the better to demonstrate to himself, critics and audiences that his talents were broader than anyone thought. When a reporter objected that Sturges was "going literary," he replied, "Movies or stage plays aren't a form of literature. They are architecture. You build them. You don't write them.'"

Yet there may have been another reason for the sudden seriousness in his style in early 1945, an impulse to consider other than comic realities. "I have been thinking recently," he wrote to an acquaintance,

> of a point of view in living which might be called Living in the Contemplation of Death. That isn't a very good name for it, but it would have something to do with a man admitting every morning that his days were numbered instead of pretending, as the majority of people do, that he was immortal. . . . It would be difficult to be too upset about the quality of the filet de sole with a coffin yawning for you over in the corner, and

missing a train becomes of no importance whatsoever if you remember that you will positively not miss the boatman on the Styx.

The living continued, as hectically as ever and without much indication that there were substantial fruits of such serious meditation as he shared in the letter. That year, Preston's gross income exceeded $450,000 and as usual almost everything he cleared after taxes was spent to keep The Players afloat, to improve it and to pay its considerable overhead.

Interviewer Bob Thomas from the Associated Press visited Sturges's office at California Pictures one day in the spring of 1945 but was turned away at eleven in the morning: Sturges, he was told, was asleep on an office sofa. Thomas returned as instructed at eleven that night to find the office ablaze with activity. From the hallway a phonograph could be heard, blaring the Spike Jones band's rendition of "Cocktails for Two." Odd characters (as if from a Sturges stock company) entered and departed his office — employees, talking animatedly about this project or that film idea. Phones rang, coffee was percolating, a secretary typed. It was the atmosphere of a pawnshop or a betting office. A press for printing The Players' menus stood in one corner, an Academy Award statuette glistened on a shelf, an elaborate model of the sailboat *Destiny* perched precariously on a bookshelf near a ten-gallon hat, a piece of sculpture and a stack of correspondence. From a rattan chair, an assistant was reading to Preston the previous pages of *The Saga of Harold Diddlebock* aloud as the author listened, sipped coffee, smiled, laughed, corrected a line, added a word, omitted a speech, inserted camera directions. Throughout the night, work continued, with interruptions for food deliveries or a quick stroll around the block to dispel sleepiness.

On April 28, Jean La Vell left a note on Preston's desk:

Dear Boss —
    This is it — I'm leaving.
        Jean

The reason was simple and understandable. She had been replaced in Preston's affection by another, a tall, wide-mouthed, doe-eyed and dark-haired siren named Frances Ramsden. In the spring of 1945, invoking his producer's privilege much as Hughes enjoyed doing, Sturges signed her to an exclusive contract at $250 per week for six months.

Born Frances Morison on March 18, 1920, in Cambridge, Massachusetts, Ramsden had a successful modeling career, and her picture could be seen hawking Lustre-Creme shampoo, Lux soap and various seasonal fashions. She then married Paul de Loqueyssie, a fledgling screenwriter.

Ramsden had first met Preston two years earlier, while visiting Los Angeles and the Paramount commissary, where a friend introduced them. "A booming voice rang out from a big round table in the room," she recalled years later,

> and this imposing man with a white scarf round his neck called to my friend. Preston was at the height of his fame and attractiveness. He had his entourage around him, and he was always "on." He insisted that I sit with him, and I didn't know what to say. Now I didn't know who was who behind the cameras in Hollywood, nor did I know anything about his credits or what he'd written or directed. But I did seem to remember something about his earlier marriage, and I asked, "Weren't you married to a Hutton?" And then he said, "You've got a very interesting face," and he wanted to test me. I told him frankly I wasn't interested in movies, that I was about to return home to New York. He said he didn't care what I said or planned, but that he was going to make the test and I'd better be there. Well, I didn't go, and that was that.

By the spring of 1945, Ramsden had relocated to Los Angeles, and one night a friend took her to dine at The Players.

> I was chatting at a banquette with my dinner companion when I heard a deep voice, "Aha, the young lady who runs away from a screen test!" Again he tried to talk me into a test — for the ingenue role in *Diddlebock* opposite Harold Lloyd. I insisted I wasn't trained and didn't want to be an actress. But he said my face was good, my voice was just right and so forth. One just didn't argue with him.

The tests on Ramsden were made and soon she signed with Sturges-Hughes.

Before the Lloyd comedy went into production — and before the agreements between the partners were renewed and expanded that year — Hughes made some of his rare visits to the company. "Everyone had warned [Sturges] against this partnership," according to Ramsden, "even Hughes's own uncle, Rupert [Hughes, the screenwriter]. But Preston thought it was a challenge and it would be lucrative."

After several business meetings, they went to The Players for dinner. Hughes's deafness and his preference for several huge salads before the main course effected a memorable evening Preston documented for the press (much to Hughes's displeasure).

"Aren't you going to eat your salad?" Hughes asked Sturges.

"No. Would you care to have it?"

"Would you mind if I ate it?"

"Go ahead."

"That certainly is very kind of you."

"I can't digest them."

"So can I."

At this point, a mistaken waiter set another salad before Sturges.

"I really shouldn't have taken yours," said Hughes contritely.

"You can have this one, too," Sturges said.

After dinner, Sturges left a slice of cake untouched.

"Aren't you going to eat your cake?" Hughes asked.

"I don't eat cake. Would you care to have mine?"

"Would you mind if I had yours?"

"Go right ahead."

"You know," said the teetotaller Hughes, washing down the cake with a water chaser next to Sturges's whiskey drink, "I don't know why we shouldn't get along pretty well together."

"Preston treated him like a younger brother," according to Ramsden.

> Howard never bought clothes, he was always rumpled and looked down on his luck, wearing sneakers and corduroys. Preston gave him his own old clothes. Also, Howard never carried any money, and Preston would peel off some bills for him. When he dined with us, Howard always ordered the same supper, steak and a baked potato, a glass of milk and a piece of pie. I remember one night — it was Lana Turner's birthday and she came with Hughes to The Players. Howard rose to go to the men's room and never returned. We found out he wouldn't open the bathroom door from inside because he was afraid of germs! He was waiting for someone to come to open the door, and he never thought to use a towel around the doorknob. He was a certified eccentric, we thought.

Preston and his young discovery dined at The Players only on weekdays.

> We had a romance, a real romance in which we were never separated. Every Friday afternoon we drove from Hollywood in the little convertible he bought for me, and we set sail from Los Cerritos Channel, San Pedro,

with hampers of food. We went across to Catalina Island, winter and summer, in his boat.

Despite his new love, Preston missed Jean La Vell, her thorough knowledge of film production, her wit and her practical assistance. And so within two months of her departure he rehired her at an irresistible salary, and she returned on strictly a professional basis.

Finally, in September 1945 *The Sin of Harold Diddlebock* was ready for shooting at the Goldwyn Studios. "I was originally going to call it *The Saga of Mr. Diddlebock,*" Sturges told a reporter, "but I think I like 'sin' better. It sort of kids those other 'sin' pictures, like *The Sin of Madelon Claudet.*"

The opening cast credits of *The Sin of Harold Diddlebock* conclude with the words: ". . . and for the first time, a young girl called Frances Ramsden" — surely the most flamboyant introduction of a new player in the history of movies.

The action begins with the final reel of Lloyd's 1925 silent comedy *The Freshman,* in which college student Lloyd — water-boy for his school's football team — wins the game, by lucky awkwardness, as a substitute player. Then, as Sturges's film seamlessly begins, an advertising executive offers Diddlebock (Lloyd) a job. The story dissolves to 1945, and Diddlebock, at the same job, is fired by the same boss.

Leaving his office, he bids farewell to a young woman at the company with whom he is secretly in love, Miss Otis (Ramsden). He then gets drunk on his first taste of alcohol and goes on a twenty-four-hour spree, returning Thursday but (shades of Trudy Kockenlocker in *The Miracle of Morgan's Creek*) entirely forgetful of what happened on Wednesday.

He soon learns that with huge winnings from a horse race he purchased a circus, complete with wild animals and sideshow. To unload it all, he approaches Lynn Sargent, a banker (played by Rudy Vallee; for whatever reason, the character's name certainly was a kind of tribute to the director's wife). But he wants to sell his own circus. There follows a wild chase with the lion all over town, ending high over the New York streets, with a sequence inspired by Lloyd's *Safety Last.* Arrested, he is bailed out by Miss Otis and learns that Ringling Brothers has purchased the circus and that on "mad Wednesday" he married Miss Otis.

Almost at once, Hollywood knew of the Sturges-Ramsden affair. The *Citizen-News* reported on October 5 that he was having only her teeth "attended to [since] he's mighty pleased with everything else." Sturges was, reported Erskine Johnson in the *Los Angeles Daily News*, "crazy about Frances Ramsden because she doesn't look like anyone else in pictures." On November 8, he gave her a newly decorated mobile dressing room and trailer for the production of the film. She rode the camera boom with Sturges and attended his meetings with actors, accountants and assistants. "While they were shooting out on location," recalled Edwin Gillette, who had returned from military service and resumed his friendship with the Sturges family, "Preston and Frances rode off into the hills somewhere and left the whole company waiting. That really teed them all off." Such escapades — unprecedented in Sturges's working life — suggest the passionate and exclusive nature of his attachment to Ramsden.

During production, Sturges did not work harmoniously with Lloyd — to their mutual surprise. "He's a little crazy," Harold Lloyd told a visitor to the set. Each had strong opinions as to the best method of shooting specific scenes, and for the first month two entirely different setups were arranged for each shot, to test the ideas of each of them. When this became technically cumbersome and exhausting for Lloyd, Sturges generally had his way, but the collaboration then proceeded only cordially and never with the sort of robust, relaxed cooperation Sturges preferred. "I couldn't make suggestions to [Sturges]," the actor said a few years later. "There was too much talk, talk, talk and not enough sight comedy."

"I have just finished with an actor [named] Harold Lloyd," Sturges wrote to a magazine editor with whom he had been on friendly terms,

> who is superstitious about everything, principally about going out of buildings, sets or anything else the same way as he went in. If I didn't want him to come on a set to help me direct another actor, I merely placed a lamp in the entrance he had used the first time and he was blocked. He is an extremely nice fellow as a matter of fact and a little insanity is the charm of the unexpected. He also won't go through tunnels. I suppose when he visited Switzerland he hopped out at the entrance to the tunnel, ran over the mountain top and rejoined the train at the other side.

In early 1946, Sturges renewed Frances Ramsden's exclusive contract. (She was, as it happened, the only actress he ever contracted.) At the same time, he received a telegram from Bianca Gilchrist in Europe. The money he was irregularly providing was insufficient in the light of postwar inflation and an increment was necessary for her survival. He cabled her

on January 7: "VERY FAMILIAR WITH DESPERATE CABLE TECH-
NIQUE FROM LIFETIME WITH MOTHER. WRITE AND TELL ME
MINIMUM MONTHLY FRANCS YOU CAN LIVE ON AND I MIGHT
BE INCLINED TO HELP."

By February 1946, *Diddlebock* was complete and Sturges turned to
the screenplay for *Vendetta*. But just as he tried to construct a coherent
historical narrative, it became clearer to him and to Louise that their
marriage had been irreparably damaged. The Sunday evening buffets were
canceled. They had been virtually the only times Louise and Mon ever saw
him during the last year.

"Preston really didn't live at home with his wife and son by this
time," according to Frances Ramsden. "He went there only when they
had big parties. Most of the time he was at the studio, or at my apartment
on Havenhurst." On March 21, the *Los Angeles Examiner* reported that
Paul de Loqueyssie, "a film writer who recently obtained a three-month
stay in the trial of divorce started by his wife, starlet Frances Ramsden
. . . yesterday gave up the idea [of a reconciliation]."

That spring, the press constantly reported the comings and goings
of Preston and Francie — so the reporters familiarly called her, taking
their cue from him. They were seen all over town together: at the Hollywood Brown Derby, at boxing matches, movie premieres, private parties. She was also seen in glamour and movie magazines — on the pages
of *Charm, Vogue, Glamour, Look, Movie World, Movieland, Screen Stars,* the
Los Angeles Times, Photoplay and *Movie Stars Parade.* Each story mentioned
Ramsden's appearance in the film and her friendship with its director.

"He knew he needed some stability in his life," Louise reflected
many years later,

> but when I discussed our failing marriage with him and told him it was
> leading to divorce, he said he had no desire for a divorce and no intention
> of marrying Frances. He wanted his home and his stability and he wanted
> the other, too. And I thought this was somewhat presumptuous. As for
> our son, Preston seemed to have everything to give him except time. He
> was, I think, a very poor father. He thought he might some day be
> interested in his child, when he was about sixteen or seventeen.

("Louise," according to Edwin Gillette, "was a very calm, very sweet
woman. He couldn't have done better, and why he threw her over I could
never understand. She got a very bad deal in that separation." In fact
Preston had few supporters that year.)

On April 29, a process server bearing Louise's petition for divorce approached Sturges while he was lunching at The Players. "Sturges's [luncheon] companion," gloated the *Hollywood Citizen-News* on May 2, "was Frances Ramsden, the talented young star of *The Sin of Harold Diddlebock.*" The suit charged the defendant (age forty-seven) with an "ungovernable temper and revengeful disposition" toward the plaintiff (age thirty-seven) — standard language of the time in a divorce proceeding, indicating the pair were incompatible. Ironically, the April issue of *Screenland* had just published an article prepared months earlier under the authorship of Mrs. Preston Sturges. Entitled "Geniuses Never Grow Up," it was a benevolent bit of cheerful, devoted-wife publicity, written by one of Sturges's assistants.

The news filled the gossip-famished press that season. *Life* magazine ran the first gleefully vulturous story on May 13, a photo-essay about Sturges's design for a casual line of women's slacks with the headline: "FRANCIE PANTS: Frances Ramsden gets some slacks, Preston Sturges a suit for divorce." Six photos of Francie accompanied the story:

> Preston Sturges, the one-man writer and director . . . is one of the few true geniuses in his field, and an eager, tireless experimenter in others. . . . His latest invention is the "Francie Pants," a kind of dungarees named after the girl who is wearing them. . . .
>
> Last week his third wife, the former Louise Sargent, sued him for divorce on grounds of "mental cruelty." But Hollywood believes that the real cause of the divorce was that Preston Sturges was being seen too much with Francie, who was herself divorced only six weeks ago.

A month later, the *Hollywood Citizen-News* announced that Preston and his starlet would marry the day after his divorce was final. This came as news to both of them. In replying to his wife's charges, meantime, Preston denied an "ungovernable temper" and insisted he needed the house at 1917 Ivar to do his best work. That, too, was a surprise to everyone, for Preston had for several years confined his writing and dictation to his offices. What he could not deny, however, was his handsome income, which that year was already $190,000. In any case Louise always insisted she ended the marriage "for my own sake, to preserve some dignity for myself and my son."

His conduct seemed unusual to longtime friends like the Woolfans. Priscilla wholly agreed with those who claimed that Preston positively worshipped women; and according to Ramsden,

> he never told a dirty joke in his life, nor did he use foul language. He respected women and never allowed people to use bad language around

women. He was very much an old-fashioned man in that sense. And he believed that if you gave your word, that was it. His word was his honor.

This was so widely held an opinion of him that it must have been astonishing to many that his behavior was so uncharacteristically unchivalrous (indeed, almost callous) toward Louise. He expected that she would sustain his open affair with Francie until he decided to return home. He was now as always a Continental husband, a Frenchman *manqué* who presumed he could always depend on a wife to make his official home and tend the child, while he freely consorted with a mistress.

Vendetta, meanwhile, went from troublesome to disastrous. Sturges saw the Mérimée story as an opportunity for satire on man's efforts to meet the postwar challenges of life; the revenge-for-love theme, the romance and the blood feud, he saw as deeper social issues he might want to explore in his screenplay.

Because of the story's European setting, he engaged the German director Max Ophüls, who had also directed successfully in France, Italy and Holland. At Hughes's insistence, Faith Domergue (his latest protégée) was given the leading role. Sturges signed a European camera crew for the Corsican background photography, hired the gifted Czech cinematographer Franz Planer and completely ignored costs that were already — before a foot of film was exposed — reaching a million dollars.

But then a serious accident occurred, and one that changed the course of many lives. On Sunday, July 7, 1946, Hughes crash-landed one of his planes in Beverly Hills and sustained severe injuries — a crushed chest, eight broken ribs, a fractured shoulder and broken nose and multiple lacerations. It was not clear for several days that he would survive. "Hughes was saved," Frances Ramsden recalled,

> by being pulled from the wreckage by the courage of a young Marine sergeant who was nearby where it happened, but Hughes never gave him a cent for reward. Preston, however, gave the man a year's free dinners at The Players.

During his long recuperation, Hughes decided to take a closer look at the movie side of his business interests. He ordered projection equipment installed in his hospital room, he viewed the daily rushes when production began in early August and he telephoned in many suggestions for changes each day. This very much irritated the independent Sturges, who wanted to supervise Ophüls and produce the picture in his own way.

Hughes's major objection, however, was the film's escalating budget. Someone, he clearly felt, had to deny the prodigal Sturges his outlandish spending. *Diddlebock* had run just over two million dollars, and *Vendetta* was going even higher — exorbitant spending for a movie in the 1940s. On his films with Hughes as in his personal and social life, according to Priscilla Woolfan,

> He was spending beyond all reason. One day he said, "Money has no meaning to me, there's so much of it around." He wasn't a gambler and he didn't spend a lot of money on things for himself. But the money went, all right — and most of it was for The Players. I remember Barbara Stanwyck telling him one evening, "That goddamned greasy spoon is ruining you!"

Sturges also reasoned that, since his actual weekly salary with Hughes was so much less than at Paramount — and because most of his income was from stock in their joint company — the lavish dispensing of funds was not exploiting Hughes. But he was indeed unmindful of the production costs. Jean La Vell (continuity supervisor on *Vendetta*) recalled that on several occasions Preston and Frances (always present although not cast in the film) took horses and rode off into the hills for a day's outing, leaving an idle cast and crew — a habit continued from the previous film, and with the same annoyed reaction from colleagues.

Hughes's solution to the financial laxity was to save the cost of Ophüls's salary: Sturges would direct it himself. And so Sturges had the unfortunate task of dismissing the man he said he had so avidly desired as director. On August 20 — only a few days after photography had begun — the cameras rolled again, this time with Sturges calling for action. The budget was well beyond two million dollars by the time the company proceeded with location shooting near Malibu Canyon.

At the same time, Sturges arranged for a sneak preview of *The Sin of Harold Diddlebock* at the Fox Westwood Village theater near UCLA. The film was timed at two and a half hours, and Hughes objected to its prolonged slapstick, the endless sequences with the tethered lion, and the forty-minute excerpt from *The Freshman*. Sturges cut an hour of footage and recommended this trimmed, ninety-two-minute version to Hughes.

"The picture, at its trade showing, got the best reviews I have ever received," Sturges accurately reported to his champion Bosley Crowther on March 25, 1947.

I was very pleased about that until I learned that Mr. Hughes took this as a cue to re-cut the picture entirely, leaving out all those parts which I considered the best.

I begged him to have a showing of both versions in New York and to ask you and possibly Archer Winsten [critic of the *Post*] to give a verdict — but he sneered haughtily at this.

For his own odd reasons Hughes continued to edit and reedit. By early 1947 there were two versions of *Diddlebock*. Retitled *Mad Wednesday* by Hughes, his version was released in 1947 for very brief runs in Miami, Fort Wayne and San Francisco. It was then withdrawn and went as a Hughes property to RKO when he bought that studio in 1948. In 1950, a much abbreviated version was released, but screening in major cities was delayed until 1951. The reviews were negative, and the film was generally forgotten until the restored picture — in its full-length version as cut to just over an hour and a half by Sturges — was released on videocassette many years later, packaged as *Mad Wednesday* but with *The Sin of Harold Diddlebock* on the print; by any name, it is an unfortunate film without many enthusiastic admirers four decades later. Except for supervising two later compilations of his silent film work, Harold Lloyd then retired forever from motion pictures. "I didn't like [*Mad Wednesday*]," according to Lloyd. "So I withdrew altogether."

On Monday, October 28, 1946, *Vendetta* was back at the Goldwyn Studios for interior shooting. While on location, the problems multiplied, as Faith Domergue complained to Hughes that she was not being given enough good closeups, and that her fledgling career was therefore in jeopardy. "Preston wasn't insisting on [the closeups] with the cameraman, on her behalf," according to Ramsden, who was present each day. "And the sparks began to fly."

Ramsden remembered what happened two days later:

Preston was at my apartment on Havenhurst when the telephone rang at seven-thirty that morning. I recognized Hughes's voice at once. Howard said to Preston: "As of this moment I'm exercising my right of taking fifty-one percent of the [company's] stock, the studio is mine. I've closed the set. Where do you want my lawyers to meet you?" Preston said at The Players.

Sturges and Ramsden drove the short distance to the restaurant and waited on the outdoor terrace, and eventually a line of cars arrived with Hughes's lawyers and their documents.

Amusing two of his actors, Ellen Drew and Ernest Truex.

With Henry Fonda and William Demarest, on the set of
The Lady Eve, 1940.

With Barbara Stanwyck
during the filming of
The Lady Eve.

The last day's filming on *The Lady Eve*.

Sturges in a typical moment,
entertaining crew and passersby at
Paramount Studios.

Paramount's most popular
director at the height of
his success.

A publicity photo of Sturges the writer and Sturges the director,
designed by himself.

At work, which also meant at play.

With Claudette Colbert, filming *The Palm Beach Story*.

With Betty Hutton and Eddie Bracken, on the set of
The Miracle of Morgan's Creek.

Jean La Vell.

Working on the ill-fated *Vendetta*, 1946. Jean La Vell holds the script; at far left, director Max Ophüls; at center (bald, wearing white shirt) cinematographer Franz Planer.

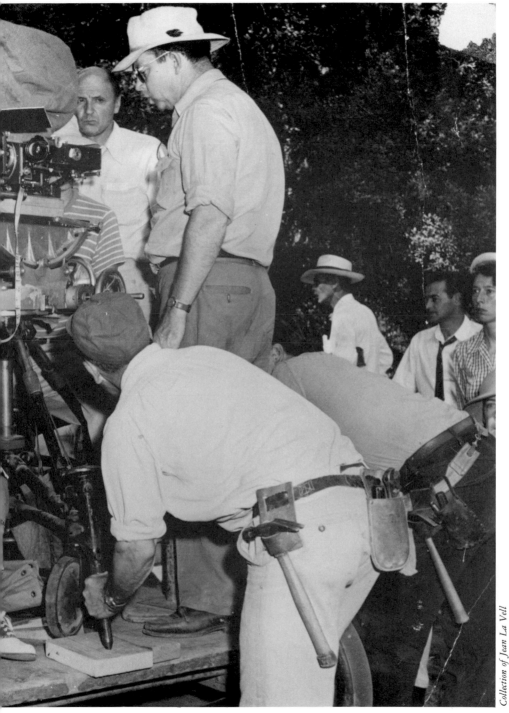

With director Ernst Lubitsch,
dining at The Players,
about 1945.

Frances Ramsden, 1945.

With Mon, during the filming of *Unfaithfully Yours,* 1948.

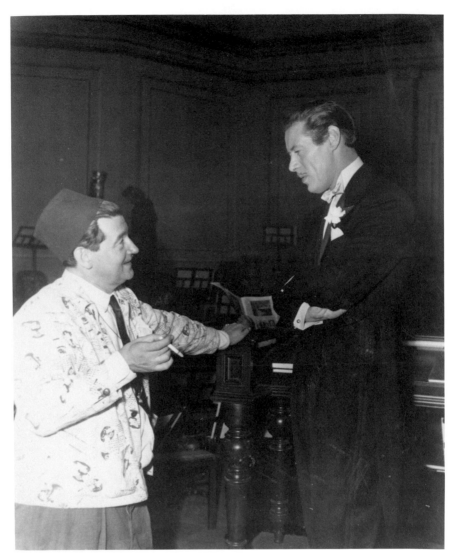

Wearing a red fez while directing Rex Harrison in
Unfaithfully Yours.

With fellow eccentric
Raymond Duncan, brother
of Isadora.

Anne Margaret (Sandy)
Nagle at the time of her
marriage to Preston Sturges,
1951.

Solomon Sturges, not long before his death.

Sandy and Preston with little Preston, London, 1954.

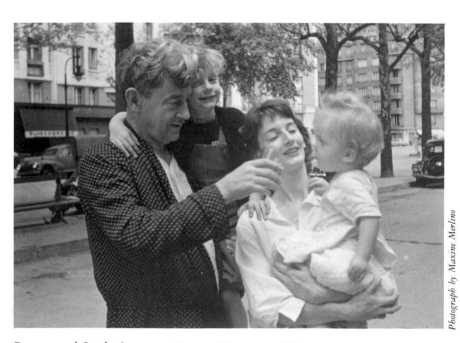

Preston and Sandy Sturges with sons Preston and Thomas — Paris, spring of 1957.

Preston Sturges in Paris, 1957.

Preston defused the situation [Ramsden continued] by charming them — offering them drinks at ten in the morning. He signed the papers in the manner of a *grand seigneur*, and they left. And with that he turned and said, "Well, that takes care of that, doesn't it?" Then he turned to me and said, "Come on, let's go sailing." And off we went.

Thus ended, after almost three years, one of the most publicized, least productive partnerships in the history of the American movie business.

The press was certainly indebted to Sturges that year, for here was another major story. Louella Parsons was first to break the news, in the *Los Angeles Examiner* next day. Sturges, it was reported, was bounced from *Vendetta* for overspending. And other angles were listed in newspapers over the next several days. Hughes had to retrench on film costs because of a major strike at TWA, of which he was major stockholder. There was also trouble at Hughes Aircraft, as the government had recently canceled a number of major contracts.

Hughes assumed control of the picture himself. He did not, however, direct the film (as he had *The Outlaw,* from which he dismissed Howard Hawks). Instead, Stuart Heisler was engaged to resume direction of *Vendetta* on December 12, with a new screenplay by W. R. Burnett; later, after continual difficulty with this apparently doomed project, Heisler was replaced by Mel Ferrer. *Vendetta* was finally released quietly the day after Christmas 1950 and died almost at once. Correctly, it nowhere bore a credit to Sturges, whose script has been entirely replaced and whose scenes had been wholly excised.

"I became an independent producer to get away from supervision," Sturges told the *New York Herald-Tribune* two weeks later.

> When Mr. Hughes made suggestions with which I disagreed, as he had a perfect right to do, I rejected them. When I rejected the last one, he remembered that he had an option to take control of the company and he took over. So I left.

All that autumn of 1946, the relationship with Ramsden turned murky and unstable. In his unpublished memoir years later, he wrote that "things got so bad after a while that when I went over to her house I never knew whether I was going to be greeted with a hug or a nightpot over my head," and the mercurial changes in the affair were documented in the press in as merry detail as the Hughes affair. "Preston Sturges and Frances Ramsden are back together again in spite of all those rumors," reported the *Beverly Hills Bulletin* breathlessly on October 10. " 'We'll probably always fight,' they say, adding, 'but we'll always make up again.' It's love, if you know what we mean." Within a week another tiff was reported, but then "Preston Sturges and Frances Ramsden are speaking again," trumpeted the *Hollywood Citizen-News* on November 9. And so it went.

Rather like his relationship with Bianca a decade earlier, Preston's with Ramsden thrived on melodrama. As of November 14, however, Preston and Frances were enjoying a pleasant interval, and he invited her to join him on his first return trip to New York since 1932. (Sturges's only departures from Southern California since that year had been for the Honolulu yacht race of 1936 and to Nevada with Louise in 1938.)

"Preston Sturges is showing the town to Frances Ramsden," reported Ed Sullivan in his *New York Daily News* column on November 21. Henceforth he would, Sturges told reporters, work only with major studios. He intended, he went on, to remain in Hollywood a half year and to spend the remainder filming with producers in Britain, France and Italy. Hughes, he said sarcastically, was "a fine partner until his activities as a plane manufacturer ceased taking up all his time."

After a month of party-going, Sturges and Ramsden departed for Los Angeles; he, however, returned via Chicago. Chronic chest pains and frequent breathing problems prompted him to check in to the Albert Merritt Billings Hospital for a complete physical examination. After three days, Dr. Robert G. Block pronounced him generally in good health, after advising him to shed a few of his 211 pounds and warning that five packs of cigarettes daily was perhaps excessive. ("He was such a heavy smoker," Priscilla Woolfan recalled, "and Bertie always tried to get him to stop, but no use. He was convinced that smoking killed Preston.")

Making good on his announced intention to work only for major studios, Sturges accepted an offer from Darryl F. Zanuck in early 1947 to come to Twentieth Century–Fox. He would receive a salary of $6,325 a week, with an increment to $7,825 on contract renewal that autumn. The studio paid him $370,000 that year — the third largest income in the nation, according to the Treasury Department — more than that claimed by either Henry Ford II or William Randolph Hearst. Since The Players was losing vast sums of money that year, the high income was very welcome in offsetting the restaurant's debts. In 1948, Sturges's salary exceeded $400,000; after taxes and The Players he was still in debt.

For his first film, there was quick agreement on a leading lady, if not on a project. Betty Grable was Fox's supreme contract star. A buoyant blonde with a superb complexion and an attractive figure (and with legs insured for a million dollars), she was the most famous pin-up girl during World War II. She was also the highest paid performer in films in the late 1940s (her 1946 salary was $208,000) and was the star of Fox's most lavish musicals (among them *Footlight Serenade, Springtime in the Rockies, Pin-up Girl* and *The Dolly Sisters*). Zanuck, ignoring Sturges's preference to create his own original stories, then decided that Sturges would direct her in a screen version of a story Zanuck had already purchased. This was "The Lady from Laredo" by Earl Felton, the story of a hard-drinking, chain-smoking, gambling swindler who is arrested on a train. It crashes and she escapes, taking the identity of a dead passenger. She then teams up with both a thief and a nasty fellow who blackmails her into marriage.

There would, of course, have to be major changes to turn the story into a musical comedy suitable for Grable's popular image, and Sturges began dictating the dialogue for what he called *The Blonde from Bashful Bend*.

Interruptions and distractions occurred, however, and Zanuck began to fret. At Fox, rumors circulated that Sturges found the entire story unappealing. "It was the truth," according to Priscilla Woolfan.

> Zanuck wanted him to do the same thing for Betty Grable that Preston had done for Betty Hutton at Paramount. In fact Preston wanted to *be* at Paramount. And he didn't want to do this Grable film at all — he hated that assignment. He wanted to make his own films from his own stories.

In addition to his indifference to the story, there was his divorce case. "The fact that we are separating is surely my fault rather than [Louise's]," Preston admitted, and he made no reply to the statement made by her through attorneys:

> Since 1941, he has been remaining increasingly away from our home. When I complained he would tell me that his work required stimulating company. He said my presence inhibited him and he didn't want to be known as a husband. He would stay out all night and said I had no right to question him. In the last two years he was home only on Sunday evenings when I entertained his friends.

An uncontested divorce was finally granted in November 1947, and Preston and Louise jointly signed the papers on the ninth anniversary of their wedding. She was to receive twenty percent of Preston's income, up to $350 weekly and forty-five dollars more for Mon — amounts that were

213

rarely paid out after 1952. Occasionally she did receive some money, but irregularly and never the entire stipulated amount.

This failure was not due to malice, but to his simple inability to come up with the funds. "He never paid for Mon's schooling," Louise said years later. "That had to come out of the very modest settlement I received. But I took my son and went to Europe, and we managed there, where living was not so expensive after the war."

Their son, then six, later recalled:

> As for the divorce, I didn't know my parents were divorced until I was about twelve. I just accepted their separation as part of life. He was usually away when I was young, that was all, and then Mother and I were in Europe.

By summer 1947, Zanuck was anxious to have a script to show Grable. "I spritz dialogue like seltzer water once I know where I'm going," Sturges wrote to his boss in a memorandum on July 21. "The French playwright Jean Racine, when asked how his new play was coming, replied happily: 'It is all finished, I have nothing more to do but write it down.' "

He knew the story and the characters, Sturges added, and he had looked at every previous Grable movie. As for Zanuck's suggestion that *The Blonde from Bashful Bend* was too long a title ("How about [the character's nickname] *Freddie?*"), Sturges cheekily counterproposed *The Beautiful Blonde from Bashful Bend.* Remarkably, the studio eventually fixed that as the title.

Sturges continued writing the script and Zanuck objected — to the "extraneous laughs" in it, most of all. Zanuck then informed him that the film, which was to have been in Technicolor, would have to be shot in black and white because there was no foreign market in 1947 to offset the high cost of color. Sturges (who had looked forward to directing his first Technicolor film) was so appalled at this news that he recommended postponing the project and proceeding with another. On October 21, *The Blonde from Bashful Bend* was officially postponed and Sturges began a story he said was about "the effect of music on a man's mind."

FOURTEEN

Transfer of Affects

T HE IDEA that certain kinds of music arouse certain images as well as feelings had first been demonstrated to Preston Sturges when he was working, in December 1932, on *The Power and the Glory*. As he wrote, a sequence took an entirely different direction from what he had originally intended. He then realized that he was being guided by music floating in from a radio in an adjacent room. Sturges had developed a variation of this treatment of subjectivity in 1941:

> We usually see ourselves as the hero or heroine of novels. Consequently one could see a family reading and then see what each was reading ACTED OUT with the reader as hero or heroine. Their real lives would be contrasted with the subject they were reading.

Now, however, Sturges was creating the story of a pathologically jealous conductor who, believing his wife guilty of infidelity, imagines ways of dealing with this, each inspired by a different style of music he conducts. Joseph Breen at the Motion Picture Production Code office rejected the titled *Lover in Law* and *Improper Relations,* and *Symphony Story* was temporarily used before Sturges finally received approval for *Unfaithfully Yours,* borrowing the title from his own unproduced 1932 farce. Zanuck, who had successfully teamed Rex Harrison and Gene Tierney in *The Ghost and Mrs. Muir,* decided to reteam them.

By early February 1948, Preston Sturges's screenplay for *Unfaithfully Yours* was complete. On the tenth, after reading it in one night, Gene Tierney begged Darryl F. Zanuck for a different assignment. Tierney had enjoyed considerable acclaim for her work in *Laura, Leave Her to Heaven* and *The Razor's Edge,* and she understood immediately that *Unfaithfully Yours* was entirely the leading man's picture. Zanuck could have forced her to acquiesce, but he felt that would have alienated her and very likely would have diminished her performance. Instead, he assigned it to Linda Darnell, a sultry brunette who after a series of supporting roles had starred in the recently released *Forever Amber.*

The film was in production from February 18 to April 20, and it was one of the most highly touted periods in the director's life. Zanuck, after all, realized that Sturges's antic personality could provide advantageous publicity for the picture already budgeted at two million dollars, of which the writer-producer-director was receiving more than three hundred thousand dollars. Both Fox studio locations were used for filming (facilities at Western Avenue and at Pico Boulevard), and reporters and columnists were not only welcome but aggressively invited to watch Sturges at work. They were amused to find him wearing a red fez and a novelty jacket with printed telephone-call mottoes ("Number please?" "Don't hang up!" "Operator, I've been cut off!" "Your time is up!"). Thus outfitted, he was featured with Darnell on the May 10 cover of *Newsweek.*

The atmosphere on *Unfaithfully Yours* could conservatively have been described as that of a madhouse. Sturges lumbered from actor to actor, shouting orders, sharing jokes, greeting visitors, checking special effects, supervising lighting patterns, stopping to pound out a jazz melody on an upright piano, ordering meals sent over from The Players for his cast, leading the crew in a barbershop quartet.

Wherever the director went, as visitors noted, Frances Ramsden was sure to follow, cradling her poodle Bobo or being tugged by Preston's Doberman, Peter. When asked by the ubiquitous press if she was going to marry Sturges, Ramsden always gave the same reply to reporters: "A girl has to wait until she's asked!" During production, her twenty-eighth birthday was celebrated with a lavish party at 1917 Ivar Avenue, catered by The Players for invited guests including the Woolfans, Harold Lloyd, Charles Chaplin, Ronald Colman, Arthur Rubinstein and three dozen others.

Fearful of the daily budget increases on the film (caused mostly by Sturges's insistent retakes and expensive slapstick interludes), Zanuck fired off nervous memoranda during and after production. "You're a day and a half behind schedule," he reminded on March 20. "We spent too much money on the picture. We shot a week longer than we should have," he scolded on May 6, to which Sturges coolly replied: "I normally work seventeen hours a day but will try to do more in the future." If twenty takes were needed before a player had Sturges's dialogue exactly right, then there would be twenty.

His cast admired and liked Sturges, to whom they were indebted for weekly gifts (comfortable slippers for everyone on the production, for example), daily catered lunches and after-work rounds of cocktails — all of which were charged not to Fox but to The Players. Linda Darnell, treated with hand-kissing deference by her director, "felt as if she were moving in a dream," according to one visitor. She was heard telling everyone over and over, "At last, I have found a director."

As for Rex Harrison, he considered Sturges "a rare genius [who] viewed life with considerable humor, and yet he was a hard taskmaster." Harrison felt Sturges was the most Europeanized American he ever knew. The work of the cast, he remembered, was immeasurably leavened by Sturges's enjoyment of his own work.

> He wanted to make it gala every day . . . and he often invited us all to his house where he ran his films for us. He loved them, and even on the set he was hard pressed not to laugh — he enjoyed his own work so, and this relaxed everyone. There was sort of a circus atmosphere.

The atmosphere during production was certainly merry, but none of this merriment is reflected in the finished work, surely the coldest, most cynical film Preston Sturges ever created. Except for a few bitterly mordant remarks about matrimony, there is little to provoke laughter.

Unfaithfully Yours concerns the internationally famous orchestra conductor Sir Alfred de Carter, who suspects that his adoring wife may have been unfaithful to him by carrying on with his assistant. While conducting the orchestra, he has a series of perfervid fantasies, which we see run through his mind.

First he leads the increasingly frenetic overture to Rossini's *Semiramide* and imagines confronting his wife with her perfidy, brutally slashing her to death with his razor and arranging for the assistant to be convicted and executed for the crime. He then conducts the lush overture to Wagner's *Tannhäuser,* while imagining himself writing a check for a hundred thousand dollars and nobly sending his wife away with it, to join her lover. Finally, he leads the orchestra in a suite from Tchaikovsky's romantic tone poem *Francesca da Rimini* and imagines a game of Russian roulette with his wife and her lover. Holding a revolver to his own

217

temple, Sir Alfred fires and kills himself. Thus the imagined sequences conclude.

At home, Sir Alfred tries somewhat halfheartedly to actualize his fantasies, but they fail — and a good thing, too, for he then learns that his suspicions were totally unfounded and his wife is worthy of his adoration.

Nothing could be farther from the frothy farce of the 1932 *Unfaithfully Yours* than this curious film from which it took its title. As a conceit — a cinematic realization of the consonance between music and imagination — it is occasionally interesting. But it is a story without a pay-off, without a third act — and one with a tone that is, from its writer-director, uncharacteristically harsh. For one thing, Sir Alfred is a maniacally high-toned monster of wounded male vanity. And worst of all, *Unfaithfully Yours* gruesomely details the wife's acute, uncomprehending pain as her husband treats her almost as appallingly in life as in his fantasies. At the conclusion, he also neatly evades punishment and correction, and his wife is as dewily devoted as ever.

Unfaithfully Yours marks a major shift in the tone of the Sturges filmography. The source of its anger and the reason for its icy misogynism are difficult to know, although it may indeed derive from the author's suspicions about Frances Ramsden, with whom his relationship was so uneven.

Ramsden, he wrote of this time in his unpublished memoir, could be

> utterly charming, kind and thoughtful, whereas two weeks before she had tried to kick my brains out from the back of a darkened automobile and [had] given me the two finest shiners I have ever seen. . . . I was always brought up not to strike women, although I've had to once or twice.

But *Unfaithfully Yours* may be more of a general collage of his life than a specific album of that year. His humor had always been whetted on the brittle stone of cynicism about human relationships, and his wit was always polished with a breezy detachment.

"A thousand poets dreamed a thousand years, then you were born, my love," Sir Alfred whispers to Daphne at the final fadeout. These were words uttered by Preston to each of his wives and to several lovers, and also written in letters — to Estelle more than once, and to Eleanor. ("They were part of his standard repertory," recalled the fourth wife of Preston Sturges, who always felt that Alfred de Carter was very much her husband.)

*　　*　　*

With *Unfaithfully Yours* completed and ready for a summer release, Sturges renewed his contract for another picture with Fox; it would be the temporarily abandoned *Beautiful Blonde from Bashful Bend*, to begin as soon as possible.

At the same time, postwar European praise of Sturges's earlier work was being reported now that the films were available there; the reviews and critical essays certainly gave him increased leverage in contract negotiating, since there would clearly be a foreign market for his pictures.

"I know of virtually no French director who has his virtuosity," proclaimed Hervé Lauwick in *Noir et Blanc,* and Henry Magnan, in *Le Monde,* spoke for many French critics when he wrote:

> Sturges always has something to say: he says it smiling, even with a somewhat bitter crease around his lips. . . . And his irony, mingled with skepticism and sometimes sadness links him to our own [French] tradition.

André Bazin, writing in the influential *L'Écran français,* hailed Sturges as "the only one who knows how to advance American comedy by renewing it at its core"; he also stressed Sturges's international appeal and suggested that his irony and sight gags were just a cover for the most potent myths. *The Palm Beach Story,* for example, he saw as an inversion of the Prince Charming tale, and the main character in *Christmas in July* he perceived as Destiny, very much as in Racine's *Athalie.* With such fascinating fancies Gallic criticism is often spiced. The following year, Bazin called Sturges a moralist, comparing him to La Bruyère and Voltaire; he also described him (more accurately) as *"l'anti-Capra."* Sturges was pleased with this French critical response, although its overstated, academic earnestness amused him.

From a Nevada ranch she was visiting that spring, Estelle wrote that after her (second) divorce from Myron Davy, she had married in 1946 a professional golfer named Harold Baer. Estelle indicated the progress of her severe illness only obliquely:

> Time flies by so fast and it won't be long before one or the other of us will be gone and phone calls will be impossible.
>
> It would be fun to sit down and talk to you sometime, but I suppose you are too busy burning the candle at both ends to have any time for an old ex-wife.

Sad news touched everyone in his professional circle that summer when actress Carole Landis, apparently grief-stricken over her well-publicized but doomed love affair with Rex Harrison, was found dead on July 16 from an overdose of barbiturates. The release date of *Unfaithfully Yours,* scheduled for that month, was immediately postponed; Fox could not present a film in which Harrison devised a scheme to murder his wife.

"Everybody liked Carole Landis," according to Priscilla Woolfan.

> She was doing well in her career and had many friends. She was in love with Rex Harrison, his picture with Preston was finished, and she thought Rex was going to divorce Lili Palmer and marry her. When he finally admitted he wasn't going to do that, and that Lili was going to stand by him as he returned to her, she killed herself. And Fox was stuck with the picture they couldn't release.

While revising the script for Betty Grable, Sturges began more construction work at The Players — for a small theater in which he planned to present simple productions for patrons before or after supper. Although he had a substantial income from Fox, the money still went for taxes, Players bills and payments to Louise and Mon. (In October, Mon was entering a Swiss school near Lausanne. Louise asked that Preston send a photo of himself for Mon; she had bought a frame for that purpose.)

That year he borrowed more than ten thousand dollars from his agent, Victor Orsatti, and smaller funds from stock players like Jimmy Conlin to cover construction expenses. "The most I can lose [on the dinner theater] is a fortune," he wrote gaily to a friend in New York. The remark was prophetic, and the loans were never repaid.

From 1947 through the 1950s, one colleague and friend who saw the varying fortunes of The Players and of its owner's life was the artist and designer Maxine Merlino. Sturges employed her first as decorator for his dinner theater, then as scenic designer for his plays. She became friend and confidante to him and to his last wife.

"Preston was like a king approaching," she recalled many years later,

> a man with great dignity, even though he always wore unpressed clothes. He was a very agreeable man to work for. My job was to carry out his dream and his ideas for The Players, which was fairly easy. He wanted to create the look of a turn-of-the-century French theater, with velvet draperies and classical columns painted on the walls in a kind of *trompe l'oeil* effect. I began working at what was then a fabulous salary, seventy-five

dollars a week. It was worth the long drive up from my home in Long Beach in those days before the freeways. Most of all I recall that Preston spared no expense. He insisted on the finest Belgian linen for scene flats — not just canvas for him. And none of them was to be painted over and used again. There were one hundred five flats finally stored away, each scene painted on this glorious European linen.

Zanuck, meantime, worried over the rushes that came in after the first weeks of shooting *Beautiful Blonde.* He strongly disapproved, for example, of the undue length of the slapstick episodes, which accounted for fully a third of the action. "You are spending more time [on such scenes] than they are worth, [and] it would be worth your while to take a look at the rushes that come in from the other [Fox pictures in production]," he wrote in a memorandum to Sturges on November 17. Throughout the autumn, Zanuck grew increasingly nervous about the protracted physical comedy, the lack of an interesting narrative and the big fight substituting for a finale.

There was also considerable tension between director and leading lady. "Betty Grable couldn't stand him," co-star Cesar Romero recalled, and Grable herself admitted:

> I was so mad I left the set after the last scene of the picture without even saying goodbye to anybody in the crew. That's the first time I've done that.

Priscilla Woolfan, who visited the studio several times, found the same friction:

> He tried awfully hard, but Betty Grable was ornery and very unpleasant with Preston. She frequently walked off when they needed only ten more minutes with her.

Grable later called Sturges "low man on the totem pole," and she was annoyed that he had been assigned to a film she called "the Sturges atrocity."

> I have everything in the world I want. The only cloud appeared when I made *The Beautiful Blonde from Bashful Bend.* I didn't want to do it . . . [and if Zanuck] ever gives me Preston Sturges again, you'll hear Grable's voice.

As for Sturges, Romero termed him "a thorough professional and a very easygoing man. But he was very particular about the words of the

script he'd written. If you changed one syllable, he called you on it."
Marie Windsor, who played a small role, agreed: "He was efficiency
itself, very pleasant and not at all temperamental. Of course everyone had
great respect for him because of his reputation, but he never put on any
airs or attitude when directing us."

The Beautiful Blonde from Bashful Bend remains, however, a disappointment, even for Sturges's most ardent partisans. Coarse humor, loud
and protracted gunfights and endless pratfalls sink this unfortunate film,
which received hardly a kind word from any critic when it was released
in the spring of 1949.

At the same time, Sturges was anxious about money, as he wrote to
Zanuck:

> My financial troubles are closing in around me so rapidly that I wanted
> some help from you . . . in the form of an advance against a [second] Betty
> Grable script I have in mind. . . . I have suitable collateral, and if you
> didn't like the story, I would write you another, and if you didn't like that
> I would write you still another one. . . .

Zanuck, however, was unwilling to pay in advance for an unwritten
story. He may have seemed obdurate to Sturges, but he was simply acting
as his own best counsel, as Sturges must have realized. The recent reviews
and poor business on *Unfaithfully Yours* — released at last in November
— were a caution for Fox.

The year 1949 began as the grimmest in Preston Sturges's career. At The
Players, financial problems were accompanied by the disappearance of
cases of liquor and sacks of produce, and it was clear that the owner was
being cheated by his employees. To pay bills, Sturges was by this time
borrowing cash in various amounts: over three thousand dollars was loaned
to him by one of his attorneys, Victor Ford Collins, but within three years
Sturges had reimbursed only five hundred dollars.

At the same time, Sturges was failing in his alimony and child-
support payments to Louise and Mon, although her reply to his excuses
was typically patient and encouraging: "You've survived seventeen years
in Hollywood without an ulcer, a heart murmur or a delirium tremens,"
she wrote on March 22, "which puts you constitutionally in a class with
Hercules." (He offered the house at 1917 Ivar as collateral for the forty-
five thousand dollars he owed her from the divorce settlement.)

Although he had thrived on Solomon Sturges's loving generosity,
Preston's early life with Mary had given him an acquaintance with un-

witting, benign neglect that passed for parenting. Thus he, too, in fact became a negligent father, uninterested in Mon. Even when his son returned from Europe to Los Angeles in 1950, no amount of pleading from friends like Priscilla Woolfan could encourage Preston to spend more time with him, or to engage in fatherly outings and activities. He had occasionally brought the boy to the set of a production, showed him *his* life and career, but of the child's emotional needs he was heedless. "He just was not an attentive father," Jean La Vell remembered, and according to Preston's fourth wife (who later saw father and son together on several occasions),

> He said he loved Mon, but I never had the impression that he loved him the way you love kids — with warmth and hugs and kisses, and who cares what they did. Somehow he thought Mon should be a replica of himself, as he'd been in *his* youth, with the same interests and curiosity and inventiveness, and when Preston didn't find it he challenged his son — kindly, but not in a fatherly way, I thought. . . . There wasn't a single weekend Mon spent with us that he wasn't just destroyed and in tears, and he didn't feel welcome. He could never measure up to his father's expectations.

"He wrote me a letter every now and again," Mon Sturges remembered many years later,

> but he never signed them "Dad" or "Pop." He signed them formally — "Your father, Preston Sturges." It was as if he wanted everything to be catalogued, remembered officially. . . . And when I was in school in Europe, he just wasn't in touch with me. He was always broke, I remember that, but he tried to send me some money at Christmastime. I remember asking my mother if she wasn't supposed to get something, too, but she just said quietly, "He doesn't have it to give." She never tried to dun him for it.

Although that year Preston had more dark moods than ever before, and although he seemed to Edwin Gillette "almost unable to take the pressures of responsibility," he still maintained an astonishing resilience. "If there's anything I dislike, it's one thing more than another!" proclaimed a sign he installed at home that year.

Publicly, his wit never failed. Invited to be a guest panelist on a radio program that year, he was asked a series of questions to which he provided his own delicious replies:

Q: Mr. Sturges, what's the best way to get over a sad love affair?
A: Wear tight shoes — you will forget everything else.
Q: What's the quickest way to get into show business?
A: Pose for an artistic calendar.
Q: Would you be interested in discovering a blonde who can act?
A: All blondes can act.

On another program, he demonstrated the same sharp humor. Again, questions were put to him as a guest panelist — this time, in the form of letters.

Q: My husband accuses me of being too friendly with our breadman just because I go out to his truck every day to buy bread. He is very friendly and we usually chat for a few minutes. If I stop buying bread from him I'll have to walk three blocks to the market. Should I give up my breadman or just ignore my husband's false suspicions?
STURGES: Bake your own bread and if you get lonely start buying ice. There are still icemen around.
Q: I'm opposed to my husband having a traveling job on the grounds that if he is away from home the children are bound to suffer psychologically. We have five children, and he is home only on weekends. His contention is that if he were home during the week the small amount of time he could devote to them wouldn't make any difference. How much time should a father be around his children for best results?
STURGES: He should stay as far away as possible, or the first thing you know there'll be ten children.
Q: We've been married a year and my husband has always been in the habit of kissing me goodbye and hello. Lately he has been forgetting this and I miss the kisses. I hate to be a nagging wife, but is there any subtle way of getting him back into that very pleasant habit again?
STURGES: Why not set him an example? Kiss all his friends while you're sure he's looking, and when he asks you why you're doing this, tell him you're just keeping in practice. But if he sees you do it and doesn't say anything, then you're really in trouble.

The wit sprang from his inveterate optimism — an attitude and outlook not at all inconsistent with an essentially cynical-realistic view of human nature. Sturges could be a whimsical and capricious fun-lover and a genial host who underwrote camaraderie (with the concomitant lack of financial responsibility), an eager, cheerful man who pitched himself into the future and always expected bad fortune to turn better.

Co-existent with his sanguine confidence, however, was a sharp instinct about the human comedy, an intuitive awareness of frailty. The optimism met the cynicism at a crucial point, however: throughout his life, Preston Sturges refused to judge or condemn the motives of anyone. He never bore grudges, he was always quick to find extenuating circumstances for ill conduct.

The generosity extended to his own estimations and expectations of himself and his talents, which he believed could never fail him. Time and again, Sturges told friends that if ever he were ultimately indigent he would sit on a curbstone, ask a passerby for paper and pen and start writing a new script. "We'll make it," he repeatedly told intimate friends like the Woolfans. "We'll get through this!" And so he always believed, even when prospects for financial survival were bleakest.

"His companion [at boxing matches] these nights is Frances Ramsden," reported columnist Hedda Hopper. Then at New Year's, Sturges and Ramsden were not speaking: "I'm not going to marry Preston," Ramsden told reporter Sheilah Graham. "It's all so embarrassing. He's never *asked* me to marry him." But then they were seen arm in arm at a dinner party. In February they apparently had ended the affair again, but next month Preston told a reporter:

> Frances and I had a misunderstanding, and I sat in The Players for a couple of days with a nice young lady named Alice Martin. But she has gone to New York and Frances and I are back together.

Maxine Merlino, who frequently accompanied Sturges and Ramsden to Catalina Island on his yacht *Island Belle,* recalled that an essential personality difference between the lovers was their different attitudes about activity.

> She was extremely active and vivacious, and she always wanted to be up and about. Preston, on the other hand, was rather lethargic. He said he was lazy, and I think Francie agreed with him. But I always had the impression that his mind was going constantly. His kind of activity was interior, you might say. He didn't have to be dashing about in a social life.

The Beautiful Blonde from Bashful Bend was a second critical and financial failure at Fox, and Sturges's contract was not renewed. For the first time in many years he found himself, in 1949, unemployed and with no indication of long-term employment.

This situation was certainly caused by his reputation as a very highly paid writer-director who did not suffer fools gladly, who insisted on as much control as he could get and who made expensive films — only three since 1944, none of them successful. "I managed to alienate every one of the seven major studios and soon found myself out of work," he admitted to a reporter about the previous several years.

Postwar Hollywood, at the same time, was being more cautious than ever. Domestic theater attendance had fallen sharply after the war — more than eighty-two million Americans went to the movies an average of once a week in 1945, fewer than fifty-five million attended in 1948 — and total box-office receipts for the same period had dropped over $200,000,000. In 1948, the major studios produced 248 feature films — almost 150 fewer than in 1942 — and the Screen Actors Guild reported an all-time low in the number of its members at work.

Everywhere there was retrenchment. The major studios were trimming production costs radically, and the first targets were high writers' and directors' fees and lengthy shooting schedules with many retakes and script changes. In each of these areas, Sturges's recent films did not warrant a studio executive's offering him a major deal. *Unfaithfully Yours* and *Beautiful Blonde,* after all, had disappointed Fox's accountants as well as critics and audiences, and this the Hollywood trade papers reported (as usual in such cases) in exact detail. The hesitation to take risks was heightened, furthermore, by the looming threat from television.

Nevertheless, Sturges was able to negotiate a commission from Metro-Goldwyn-Mayer in early 1949, for a script he was writing for Clark Gable. Sturges was to receive twenty-five thousand dollars for the first draft, and the same amount after a revision. During that year, MGM continually advanced him portions of the money as he made frequent, fervent protests of poverty.

Throughout the spring and to summer's end, he worked on that screenplay, called *Mr. Big in Littleville,* later retitled *Nothing Doing.* The story concerns Charles "Big Kim" Kimberly, a famous business tycoon who goes on a long vacation. He goes incognito to a small town and stays at a boardinghouse owned by a lovely war widow named Mrs. Jones, who has a young son. He assumes the name Mr. Jones and although he falls in love with her, he refuses to marry:

BIG KIM: Did it ever occur to you that there are some men not
  made for marriage? Men who've already tried it and found that, in
  their particular case, it didn't work? Men who jump around too
  much? Men who are never home? Men who need that certain
  stimulation they can get only out of —
MRS. JONES: New faces?
BIG KIM: Something like that.

The dialogue certainly suggests a Preston-Louise basis, or a Preston-Eleanor, Preston-Bianca, Preston-Jean, or a Preston-Frances basis. *Nothing Doing*'s title refers not only to a man on holiday from work but also to the response to a marriage proposal.

Big Kim helps the Joneses expand the premises with a bar and dining room, supervises the construction work and renovations and installs a swimming pool and barbecue grill. (These sequences seem directly inspired by Sturges at The Players and Ivar Avenue.) He then revives and improves the town as well.

At the conclusion, Big Kim decides to live permanently with Mrs. Jones and her son, hoping at last to love "without fear, without reservation, generously — because you were made to love."

"You're not getting any bargain," Big Kim tells the widow Jones. "Half the time I don't seem to know where I am, the other half *nobody* knows where I am." She will take her chances.

Diffuse and talky, *Nothing Doing* is remarkable as a spiritual testimony of Preston Sturges's feelings in 1949. At the age of fifty, he wrote a script that may reflect his own deepest feelings at the time. It was too late for him to establish a family life with Louise and Mon, but the sequences with Mrs. Jones and her son are a kind of elegy to what he almost had with his own wife and child, and what he may have hoped for again. Nowhere else in his writing is there so plain a desire for a settled, loving life, nowhere is the acknowledgment of a man's wandering so poignant.

Clark Gable, however, was not keen on the script, and MGM instead put him that year in films with Loretta Young and Barbara Stanwyck. The screenplay was never realized on film.

Late that summer of 1949, Estelle died at her home in Santa Barbara at the age of forty-seven, after a dreadful final ordeal with cancer. Preston was deeply grieved at this news. Their correspondence had never been interrupted for longer than a month or two over the years, and he always cherished her belief in his talent, her unfailing encouragement, her perpetual good cheer, her style, wit, optimism and her sense of fun. She had loved his father and been loved by him in return, and even Mary — initially so indifferent to her — had finally to admit that Estelle's charm and sweetness were genuine.

Certain of Preston's friends and mistresses (and even his last wife) were convinced that he never stopped loving Estelle, never stopped regretting the loss of her love more than twenty years before her death. Forever after he referred to her as "the young woman I loved so much," and so he described her just weeks before his own death a decade later.

But no news depressed him for very long, and by late autumn of 1949, with no fresh movie prospects, he turned his attention to the developing medium of television. From the American Broadcasting Company's Los Angeles affiliate there was that year a live melodramatic series called *Mysteries of Chinatown,* seen by the rest of the country via kinescope relay. Sturges, perhaps aware that ABC's Television Center had once been the Warner Brothers Vitagraph Studios, with an especially fine sound system, visited the rehearsals at least twice that season. He had no specific proposals for television, nor did he yet think it might have a future for him; the latest technology fascinated him, however.

"He watched the rehearsals from the vantage points of the studio floor and the control room," recalled Richard J. Goggin many years later; in 1949, he was the station's senior director. "He was naturally very interested in all aspects of production: sets, costumes, lighting, sound, multiple camera work . . . and of course staging and television direction."

The atmosphere, Goggin remembered, was high pressure in those days of live, one-chance-only television dramatic broadcasts. But after a dress rehearsal, Sturges

> quietly and graciously pointed out to me that in one scene I had "crossed the line" — I had reversed screen direction between two camera shots.
> A reversal of this kind was taboo in direction and editing for film, and it was equally to become a taboo in television [since it disoriented the viewpoint]. I never let it happen again.

A week or two later, Sturges again visited Goggin's production of *Mysteries of Chinatown,* and he brought a present for me. It was something, I assume, that may have been peculiarly his own — a wooden "shot framer," in size and construction somewhat resembling the old stereoscope viewers.

Goggin recalled feeling pleased and flattered "by this special gift from a famous film director to a young television director."

That spring, the relationship with Frances Ramsden finally ended. They had one acrimonious disagreement too many, as he wrote to his New York friend and benefactor John Hertz, Jr., on July 19, just after Ramsden's marriage to a writer named Bill Jacobson in New York:

> Our memories are bookkeeping systems with a separate account for every single person. . . . It is very dangerous for newly in love couples to permit themselves the slightest discourtesy or anger toward each other. They may say, after wiping away the tears, that they have forgiven and forgotten the incident, but they are wrong. It is written forever in indelible ink on the debit side of their ledgers. The trouble with Francie and myself is that our ledgers were overflowing.

Before she departed, however, she loaned him $1,350, in return for which he promised to pay her final Los Angeles expenses. "It has never bothered me to pay up a few bills for a lady who was kind enough to join her lot with mine," he wrote to Ramsden on August 4, "[but] I have still no money at all so there is no use writing to me about your debts."

But by this time Preston Sturges was in high spirits. That season he had met a slender, energetic woman with great blue eyes and a quick intelligence. He turned fifty-two that summer of 1950; she was twenty. This was not, however, to be a transient love affair.

FIFTEEN

Return to France

O F ALL the women in his life," said Priscilla Woolfan, who by 1950 had known Preston Sturges almost twenty years, "Sandy was the closest to what he was seeking. She was the one he cared for most. She was so young and so sweet, and she was awfully smart — and that was what he wanted a woman to be for him."

Anne Margaret Nagle — always known as Sandy — was born January 3, 1930, in Washington, D.C. She had been married for a short time and had moved to Los Angeles but by 1950 was separated from her husband and held a clerical job. On her way home one evening to the apartment Sandy was renting above Sunset Boulevard, she noticed The Players' electric sign was sparking, and she went to warn the proprietor of possible fire. He reassured her that the simple short-circuit would soon be repaired and then invited her to see the small dinner theater he was constructing. "He described his dreams for a wonderful acting space," she recalled years later,

> and I remember there were books on theater all around. Nothing in the world was as exciting as this for him, but soon I learned that everything he touched evoked that kind of enthusiasm from him. All his considerable energy was in it. He saw visions about things and counted on the fruition of every project. If someone came along with a cooling caution — that a plan was off-base, or that a contraption wouldn't work — he heard the words. But if he had decided to do it, the words made no dent in him.

Preston Sturges did not announce himself as the owner of The Players, nor as a movie director, nor as an Oscar-winning writer. He invited the young lady to return several times to watch the progress of the theater, and at last she learned his identity.

> Initially, I thought he was a work supervisor, and when I finally found out who he was it didn't make any great impression on me. As a child I had rarely seen anything other than Disney or Sherlock Holmes [movies].

Over the next several months, Sturges showed her several of his films, and she was an eager and appreciative audience. She also learned that The Players theater was an attempt at a money-making venture, since for the first time in many years Sturges had no regular salary. "The little theater was not built," Sandy said, "for him to stake a reputation as a man of the theater, nor to stage plays he would write himself."

At the same time, he was working on a screenplay, and he asked Sandy if she would consider working as his secretary.

> So I quit my job and we began working at The Players each night, after it closed to customers. At three or four in the morning, we began work, he dictating and I typing, and at dawn I made my way to my apartment up the hill.

He also asked her opinion of the plays and portions of plays he was selecting for his little theater.

> His goal was to open with five one-act plays, the idea being that customers would eat, drink and enjoy the plays. But the food costs were always between sixty-five and eighty percent of the budget, and with salaries and other operating expenses, it just continually lost money. He was simply not a good businessman, and he signed checks without even looking at them.

The debt incurred at The Players was so consistently overwhelming — with perpetually unpaid wages and taxes, mortgages in default and creditors often bringing suit — that Preston continued to borrow. His creditors included Louise, who in early 1951 loaned him six thousand dollars (although she herself was already owed substantial sums by him); he eventually repaid her with a tax refund. At the same time, friends suggested he raise the menu prices — which were almost at wholesale — but he was convinced this would drive customers away. "What customers?" asked one distraught employee.

In addition, according to one of Sturges's attorneys, Marvin Chesebro:

Some of the people who worked for him siphoned off the profits, walking out the back door with cartons of liquor while Preston was sitting, chatting and drinking with friends after hours. He believed that others would act as he did — that their word was their honor. The characters of his movies show that he was not oblivious to the other side of people, but in life he had a sort of grand naïveté. He wasn't a businessman, he was an artist, and he should've stayed with the writing.

Throughout 1950 and every year for the rest of his life, Sturges tried to do just that, to negotiate for screen work as writer or director or both; of more than three dozen movie projects, only one was brought to completion.

As he admitted, by then he had alienated every studio in town, and his last several films had been unsuccessful. "You always want things your own way, Preston," wrote Paramount's vice-president Y. Frank Freeman in 1950 when Sturges tried to recontract with that studio. "Every collaboration [you undertake] seems to lead to a fight. We're sorry, but . . ."

According to Rudy Vallee, Preston's habit of correcting people's grammar and pronunciation did not endear him to colleagues, either — especially studio executives, whom Sturges blithely mimicked, suggesting better tones and inflections and methods of eradicating an ethnic accent. "The only amazing thing about my career," Sturges wrote later, "is that I ever had one at all." And not long before his death he noted in his appointment book: "As I know only too well, intelligence and good judgment do not always walk hand-in-hand."

Indeed, it seemed then (as it has seemed to many since) that Preston Sturges peaked from 1939 to 1943. His output since then had not invited impressive negotiations, but in spite of almost constant rejection by executives — as well as the disappointments of several deals that were promised but eventually lapsed for want of production funds — he continued always to create around himself an atmosphere of buoyant expectation.

At the end of 1950, a Broadway musical based on his script for the 1935 film *The Good Fairy* was planned — called *Make a Wish* — and Sturges was invited to write the book for it. He and Sandy went to New York in March 1951 for work with the producers, lyricist and composer, but the show encountered considerable production difficulties.

"I stayed with *Make a Wish* as long as I could," Sturges told a reporter, "and helped as much as I could within the limit of my somewhat restricted time" — the restriction being caused by the imminent deferred opening of The Players theater. Before the April premiere of *Make a Wish*, Abe Burrows (without credit) rewrote almost the entire text. Still, only the vivacious performance by Nanette Fabray saved the show from an early demise. (It had a modest run of 106 performances.)

Back in Los Angeles, The Playroom at The Players, as it was called, opened with three one-act entertainments: Sturges's own version of W. W. Jacobs's "The Monkey's Paw," Sturges's free rendering of Chekhov's "The Boor," and Sturges's restaging of William Saroyan's "Hello, Out There." Reporters and patrons were impressed with the mechanized floor that swiftly converted from ballroom to tiered seating plan for two hundred; with the simple scenery that swung into place on overhead tracks; and with an ingenious acoustical system that made onstage whispers audible through the hall. Eventually, Eddie Bracken appeared in a scaled-down version of the Marx Brothers' *Room Service,* and Carolyn Jones appeared in "Live Wire," directed by Aaron Spelling (later her husband and a well-known television producer).

The problem, however, was still cost and profit. "It never worked," according to Marvin Chesebro.

> He was really a visionary, and so he saw things not as they were, but how he thought they should be. He saw The Players as a place for wonderful meals and marvelous entertainment — just like his home. Customers marched in on time to see the show, but they never ate or drank very much, and that was to have been the source of the profit.

"People did not want to stay in one place all evening," Sandy added. "Weeknights the audience was sparse, and weekends people came for supper or the plays, but not both."

Besides other restaurants on the Sunset Strip, additional competition came that year from America's nascent television culture: for the first time, people were remaining at home during the week for their evening's entertainment. In huge numbers, Americans were watching Arthur Godfrey's *Talent Scouts* and *I Love Lucy* on Mondays; Milton Berle, the *Fireside Theater* and *Armstrong Circle Theater* on Tuesdays; the *Kraft Television Theater* on Wednesdays; George Burns and Gracie Allen and the popular quiz show *You Bet Your Life* on Thursdays.

Working with her for long periods, Preston found Sandy intelligent and attractive, and nothing like an immature, inarticulate admirer. He found her suggestions on the mark (notes appended to manuscript drafts approve her emendations and proposals), and her energy and enthusiasm matched his. "Sandy was a brilliant girl," according to Maxine Merlino, "one quite capable of having a successful life and career on her own. But her one wish was to completely submerge herself in Preston's life and work. She was also very generous and attentive to little Mon when he came to visit, and she played with him and kept him occupied for hours. Many times Preston looked at her from a distance and turning to me, he asked, 'Isn't she wonderful?'"

"After hours, at The Players, he began to work," Sandy recalled.

> It took him time to get the engines going, but when he found the rhythm — what a change! He became the character he was writing. His voice broke and tears coursed down his cheeks, and your heart would be gripped. And just as suddenly the voice of an angry character would turn his face red. It just didn't seem as if he were plotting a story. Characters came alive through him.

He was unaware, she remembered, how a story would conclude until it actually ended.

Soon he was stopping occasionally, in the middle of dictation, to say how deeply attracted to her he was. "I don't know whether to marry you or adopt you," he added one day. Sandy knew that his friends were asking his intentions regarding her.

> The fact that I didn't look my age made it all the more difficult, because his friends saw me as a teen-ager. I assumed he thought of me as a child, and I certainly didn't think of him as a partner. Then he began to say, "If only we could be married," and I thought it was just kidding. I never took it seriously that I would be Mrs. Sturges.

By spring 1951, he was introducing her to friends and restaurant guests as "the girl I'm going to marry." When her first marriage was at last formally dissolved, she still did not believe Preston was serious about a wedding. "I had grown to love him, yes, but I was not yet in love with him. But that changed, too," and on the stage of The Players, on August 15, 1951, they were married.

The construction of new roads in Los Angeles brought a sudden, welcome windfall to the Sturgeses, for the county needed the land at 1917 Ivar Avenue for the new Route 101, the Hollywood Freeway. The house, however, was to be moved to property Preston bought at 7420 Franklin

Avenue, at Vista Street. While complicated relocation permits were arranged, while the Ivar house was subdivided and prepared for the difficult
move, and while it was (very slowly, over the course of two years) reconnected at Franklin Avenue, the Sturgeses were invited to live in an empty
house owned by their friend, pianist José Iturbi, at 707 North Hillcrest,
Beverly Hills. Their tenancy (for which Sturges could not pay the contracted minimal rent) was to have been for a month or two.

"But it was two years," Sandy recalled, "before the house was put
back together, by which time nobody remembered where the plumbing
and wiring attachments were supposed to go." He was never much concerned, according to Marvin Chesebro,

> that the foundation [at 7420 Franklin] wasn't firmly fastened. When there
> were all kinds of trouble with it, he didn't brood — it was like everything
> else: it was just the way things were for the present.

During that time (1951 to 1953), a number of projects were hope-
fully begun but sadly unrealized: a television series based on productions
from The Playroom, but in which there was no network interest; a film
version of a Broadway musical he wrote for Paramount and Betty Hutton,
called *Look, Ma, I'm Dancin'*, which was cancelled when she withdrew
because the studio would not engage her husband, choreographer Charles
O'Curran, as director; a complete revision Sturges unnecessarily offered
for William Wyler's upcoming film *Roman Holiday* (for which Wyler —
to provide Sturges some quick cash — had requested only a quick reading
and a few lines polished in the completed script he already had); and
another complete but unwanted revision of Billy Wilder's soon-to-be-
produced *Sabrina*. "I knew he needed the money," Wilder recalled years
later, "but it didn't work out. He was not a collaborator," and there was
never any thought of abandoning the first-rate screenplay by Samuel
Taylor and Ernest Lehman. Another unrealized project was an original
script called *The Great Hugo,* a satire about a European monarchy in need
of an heir.

"In all these," Sandy confirmed,

> he was trying to make a good impression on Paramount, trying to show he
> was capable of submitting good work in short order. More than once, we
> worked around the clock, three and four days at a time, with only short
> breaks for meals. He did that with his astonishing energy, his hope — and
> with pots of coffee and packs of cigarettes. And somehow I just kept up
> with him. He did so much every day!

Perhaps one of the reasons for Preston's choice of a young spouse — in addition to her obvious attractiveness, her intelligence, energy and wit — was that (very like Big Kim in *Nothing Doing*) he wanted at last to participate in a secure family life. "Around that time he started talking about raising a large family," Priscilla Woolfan remembered. "Six six-foot sons, he said, to bear him to his grave one day!" At precisely the time of his life when his creative energies were still keen but the application of them was no longer welcome among his Hollywood colleagues, his offspring would be tangible proof of a heritage none could ignore.

On February 22, 1953, Sandy gave birth to a boy they named Preston — but without the "Junior," his father insisted. "He was shameless with pride about little Preston," according to Sandy.

> He always carried a pocketful of photos he took out at the slightest inquiry, and heaven forfend if someone didn't notice the child's intelligence and muscular development and everything else.

Preston's birth, and that of Thomas Preston three years later, were the happiest events in the last years of their father's life and compensated for further financial heartbreak. That same year, creditors and the government judged against Sturges and The Players, a lien was put on all income, the contents were put up for auction, and the restaurant was rented and eventually sold for debts. (In 1954, a Japanese family purchased it and the funds were turned over for taxes and creditors; The Players became the Imperial Gardens restaurant and nightclub.)

There were other disappointments. In the summer of 1953, Preston worked on a rewrite of the book — and eventually also took over the direction — of the Broadway musical *Carnival in Flanders* (based on the film *La Kermesse Héroïque*). The star of the show, Dolores Gray, recalled that he was "elegant but autocratic," and that his long absence from stage work may have accounted for the fact that

> he had no idea what he really wanted from us. . . . He continually brought us new pages, and then still more new pages of material he was constantly rewriting, and he seemed to cover his own fear by becoming more and more imperious with us all.

But the show's problems cannot be entirely laid at Sturges's feet. Herbert Fields and George Oppenheimer had written the original text, and Bretaigne Windust was its first director. After the producers realized (following the Philadelphia tryout) that James Van Heusen's score and Johnny Burke's lyrics required a stronger book, Sturges (known to them from Paramount days) had been invited to submit revisions. This he did with remarkable speed, but *Carnival in Flanders* was in fact too complicated and lavish a musical to admit of a quick fix. The show closed after six performances in New York.

Cesar Romero met Sturges in New York that month and found him "in pretty tough straits financially, since his fortunes had really changed. But he was greatly elated because he said he was about to leave for Europe."

That trip was scheduled because there were plans for Sturges to direct his film version of George Bernard Shaw's *The Millionairess* with Katharine Hepburn, who had played the role in London and New York the previous year. Producer Lester Cowan was attempting to arrange financing for an Anglo-American co-production, a venture that seemed promising if the film could be made in London. The last months of 1953, Sturges worked incessantly on the screenplay and pronounced it the finest of his career — a judgment with which Hepburn, for one, wholly agreed:

> It was a marvelous piece of work, expertly written and I thought years ahead of its time. Sometimes it was more Sturges than Shaw, but it was very well constructed and it would have made a terribly good film.

Considerable additional work was done on the screenplay that winter, and Katharine Hepburn encouraged Sturges, welcomed him to her Manhattan home for lunch, listened to portions of the script, asked questions and made suggestions. "I never had the feeling that his talent was in any kind of decline," she reflected years later.

> In fact I thought he was working very well. But he was a strange, curious figure — brilliant, certainly, but strange — and I thought he was not entirely happy at that time, and that maybe he was sometimes drinking a bit too much.

On January 23, 1954 — Sandy and the baby having joined Preston in New York — the family sailed aboard the *Queen Mary* for London, where Preston hoped to begin production on *The Millionairess*.

Cowan had told them he had signed Alec Guinness and Alastair Sim for supporting roles, but in fact neither actor had any idea about such a film. "Cowan was not a conscious liar," Sandy said. "He conceived of what was ideal and voiced it as a fact — rather like Mary Desti." But Cowan could raise no additional English funds, and so much time had elapsed that Katharine Hepburn, greatly disappointed, had to honor another commitment. *The Millionairess* became another dashed dream.*

With his uncanny resilience, Sturges proclaimed a holiday for his wife. He found a 1922 Rolls Royce designed to accommodate large parcels, and, on April 23, they headed south for Dover and the Continent. "He bought an array of toys for the baby," Sandy recalled, "and he was looking forward to showing me all the places of his childhood in France, from Fleurines to Paris. This was only to be a short vacation for me, with no intention of staying." The short vacation extended to more than three years, none of it a holiday.

Before proceeding to France from the port of Ostende, they spent several days with Vely Bey and his new wife and son in Brussels. "By this time, Vely Bey was very courtly," Sandy said. "He frequently bowed, but he was suave without being the least bit sophisticated. At one point, when Preston left the room, Vely Bey leaned over to me and whispered, 'Of course, I always thought Mary was quite crazy.' "

In May, at Deauville, Preston at last met Marcel Pagnol, whose *Fanny* he had adapted almost twenty years earlier, and with whom he had regularly corresponded. A true friendship was formed immediately, and Sturges offered to prepare as a favor for Pagnol the English subtitles for Pagnol's imminent screenplay of the Alphonse Daudet story cycle, *Les Lettres de mon moulin* (*Letters from My Windmill*). Later, he begged that his name be removed from the credits: he feared it would be a signal to Americans that he could find work only as a translator of foreign films.

After a tour of the provincial locales of his youth, Preston took Sandy and the baby to Paris, where they checked into the modest Royal Malesherbes Hotel. Before long (and after a complicated round of negotiations), the Gaumont Company offered Sturges the opportunity to adapt and direct the film version of a best-selling collection of humorous essays by Pierre Daninos, to be called *Les Carnets du Major Thompson*. The pieces had as their focus the retired Englishman Major Thompson, who lives in Paris with his French wife and their son.

"I had to write two scripts for it," Sturges said in an interview.

First I wrote what I think was a rather amusing story about a French author having invented a fictitious Englishman, and one day the fictitious En-

---

* The 1960 film of that title, directed by Anthony Asquith and starring Sophia Loren, Peter Sellers, Alastair Sim and Vittorio De Sica, did not use any of Sturges's screenplay.

glishman appeared in Paris . . . and it came out that he was a war hero who had lost his memory fighting for France.

That, as it turned out, was a pleasant story, but it extrapolated wildly from Daninos.

> So I took one chapter . . . and from three pages I made a conjugal comedy about the English major and his French wife and the dispute as to how they will raise their child, whether he will learn the facts of history from the English or the French point of view.

The essential structure and much of the intended humor derived from Sturges's apparent attempt to use the technique of *The Power and the Glory* in *Les Carnets*. Thus Major Thompson (Jack Buchanan, in the finished picture) often narrates in voice-over the scene shown onscreen, dryly commenting on the habits of his French friend Taupin (Noël-Noël) or his French wife (Martine Carol).

While Gaumont concluded casting and pre-production and Sturges polished his script during the autumn and early winter of 1954, the Sturgeses leased an *hôtel particulier* built by an English painter at the turn of the century. The house was at 61 boulevard Berthier, a wide thoroughfare lined with chestnut trees in the seventeenth *arrondissement* of Paris, not far from the Parc Monceau. There was an old kitchen (in the *sous-sol*, a huge room just below ground level, with white tile, sinks and cabinets) and here Sturges set up an office, where he worked with Marie Fumal, a secretary provided by Gaumont. "Esthetically, the apartment was very pleasing, even to the baby's antique crib," according to Phyllis Feldkamp, whose husband Fred (a former editor at *Life* magazine and by then an independent producer) discussed various film possibilities with Sturges in Paris. "It was the kind of artist's place an artist without great means would have."

The owner of the house lived on the first floor with her two poodles, and the Sturgeses occupied the upper studio, two stories and twenty feet high. This level also contained their kitchen and a toilet and was large enough for a piano, a huge oak table, a four-poster bed, chairs, sofas and playroom for Preston (and later his baby brother Tom). Off the loggia on an upper level they arranged a small bedroom for baby Preston and had a full bathroom installed. Two small top-floor rooms were reached by a winding staircase.

* * *

Living in Paris again was at first undilutedly joyous for him: here was a chance to show Sandy the places of his youth. There were also frequent Sturges festivals in Paris. "He's the only real satirist to come from Hollywood," proclaimed critic Pierre Kast after visiting him in January 1955. Sturges of course spoke their language splendidly, and he was welcome at clubs as a guest speaker and at parties and bars simply as a guest. "He had," Phyllis Feldkamp remembered, "a well-honed French and was perfectly at home in any company in Paris."

His humor intact, he developed for the amusement of friends his own list of "fractured French" phrases:

Allons enfants de la patrie
Go away, children, I am not your father.

Fromage de brie
This cheese is garbage.

Sole à la bonne femme
A good woman is lonesome.

Fille de chambre
There is a steak in the toilet.

Toujours l'amour
A two-day honeymoon.

Après moi, le déluge
Everywhere I go, it rains.

Tant pis, tant mieux
My aunt goes to the toilet, my aunt feels better.

In August 1955, the much-delayed shooting of *Les Carnets du Major Thompson* began. Sturges had prepared both French and English scripts, and he impressed Gaumont executives by planning to shoot each scene in French and English with the same cast.

"I find working in French studios perfectly delightful," Sturges told an English reporter at the time. "The system in France is called *débrouillard* — which means, now you're in it, get yourself out of it [literally: one has to be "resourceful"]." He proved himself just that when he summoned a passing cabdriver to play a cabdriver, used loose manhole covers from the street as counterweights for a heavy camera boom on location and borrowed stockings from a wardrobe lady and shoes from Sandy for a quick, improvised insert shot of a character's feet when the right actress, unprepared, had neither nylons nor the proper footwear.

On their side, the cast found him genial and ever *débrouillard*. "He's the smoothest director I've worked with since Ernst Lubitsch," said Jack Buchanan. The director's poise was certainly evident when the company was photographing a fox-hunting scene in the Bois de Vincennes. Actors, crew and horses were all ready, but the hounds failed to arrive. After a long delay but unwilling to lose the sequence, Sturges asked for a pad and pen and rewrote that portion of the script. Now it began with a voice-over narration: "One day, when we had lost the pack of hounds. . . ." The scene is one of the (very few) truly funny moments in the finished picture. (When it was finally released in New York as *The French They Are a Funny Race* in May 1957, the critical response was dreadful and moviegoers ignored the picture.)

Several sequences combine a coolly confessional tone with a sort of self-righteous indignation, and everywhere the self-exiled Thompson mostly resembles his filmic creator. (Like Sturges, the major depends on a secretary to take dictation.) A flashback to an earlier time, for example, reveals Thompson's former tippling, horse-loving wife Ursula (Catherine Boyl), clearly modeled on Estelle — except that Ursula (not the paradigmatic Sturges) is the cool, lazy, financially dependent spouse. Thompson, a sloppy drinker, argues endlessly and unfunnily with his wife and is seen wandering through Paris, a lonely exile "no longer an Englishman, but never quite a Frenchman." Only a gratuitously happy ending, with his wife announcing a new pregnancy, reverses the prevailing cloudy atmosphere.

That summer of 1955, Sandy took baby Preston and her mother (who was visiting from America) to Deauville, and Preston joined them each weekend. On Sandy's return in the autumn, she made a painful discovery from an open letter accidentally placed with other mail. It bore the signature of the actress Gaby Sylvia; its contents made clear that she and Preston were lovers.

A slim, brown-haired, Italian-born beauty then thirty-five, Gaby Sylvia (born Gabrielle Zignati) had a warm, sometimes seductive smile and dark, expressive eyes. She appeared often on the Paris stage, and had just been hailed for her performance as Estelle in the 1954 film of Jean-Paul Sartre's *Huis-Clos* (*No Exit*); she had also appeared in Italian and French films. How she and Sturges met and just when the affair began remains unclear, but it is certain that Sylvia had temporarily complicated her life with her lesbian lover by succumbing to Preston's persuasive charm. Gaby called Sturges "one of the two men I've known who really likes women — to talk [to] and to be with them."

Sandy, by now pregnant again, was devastated.

> Everything in my life seemed to collapse, and when I discussed the affair with Preston, he insisted that he loved me and would never leave me, and then he said, "There's only one thing disturbing you — that I got caught." He didn't think it was a big deal at all. Well, I wasn't quite so casual about it. I was completely taken by surprise, and I believed then and now that this was his first infidelity in the years since we'd been married. But in 1955 it just hurt me terribly. I wanted to leave, but where could I go, with not a cent or a sou, with one child and another on the way?

Years later, Sandy understood the rationale for the infidelity.

> Everything kept falling through the cracks, and he needed something, someone new who adored him — the rush of sudden romance with someone who thought he was just marvelous, a wonderful playwright. He was never a promiscuous philanderer, and this affair just happened.

(She remembered once, in Paris, that Preston was "always calling me 'darling' — it was 'Darling, you know . . .' and 'Darling, have you seen . . .' all over the place. I stopped and said, 'How fortunate for you that 'Darling' works, because you never have to remember to whom you're speaking!' That really touched something in him, because he got furious!")

Jean La Vell had regarded Sturges as an idealist whose affairs bespoke a romantic constantly seeking the perfect woman. But Sandy felt that Gaby Sylvia was not only a new romance: Gaby was also an exciting stage actress Preston hoped to star in his work.

He had especially counted on Gaby playing in his farce *J'appartiens à Zozo,* which he wrote in French and also in English as *I Belong to Zozo.* This was to be another Sturges work that recalled Feydeau — with elements uncannily like both *Un Fil à la patte* (variously translated as *Cat Among Pigeons* or *Not by Bed Alone*) and *La Puce à l'oreille (A Flea in Her Ear).* His appointment books for the last five years of his life contain pointed references to Feydeau, with detailed notes of that playwright's French stage directions.

Zozo was the story of a girl whose one true love quite suddenly is engaged to marry another. For revenge, she plans to marry a famous bullfighter. The first man is miserable and does not intend to lose her; he will marry his fiancée but keep the girl for a mistress. She then decides she does indeed want to marry him: her decision, however, is made after her wedding to the bullfighter but before the wedding night. The only way to resolve the crisis, they figure, is to have the bullfighter discovered with another woman in bed on his wedding night — thus an annulment could be effected, and the lovers would be free to marry.

Sturges completed the manuscript, but every French producer objected, since in France the disclosure of adultery was not grounds for annulment. Sturges then rewrote the play so that the girl (who had a tattoo on her backside that read *"J'appartiens à Zozo"*) sets in motion even wilder romantic complications, with revenge fantasies, slamming doors, changes of costume — all the characteristics of farce that had attracted him since he had seen *La Prise de Berg-Op-Zoom* and the vaudeville and burlesques of New York over forty years earlier.

"Preston's attraction to Gaby was not just soulful, therefore," Sandy continued. "He also thought it would have professional benefits, for *Zozo* was a pet project." The liaison with Gaby Sylvia was over — and she returned to her lover — before the Sturges's second child was born in June 1956. But the possibility of professional collaboration remained, and he hoped she would act in two of his plays and in his adaptation of Robert E. Sherwood's antiwar comedy *The Road to Rome.* "I had the impression," Sandy said, "that he didn't want to lose her."

On June 22, 1956, Thomas Preston Sturges was born, named (as his father wrote to young Preston's godmother, the family friend Grace Barrett in New York) "after Sandy's father, my mother's brother, the central character in *The Power and the Glory* and the speakeasy proprietor in whose joint I laid the play *Strictly Dishonorable.* We threw in the Preston for good luck." Like his brother who was christened in New York at St. Patrick's Cathedral, the new baby was baptized Catholic (Sandy's faith) at Notre-Dame. "You will notice," Sturges continued impishly in the same letter, "that nothing less than a cathedral goes for my sons. I don't know exactly what St. Thomas did in his life, but I hope he was a nice fellow. I believe he came from somewhere in Missouri but I am not sure of this fact."

A doting and attentive father in Paris as he had not been earlier in Hollywood, Sturges made it clear that his family life was the happiest he had known: "Marriage," he wrote to a former studio colleague, "is a very nice institution although you don't always find the perfect mate the first few times out." Of his devotion to what he called his "three little darlings" there was no doubt in anyone's mind; the devotion had been neither diminished nor contradicted by the affair with Gaby Sylvia.

Nevertheless, it was clear to (among others) Maxine Merlino — who visited the Sturgeses in Paris that season — that

> the marriage was not a happy one at that time. Sandy had had enough of his interest in Gaby Sylvia, and she confided to me that she was going to leave him but not divorce him, to try to bring him to his senses. . . . "She's disenchanted with me," Preston told me. He was right, in a way. But she was also extremely loyal, very forgiving and understanding, and she certainly wanted the marriage to last, for all their sakes.

On May 5, 1957 (with his wife and sons remaining in Paris), Sturges flew to New York for the American premiere of his film. At the Algonquin, he happened to meet Muriel Angelus and her husband, the musician Paul Lavalle. They reminisced about *The Great McGinty,* and he was delighted with her company again. "But it was so sad," she recalled later, "to see this wonderful man at that point in his life. He was brave but obviously not very happy, in that tiny little hotel room and with no great prospects before him."

Film critic Andrew Sarris interviewed Sturges in New York that month, and he found "his eyes still retained their thoughtful glitter, and the grayness of his fifty-nine years was more an imperial gray than a sparrow gray. What Sturges understood . . . was that he needed Hollywood more than Hollywood needed him." American film, indeed, had so drastically altered its style by the late 1950s (with wide-screen formats and increasing use of color among the responses to the threat from television) that the intimate and talky Sturges stories seemed obsolete to many critics.

He returned to Paris two weeks later and made a serious effort to stop his sometimes excessive drinking, which had caused Sandy concern. He had, of course, been accustomed to alcohol since his Paris schooldays and throughout his life he was frequently a heavy social drinker. Now, this was occasionally a problem.

Early in July he worked for one day and a thousand dollars, filming a cameo appearance in Bob Hope's *Paris Holiday;* in a single outdoor sequence, he spoke a few lines as Serge Vitry, a mysterious character who offers Hope luncheon on his terrace, is summoned to the telephone and —

Sturges would never have been so ungracious — never returns. Only his accurately French-accented English is remarkable.

On July 28, Sandy and the boys departed Paris on a flight for Los Angeles, via New York. The journey, she insisted to friends, was occasioned by Preston's need for some old script material he hoped to rework — notably, the original draft of *Matrix* — that had been carefully packed away at Franklin Avenue. He wanted to see what other projects might be worth resurrecting "in case of a hasty return" to Hollywood, as he wrote to a friend from Paris on August 8. In addition, a change of climate would benefit young Preston, who was developing a childhood respiratory ailment from the Paris weather that year.

But most of all, as Sandy later admitted,

> It was difficult watching him suffer so in Paris. He fought for contract after contract, and we went out evening after evening. To me, it was all to no purpose, but to him it was very important to be seen so he wouldn't be forgotten. American producers like Darryl Zanuck were frequenting Paris, and Preston wanted to meet the right person with all his stories ready to go. He figured that if he wasn't seen every night at the Élysée Matignon [a bar-rendezvous for movie people at 2 rue Matignon, near the Champs Élysées] or at the Bar Alexandre [at an hotel], that would be the night that "X" would be in Paris seeking just the script he could provide.

"It was very sad for us to see," according to Phyllis Feldkamp. "Sandy was so young, and it was a very precarious life in Paris. And I'm afraid Preston was not always terribly nice to be with."

Not long after Sandy's departure with the children, Sturges engaged a gifted young secretary named Bernard Hiatt. An American who had graduated Boston University with a master's degree in theater directing, Hiatt had come to Paris on a Fulbright grant for advanced studies in theater, and in 1957 his year of study had concluded. Sturges saw Hiatt's classified newspaper advertisement as an expert typist (in French and English) and hired him in September. Because Hiatt's Fulbright stipend had ended with the academic year and because he did not want to leave Paris, he needed both work and living quarters, and he accepted Sturges's offer of a room in the apartment on boulevard Berthier.

Years later, Hiatt recalled the time he worked as Sturges's secretary.

> I was paid very little, but at least I had a place to live. At first everything went very well. He dictated at least a half-dozen drafts of *Zozo* during the

245

year, and he intended it as a major comeback for him. He wanted to regain the standing he felt he had lost, and he wanted desperately to make life better for Sandy and the boys.

By the end of 1957, however, it was clear to Hiatt that the living-working arrangement was problematic.

> I began to feel like an indentured servant, since he expected me to be available twenty-four hours a day, whenever he felt like working. And so I told him I could continue to work for him only if I moved to a small hotel. This occasioned a terrific fight between us, since he seemed to presume that I could turn over my entire life to him, and he saw my announcement as an act of rebellion. But he really had no choice because he needed my services and because we really worked together very well. And so I moved out and came to work every day, from early afternoon to early evening.

In the evenings, Sturges invariably went out to the Élysée Matignon "to hustle the script [of *Zozo*]," as Hiatt recalled. "Gaby Sylvia, he said — more out of hope than guaranteed conviction — would play the leading role of Gina."

During the many months of revisions on *Zozo,* there were several setbacks. "One evening he went out with a recently revised script — it was the only copy we had, I had just completed typing it — and he lost it in a taxi or at a bar. But he was indefatigable. We just began all over again, and he tried to remember all his revisions and recreate what he had lost."

Another obstacle, however, was more deeply affecting, as Bernard Hiatt remembered. Sturges completed another French revision of *Zozo* and gave it to his old friend René Clair, who read it but then said that the play was very charming, but that it wasn't French, either in language or spirit — a criticism Sturges took very seriously, since it threatened his confidence that the play could be successfully produced for French audiences. "That just about devastated him," according to Hiatt.

Like so many others, Bernard Hiatt had seen Sturges's social grace and polish, his bluster, his gaiety, his ego — "and the tyranny, too. He was a sensitive, smart man, but his sense of himself as a writer had been severely tested by this time — especially after Clair's reaction."

Nevertheless, Sturges continued dictating revisions to his secretary every day.

But one day, as we were working, he suddenly stopped. I looked over at him, and then he burst into tears, and he was sobbing uncontrollably. It was so terrible, so moving, I'll never forget it. Here was this big, imposing man — large in every way — and he was just helpless. He fell on the sofa and sobbed his poor heart out, crying that it was all over, that he had lost it, that everything was gone, that his life was finished.

At that moment, all Preston Sturges's latent vulnerability poured out with his tears. There had just been one failure too many, and he could no longer endure stoically. For so long, deal after deal had not materialized, project after project had been subsidized but eventually stymied. In spite of his tireless energies to produce work that was full of promise (and often astonishingly good), and in spite of his willingness to try different kinds of plays, to work in television, to polish scripts by others sent to him by French or German producers, the business elements had too frequently failed. The single essential ingredient for success in film or theater had eluded him for a decade — luck, however it is defined or nuanced.

"I think he was in a terrible position," Phyllis Feldkamp reflected. "He had been a genius at what he did in the past, and suddenly wherever he turned and whatever he tried slipped through his hands."

For Maxine Merlino, there was an added dimension to Preston's anguish. "He told me over and over again," she recalled years later,

> that he had made and lost three fortunes, and at the end he was depressed because he wasn't sure whether he would be remembered or not. I remember that in Paris he seemed to have an obsession with death — nothing suicidal or anything like that, and any morbid tone didn't last very long. But he wondered whether death would mean oblivion for him, his name and his reputation.

And then a frightening moment occurred.

One afternoon Bernard Hiatt arrived at the apartment to find Sturges wide-eyed and drained of color. He had sat up all night with such severe chest pain that he could not lie down. An examination at the American Hospital, Neuilly, revealed a transitory heart spasm brought on by stress.

SIXTEEN

The Closed Circle

PRESTON'S letters to Sandy in 1957 — mostly dictated to and typed by Bernard Hiatt — alternated fervent protestations of love ("You are the love — the joy — the companion of my life . . . I love you dearly . . . I don't deserve you, or [my] sweet sons") with severe, paternalistic reprimands if she failed to write as often as he deemed necessary ("You're still only a kid, and kids need to be trained. God willing, I will live long enough to train you properly! . . . You need some hints on deportment, [but] you might turn into a hell of a wife with ten or fifteen years more effort").

There is no doubt that his infidelity had hurt her; she had neither expected it nor could she accept it as routine. "I will attempt to explain the differences between the lapses in faithfulness of the male as opposed to those of the female," he wrote to her January 26, 1958.

> By far the greater part of the world is still polygamous. . . . In other words, whereas the number of conquests a man has *made* in his lifetime is to some extent the gauge of his success as a male, the number of conquests a woman has *resisted* is probably the gauge of her success as a female. It is doubtful that you will agree, considering your age and upbringing.

She fired off an articulate response:

> Your contention is a complacent and comfortable theory for a husband to advance, but plainly untenable. . . . Perhaps you are confusing resistance and coquetry. Resistance implies the ancient Iron Virgin while coquetry is

248

a *game* of resistance that will with proper effort and delicacy lead eventually to the surrender of the citadel.

Worse, if total resistance implies true femininity, with what, pray tell, have you been consorting all your life?

Sandy felt, however, that there was no question of permanent separation, much less of divorce. They were enduring a rough patch, but they would triumph. Her letters clearly indicate that the journey to Los Angeles was planned as temporary, and that she and her sons had no return tickets only because they lacked the funds, which would, they thought, be soon forthcoming. During their absence, Sandy was ever his staunch ally, however, and she was not eager to abrogate her marriage promises: "Come home," she pleaded with him that spring,

> and let's write a few shooting scripts. Let's write *one* shooting script. The restaurant won't be there to drag you away every night. . . . Everything is here, darling. . . . Your little boys need you. . . . Don't waste too much time thinking it over, just come.

But he did not — "perhaps," Sandy said,

> because there was always something "about to happen," and coming back would be a last resort. He wanted to come back with a hit — just as he hung onto The Players and wanted to sell it only when it was solvent, not when it was losing money. He thought it was unmanly to abandon a place when it was going down, unmanly to give up on a failing career and do something else. In his letters he wrote of endless Paris meetings and nights out, always hopeful. I thought it was just foolishness.

He could indeed have returned to a number of alternatives, had he chosen to do so. Even in these dark times, Preston never lacked a fund of story ideas, and television was regularly engaging playwrights and film writers for its expanded hours and new markets. There could also have been (had he tempered his desire for sole control over a project) collaborations with movie producers, directors and other writers; he would not, however, yield to that stipulation. Perhaps it, too, seemed somehow "unmanly," a change of course springing from weakness. "Sometimes I feel," he wrote in his appointment book on June 26, 1958, "like a ghost who has come back and is trying unsuccessfully to make contact."

He also noted in his appointment book the deaths of film people he knew. On July 31, 1957, he had clipped the obituary of A. C. Blumenthal, dead at seventy, the man "who robbed me of my *Child of Manhattan* picture rights in 1932 . . . a filthy crook." But there were happier memories when he marked the passing of colleagues like Bill Le Baron and of Jesse L. Lasky.

"I met Sturges at the Bar Alexandre in 1958," Rex Harrison recalled, "where he was regularly holding court. He seemed very depressed to me." Billy Wilder also visited Paris that year:

> I was trying to put in a good word for him with Paramount's man in Paris, Ilya Lopert. How could we have a great man like Sturges sitting there and drinking brandy all night? This guy must work!

Sturges was not invariably morose, however. "He had a powerful sense of history," according to Phyllis Feldkamp,

> and he loved bringing it to life as we drove around Paris. He couldn't suppress his excitement [and] the immediacy of his voice-overs as we'd go past the ruins of the Roman wall or some other thrilling vestige was like having your own *son et lumière*. One night, going across the Place de la Concorde towards the rue de Rivoli, Sturges, who was driving, suddenly grabbed my arm, exclaiming: "Do you realize where we are? It's the route of the tumbrils! Do you realize that right here the guillotine stood? Here, on this spot, the cobblestones were running in blood!"

And Bernard Hiatt — who left Sturges to return to America in the summer of 1958 — remembered his employer's inexhaustible ability to revive himself:

> He had a sense of gaiety and fun in spite of everything that was difficult in his situation. Sometimes he just stopped and said, "Oh, the hell with it, let's have some laughs, let's have a party."

His tone might at first have seemed uncharacteristically grim when he wrote to Grace Barrett in October:

> The best thing for everybody would probably be my demise. Sandy would have no trouble finding a new and well-to-do father for the little boys — and my creditors could take me off their income tax as debits impossible to collect.

But the old spark was still there, ready to be encouraged:

> Do not gather from this, however [he continued in the same letter], that
> I have the faintest intention of doing myself in. I am much too curious to
> see what further punches in the nose Fate has in reserve for me.

The doldrums did not last, of course, and there is a jotting in his appointment book that suggests (for the first time) a sense of spiritual quest and gentle affirmation: "There has to be a God," he wrote on October 13. "I just don't think we've found out much about him up 'til now."

He continued, in December, to work on the adaptation of *Matrix*, which Sandy had forwarded from Los Angeles — a story, he noted, "in which the young man's weakness has always been his strength, and the reason for his strong hold on the maternal instinct of this lovely girl." He might have been writing of himself.

As the holidays approached — the second Christmas he was separated from his wife and sons — Sandy remembered feeling

> that I was never going to see him again. Not because I thought he was
> going to die, but I began to feel a distance from him. When I mentioned
> this on the phone to him, he said he adored me and this was just a woman's
> fantasy. But by this time the relationship just didn't seem as real as it had
> once been. I was working, taking care of the boys, trying to run the
> house — it was a very different life from his, and far away.

And although they both continued to hope there would soon be enough money to bring him to Los Angeles or her back to Paris with the children, they simply could not afford either alternative.

At the end of 1958, however, came an opportunity that brought him to America and to the possibility that he would soon be reunited with his family. He arrived in Manhattan two days before Christmas and checked into "my favorite old room number 200" at the Algonquin Hotel. He had been invited to direct a farce by Lorenzo Semple, Jr., *The Golden Fleecing*, for which rehearsals began at the York Theater on January 6, 1959. "But [with Sturges as director] we never got out of rehearsals," recalled Peter Turgeon, an actor in the play. "We never got to the second act. Sturges was a sad shell, quite unable to cope with this simple comedy. It was tragic."*

* Courtney Burr, the original director, resumed his duties, and the play finally opened.

But although the direction was an unfortunate experience — Sturges kept trying to rewrite the playwright's dialogue — his dismissal did not suppress his desire to exploit New York contacts for work. When he was invited to appear on David Susskind's new local television talk show *Open End,* he readily accepted. On the air, he told of the time he had been in a restaurant when a beautiful woman approached him and asked, "Aren't you Preston Sturges? The one who wrote *Strictly Dishonorable?* The one who gave us all those wonderful movie comedies?" He replied yes to these questions and was then shocked to hear her say, "Dammit! I spent the weekend with the wrong Sturges!"

Watching that program was Robert Lescher, an editor with the publishers Henry Holt and Company. Lescher felt, listening to Sturges's repartee, his colorful anecdotes and his tales of Broadway and Hollywood, that his memoirs would be a valuable and entertaining book. He and literary agent Sterling Lord (who represented, among others, Jack Kerouac and James T. Farrell) approached Sturges, they discussed the project at a luncheon on January 8, 1959, and before the end of the month a contract was offered. Sturges received a thirty-five-hundred-dollar advance on signing, with another four thousand dollars due on submission of a complete autobiography.

"He was certainly one of the most sophisticated men I ever knew," Lescher recalled years later,

> and he was wonderful at putting people at ease — especially shy people, like my wife. That he could do very graciously. . . . One night we dined with him, and when we were seated at a restaurant, he said in his rotund voice, "Tell me, my dear, where are you from?"
>
> "Oh, just a little state — you wouldn't have heard of it," she replied.
>
> "Which is that?"
>
> "Rhode Island."
>
> "Where in Rhode Island?"
>
> "A tiny town you wouldn't know — Bristol."
>
> "But my first wife lived on Popasquash Road in Bristol!"
>
> I never forgot how gracious he was, how he found out just what to ask and how to put her at ease. He was just a charmer.

On February 8, Sturges interviewed a young lady named Toni Wheelock, who would be his nighttime secretary and typist, and three nights later, at 12:10, he began dictating *The Events Leading Up to My Death,* for which he had collected random notes over the years. They worked in room 207, the hotel's accounting office, loaned to him without charge after hours by the owners of the Algonquin.

His appointment book confirms his mother's presence in his thoughts on April 12, the twenty-eighth anniversary of her death at 603 Fifth Avenue. "My [step]father is still very close to me although he died years ago," Preston had written to a friend when he was still in California,

> [and] my mother who died in 1931 practically overflows this house. Her pictures and possessions and ideas and witticisms are everywhere. Not a day passes that she is not mentioned many times. At night I sleep on her bed.

For relaxation, he paid forty dollars for a new classical guitar and taught himself to play some folk tunes. Charles Abramson, his old friend from the 1920s, was then living at the Royalton Hotel, directly opposite the Algonquin; he and Preston shared a drink, a song, occasionally an exchange of notes and ideas for television productions.

At first the memoir proceeded roughly, but then Sturges became convinced it was going to be a great success. By June 22 he had dictated three hundred sixty-eight pages, but there was a problem: he was only up to 1927.

That was not the only difficulty. "The result was an unfortunate manuscript," Robert Lescher remembered. "The pages were prolix, repetitive, often distasteful — really just terrible."

That does indeed describe much of the manuscript, which may have been (at least in part) a therapeutic act for its author. The style is conversational rambling, with one thought leading by association to another and then another. Some of it is acutely amusing, much of it is needlessly detailed and most of it is terribly overwritten. Had he finished the memoir to 1959, it certainly would have run to well over a thousand pages and required major surgery.

Lescher, however, was prepared to work with Sturges.

> I took him to lunch one day, dinner another, tried to cheer and encourage him. I wrote to Sterling Lord about the problems with the first several hundred pages, and assured him I was prepared to work. But Preston was full of himself, and criticism was not exactly mother's milk to him. What I said meant nothing to him. He just couldn't focus, or didn't want to.

In his appointment book Sturges confided that "they did not seem to care much for what I had written of [the memoir]. But after my first dejection, I did nine pages anyway — finished on [page] 324." Four days later, at the end of June, he added, "I don't know why, but [prizefighter Ingemar] Johansson's pulverization of [Floyd] Patterson . . . feels like a personal victory to me. I think I will win by a stunning K.O., too."

As he reviewed his life for his memoir, there were simultaneously a mellowness, a warmth and humility in his correspondence that year. On April 6, he addressed a letter to Louise, "My dear old friend," and inquired about her health and welfare: "We were very close friends at one time, we went through much together, and we had pretty much the same hopes and aspirations." He was thinking of their son, to whom he had recently written, "I regret bitterly that *your* father is not the oak tree that mine was." It was his plain apology, unexpected and unselfconscious. Now, as he wrote to Louise, he wondered

> how, if [Mon and I] were intimately connected by correspondence, for instance, I might attach my wisdom . . . to his young exuberance and make, out of our two halves, one individual of great value. And then a voice within me said, "*What* wisdom? Gained from *what* years of experience? You are as inexperienced and impulsive at 60 as you were at 16 — so shut up!"

As for Sandy, little Preston and Tom, they were all full of excitement about a reunion that coming autumn, as she recalled:

> The children and I were set to join him in New York that September, when there was a project definite. We had selected a school for Preston, who was then six, and we were going to rent a place in Turtle Bay [on East Forty-eighth or Forty-ninth Street], near our friend Katharine Hepburn.

He maintained a crowded writing schedule, met with old acquaintances (among others, actress Paulette Goddard and her husband, writer Erich Maria Remarque) and kept appointments with producers. Sturges also made time to counsel novice writers. When a New York writer named Harold Cohen wrote to Sturges asking him to read a first play he wrote called *A Piece of Pie in the Sky,* he replied (on May 9):

> When I started out as a playwright, a number of people were kind and polite with me and read my first effusions. I have always tried to pay back the debt I contracted. . . . Perhaps what I have to say may actually be of some help to you.

254

Also in May, he went to a physician for a complete examination. "I am in *perfect* health," he noted in his appointment book on the twenty-fifth. "25 more years to live, so there is time for everything. Very, very slight [high] blood pressure."

In a letter to Mon on his eighteenth birthday, Preston elaborated:

> I took a complete physical check-up the other day and to my horror the doctor told me I was good for another twenty-five years. This gives me time to take up another profession, such as dentistry. . . . Please felicitate your mother on having brought you into the world so safely 18 years ago, and in such trying circumstances, and have a cheerful thought occasionally for
>
> Your affectionate father

In July, Nel King, who had been an assistant film editor at Paramount in the 1940s, invited Sturges to come to a private party in New York. He brought a print of *The Palm Beach Story* and, she remembered,

> gave us a running commentary on the skill of the film editor, the admirable score, the deftness of the actors — as if *he* had not made the picture at all. I think of that as typically Sturges — his generous perception of others' talents and his unselfconscious acceptance of his own.

Toni Wheelock, at the end of July, departed for her wedding trip, and a temporary replacement was found named Elena Long. On the thirty-first, she took dictation from an energetic Sturges from five in the afternoon to one in the morning.

On August 3, the estate of Robert E. Sherwood at last approved Sturges's revisions to Sherwood's *The Road to Rome*. He also contacted the agent for actor Don Ameche, to confirm Ameche's interest in a screenplay Sturges was simultaneously writing about a gentleman crook, and he made additional notes for a film to be called *The Gentleman from Chicago*. That same evening, he screened *The Great McGinty* for producers at CBS who had responded favorably to his suggestion of a new documentary television series. Charley Abramson accompanied him.

The day had been a flurry of activity, and in his appointment book, Sturges noted: "Next week — wedding anniversary!" His projects seemed bright with promise, and he was back on course — he was certain of it.

"I always thought," he wrote in a note to himself that summer, that I was going to die at 56 — [but I had] a physical exam at 60 and result: Well, I'm just starting! I know that my life, even in these disagreeable, trying times, is COMPLETE — although I don't know exactly *why*. Is it because my hopes and disappointments, and renewed hopes, and ideas, and intentions, go *all the way* — the full swing of the pendulum? Is that what energy and vitality really mean: mental energy and vitality?

Shortly before midnight on August 5, 1959, as he was dictating pages of a new script to Elena Long in his room at the Algonquin Hotel, he suddenly stopped, complaining of severe chest pain. Then he became short of breath, but he would not leave his hotel room to go to a hospital; this was merely heartburn after a hastily eaten late supper, he insisted. Elena was frightened when he lay down and did not respond to her questions. Anxious, she rang Charles Abramson and asked him to hurry across the street.

Abramson found the room cluttered with pages of Sturges's memoirs, of a new script he had been dictating, with notes for a play he was revising and with the first draft of still another film. A physician was summoned, but nothing could be done for Preston. At 2:15, on the morning of August 6, 1959, a heart attack stilled his remarkable vitality.

SEVENTEEN

Coda

"HE GOT BETTER after his death," Preston Sturges once wrote as a possible line of dialogue to describe a painter's or composer's reputation. With a savage irony, it also applied to himself.

By April 3, 1975, he was getting very much better, in fact. That evening, the International Ballroom of the Beverly Hilton Hotel in Beverly Hills was filled to its capacity of seven hundred. The Writers Guild of America convened for its twenty-seventh annual ceremony, a formal dinner at which awards were presented in nineteen categories of writing for film and television.

Up to that year, the Laurel Award for Writing Achievement had been given only to living persons who had, in the words of the Guild citation, "advanced the literature of the motion picture through the years, and . . . made outstanding contributions to the profession of the screen writer." Previous honorees had included Charles Brackett and Billy Wilder, Joseph L. Mankiewicz, John Huston, Dalton Trumbo, Ernest Lehman and Paddy Chayefsky.

But Wilder, Preston Sturges's colleague at Paramount, had asked the Guild to reverse its regulation that year. "I fought for Preston Sturges to receive it, and although there was some negative reaction to the suggestion of a posthumous award, it finally carried."

Writer and former Guild president Melville Shavelson eulogized Sturges that April evening, admitting that the award from his peers was "too little and too late," for here was the first true *auteur* in Hollywood, the man who led the way for such as Billy Wilder and John Huston and all the others. In five hectic years at Paramount, he wrote nine solo original screenplays and directed eight of them, winning an Academy Award and two nominations, all for his writing.

And then, as if forestalling the usual assault of vapid criticisms about creative longevity, Shavelson said:

> Certainly the apex of his career was brief, but how many of us would not be willing to burn out as fast if we gave, in Edna Millay's words, such a lovely light?

Shavelson was on the mark, addressing the charge of creative decline which for over twenty years had been so often ascribed to Sturges by American critics. For more than a decade before his death, ran the typical negative comment, he did not produce anything resembling his former achievements; the implication was that somehow the output of his golden years was diminished (if not negated) by the slimness of what followed.

But comic filmmakers and satirists rarely have long careers; their tones and concerns are ordinarily topical, their voices emblematic of a specific time, place and style in cultural life. The charge of "decline" is not, for example, generally applied to Charles Chaplin, whose great period lasted from 1914 to 1931 and who in the last forty years of his life directed only five controversial films of uneven quality. Nor is "decline" ascribed to Leo McCarey (born the same year as Sturges), another director of classic comedies such as *Duck Soup, The Awful Truth* and *Going My Way* and a man who in the last sixteen years of his life managed only three less impressive films.

Sturges's talents had indeed peaked. But the zenith of his career spanned from 1929 (*Strictly Dishonorable*) through the scripts he wrote in the 1930s and those he directed thereafter, especially the intensely agile, popular pictures from 1939 to 1943. True, he no longer created works of this quality thereafter, but it is hard to escape the feeling that if he had died in 1945 he would perhaps have been immediately hailed as one of the titans of the cinema. Instead, he had the audacity to live and to attempt work, without either apology or self-pity. "He made his life one long adventure," said Nel King, his former colleague at Paramount, "and he left us wonderful things to remember him by."

"You can't replace someone like Sturges," Billy Wilder reflected in 1988.

When he died we suffered not only the loss of a human being we liked and admired, but also a whole category of pictures. You can't replace someone with that original a mind. A whole species went with him. And when the history of movies is impartially written, Preston Sturges will have a place of honor. He was a superman in the craft.

"I am the most cheerful of men," he had written. "I enjoy every moment and every opportunity. . . . I have had flops, like everybody else, [but] like Carnation's contented cows, I have been a happy writer, and this happiness came from hope."

Hope was an outlook that gave him strength, a confidence that gave him energy, an attitude that had become a habit, maybe even a virtue. Very likely without knowing it, he had learned this from his mother — a woman more memorable than any of the characters he created, more unpredictable, and finally more courageous, too. Mary Desti had always urged him to hope, and to *learn* from hope — as Sabrina (in Milton's *Comus,* which he had read and remembered) was asked to "listen and save."

In her last days, Mary told him that there was no tragedy in dying, the only tragedy was never to have lived. She wanted him to know that she had tried to live well and fully, despite mistakes and maybe even because of them. But he knew her words were counsel for him, too: above all, he must *live.* He listened and saved.

Notes

CHAPTER ONE

4   in a loathsome   Preston Sturges, unfinished and unpublished memoir, *The Events Leading Up to My Death,* p. xviii. Hereinafter, MEM.

4   My mother was   MEM, pp. xii–xiii.

4   conclusion that   *Ibid.,* p. xiv.

5   a drinking man   *Ibid.,* p. xxvii.

5   was a confirmed   *Ibid.,* p. xxxiii.

5   but how   *Ibid.,* p. xxxiii.

7   This goddess   Mary Desti, *The Untold Story* (New York: Horace Liveright, 1929), p. 17. Hereinafter, Desti.

7   In January 1901   Desti, p. 22.

8   one Frenchman   *Ibid.,* p. 23.

8   This really meant   *Ibid.,* p. 24.

9   Before I was born   Isadora Duncan, *My Life* (New York: Boni and Liveright, 1927), p. 9.

9   Mrs. Duncan came   Desti, pp. 27–28.

10   became the carefree   Fredrika Blair, *Isadora* (New York: McGraw-Hill, 1986), p. 44.

10   You [were] an antique   Desti, p. 26.

10   a robust woman   Victor Seroff, *The Real Isadora* (New York: Avon, 1971), p. 73.

10   But Mary   *Ibid.,* p. xii.

11   Isadora, I thought   *Ibid.,* p. 34.

11   Desti told me   Ilya Ilyich Schneider, *Isadora Duncan: The Russian Years* (New York: Harcourt, Brace and World, 1968), pp. 104–105.

11   worshipped   Mercedes de Acosta, *Here Lies the Heart* (New York: Reynal, 1960), p. 80.

NOTES

CHAPTER TWO

13　I revere　MEM, p. xxvi.

13　whose love　PS to Eleanor Bailey Johnson, Feb. 12, 1946.

14　But you haven't　MEM, p. 17.

14　conventional life　Desti, p. 34.

16　In my boyhood　PS appointment book entry, June 5, 1959. Hereinafter noted as PSd.

16　The children　Desti, p. 44.

16　danced gaily　*Ibid.,* p. 46.

18　I was terribly　MEM, pp. 79–80.

18　You wore the Grecian　Maria Theresa Bourgeois to PS, May 10, 1941.

20　Mother is going　MEM, pp. xxv–xxvi.

20　leapt upon　*Ibid.,* p. 81-F.

21　The bath　Frederic Ernest Farrington, *French Secondary Schools* (London: Longmans, Green, 1915), p. 157.

22　a kind of　André Moldavan to PS, Apr. 26, 1945.

23　Sometimes　MEM, p. 96-D.

23　I very rapidly　*Ibid.,* p. 96-F.

24　a vision of you　*Ibid.*

24　Why don't you　*Ibid.,* p. 98-A.

27　I do not know　Solomon Sturges (henceforth SS) to PS, Apr. 19, 1933 and Jan. 15, 1930.

CHAPTER THREE

28　a most powerful　Aleister Crowley in John Symonds, *The Great Beast: The Life of Aleister Crowley* (Melbourne: Rider, 1951), pp. 110–111.

29　a sinister buffoon　MEM, pp. xxii, xxiii-B.

29　I wrote this　Soror Virakam (Mary Sturges) in Aleister Crowley, "A Note," *Book 4* (New York: Samuel Weiser, 1980), n.p.

30　When [Mother]　*Ibid.,* p. 153.

30　You have no　MEM, p. 168.

31　terribly funny　*Ibid.,* p. 158.

31　I howled　*Ibid.,* p. 2.

33　there was always　*Ibid.,* p. 167.

33　a very high-toned　*Ibid.,* p. 175.

35　Isn't he *big*　*Ibid.,* p. 192.

38　Mary! If you　*Ibid.,* p. 219.

38　My friend Mary　Duncan, p. 319.

39　She never even　MEM, p. 233.

39　the name of　*Ibid.,* p. 231.

39　first and rather　*Ibid.,* p. 258.

39　and my progress　*Ibid.,* p. 260.

42 the usual collection *Ibid.,* p. 271.
42 Why some *Ibid.,* p. 280.
42 a rather versatile Marion G. Denton to PS, Mar. 21, 1941.
43 I obliged MEM, pp. 306–307.
43 We were fed *Ibid.,* p. 310.

CHAPTER FOUR

44 I didn't care MEM, p. 320
44 I was so *Ibid.,* p. 322.
45 of unpredictable temper *Ibid.,* p. 324.
45 You goddam fool *Ibid.,* p. 325.
46 new-rich *Ibid.,* p. 331.
47 Oh, Preston Mary Desti, quoted in Iles Brody, "Man the Kitchenette," *Esquire,* Oct. 1945, p. 124.
48 I am not PS to Jesse H. Finkler, Feb. 2, 1932.
54 [it] was run MEM, p. 356.
55 fishing the same *Ibid.,* p. 358.

CHAPTER FIVE

63 She was a Sidonie Lederer to DS, Jan. 16, 1989.

CHAPTER SIX

72 I laid MEM, p. 361.
77 a well-nigh J. Brooks Atkinson, "The Play," *New York Times,* Sept. 19, 1929.
81 a mysterious figure *New York World,* Jan. 18, 1930.
81 dramatic but S.S.B., in *"Recapture, A Play by Preston Sturges, at Werba's Flatbush," Brooklyn Daily Times,* Jan. 21, 1930.
82 for enlivening *The Nation,* Jan. 8, 1930: 35.
84 quite weak PS to SS, Jan. 7, 1930.
90 There was little Arthur Ruhl, *New York Herald-Tribune,* Nov. 8, 1930.
90 The more young Robert Benchley, in *The New Yorker,* Nov. 22, 1930.
92 I know Quoted by PS to Priscilla Woolfan; Woolfan to DS, Aug. 11, 1988.
92 Always keep Quoted in PS appointment book, Apr. 25, 1959.

CHAPTER SEVEN

93 She certainly SS to PS, Dec. 13, 1931.
94 insane and sadistically MEM, p. xxviii.

94 awfully fat   PS to SS, Sept. 9, 1931.

95 I think   SS to PS, Jan. 10, 1931.

96 a mild little   PS to Eleanor Hutton Sturges, Sept. 11, 1931.

96 I guess   SS to PS, Aug. 20, 1931.

96 sensational   PS to SS, Aug. 24, 1931.

97 one year   PS to SS, Sept. 9, 1931.

98 It seems   PS to SS, Sept. 23, 1931.

107 a very charming   PS to Sidney C. Love, Aug. 30, 1933.

108 I raised   Jesse L. Lasky, Jr. (with Don Weldon), *I Blow My Own Horn* (London: Gollancz, 1957), p. 246.

109 This is unusual   *Hollywood Reporter,* Feb. 22, 1933.

CHAPTER EIGHT

114 Living alone   SS to PS, Apr. 19, 1933.

116 exploited for dramatic   René Clair, *Cinéma d'hier, cinéma d'aujourd'hui* (Paris: Gallimard, 1970), p. 292 (trans. DS).

119 I have carried   PS to Darryl F. Zanuck, Feb. 24, 1947.

122 He could talk   Axel Madsen, *William Wyler* (New York: Crowell, 1973), p. 104.

123 [Sullavan] was   *Ibid.,* p. 109.

124 What would you   *Ibid.,* p. 110.

CHAPTER NINE

130 Uncle Carl   Odgen Nash, in Clive Hirschhorn, *The Universal Story* (New York: Crown, 1983), p. 54.

132 The chief villain   John Douglas Eames, *The Paramount Story* (New York: Crown, 1985), p. 37.

137 A pretty girl   PS, undated notes in UCLA archives.

138 He was very   Edwin Gillette to DS, Aug. 23, 1988.

140 leaves me cold   PS to Sidney Biden, Feb. 13, 1939.

142 She is tall   *Ibid.*

142 she is much   PS to Eleanor Hutton, Jan. 23, 1939.

143 I admire   SS to PS, Aug. 25, 1938.

145 He was put   Louise Sturges to DS, Aug. 29, 1988.

149 When a picture   PS in *Time,* "The New Pictures," Oct. 21, 1940:92.

CHAPTER TEN

151 When I came   Billy Wilder to DS, Sept. 28, 1988.

153 Since there is no   John Lee Mahin to Jack Karp, Dec. 20, 1939.

154 He was so   Muriel Angelus to DS, Oct. 17, 1988.

156   We never stopped   MEM, p. xxvi.

157   this life   PS to Richard de la Chappelle, Feb. 12, 1946.

159   There's nothing   "Director Sturges Tells How It's Done," *Detroit News,*
Nov. 10, 1940.

161   I try only   PS in "Hedda Hopper's Hollywood," *Los Angeles Times,* Dec.
22, 1940.

161   so he'd have   *Photo Story,* Mar. 1943.

CHAPTER ELEVEN

163   [He] is the sensation   "Paramount's Pan-American Convention at Pan-
ama," *Buenos Aires Herald,* Feb. 16, 1941.

164   In these days   Quoted in *Hollywood Reporter,* Feb. 28, 1941, p. 3.

165   Mr. Sturges   Mason Wiley and Damien Bona, *Inside Oscar* (New York:
Ballantine, 1987), p. 109.

167   Preston Sturges suggested   Veronica Lake, *Veronica* (New York: Citadel,
1971), pp. 83–84.

171   He was   *Ibid.,* p. 90.

171   I directed   Quoted in Barry Pattison and Christopher Wicking, in *Screen,*
July–Oct. 1969, included in Jay Leyda, ed., *Voices of Film Experience* (New
York: Macmillan, 1977), p. 298.

171   That touched   Jean La Vell to DS, Mar. 2, 1989.

172   I was the child   Solomon ("Mon") Sturges IV to DS, Sept. 29, 1988.

173   How is it?   in Sidney Skolsky, *Hollywood Citizen-News,* Oct. 21, 1941.

178   This was a dream   Robert Pirosh to DS, Nov. 30, 1988.

179   Preston is like   René Clair in *Time,* Feb. 14, 1944.

CHAPTER TWELVE

182   The prices   Elsa Maxwell, in *Photoplay* and *Movie Mirror,* Jan. 1944.

182   If allowed   PS to Bosley Crowther, July 22, 1947.

183   a perverse piece   C. A. Lejeune, *Observer,* Jan. 4, 1942.

183   a confusing mixture   *Time,* Feb. 9, 1942.

187   She was about   MEM, pp. 329–330.

192   He's a wonderful   Eileen Creelman, in *New York Sun,* May 24, 1943.

CHAPTER THIRTEEN

196   the funniest   F.C., "Miracle on the Gallop," *Wall Street Journal,* Jan. 21,
1944.

197   I can't devote   Hughes, in *Time,* Mar. 6, 1944.

197   I am merely   *Ibid.*

198   Sturges-Hughes   Philip K. Scheuer, "Sturges Puts Initiative into Film Making," *Los Angeles Times,* Mar. 26, 1944:1.

200   It's sort of   In Harrison Carroll, *Los Angeles Herald and Express,* Apr. 3, 1945.

200   Movies or   PS to Thornton Delehanty, *New York Herald-Tribune,* Apr. 1, 1945.

200   I have been   PS to John McCutcheon, Jan. 3, 1945.

202   A booming   Frances Ramsden to DS, Dec. 11, 1988.

203   Aren't you going   PS, "Howard Hughes Is Salad Champion," *Los Angeles Herald,* Aug. 12, 1946.

204   I was originally   PS to Thornton Delehanty, *art. cit.*

205   He's a little crazy   Jeanne Yount, "In Our Town," *Portland Journal,* Oct. 21, 1945.

205   I couldn't make   Harold Lloyd to Bob Thomas, "Hollywood Today," *Burlingame Advance,* Nov. 23, 1948.

205   I have just   PS to Iles Brody, *art. cit.,* p. 124.

212   a fine partner   *Variety,* Nov. 18, 1946.

213   The fact   PS to Vely Bey, Sept. 9, 1947.

CHAPTER FOURTEEN

215   We usually   PS, idea book, Sept. 27, 1941.

216   A girl   e.g., Hedda Hopper's syndicated column in *Los Angeles Times,* Mar. 10, 1948; Sheilah Graham in *New York Mirror,* same date.

217   felt as if   Seymour Stern, "Maestro's Return," *New York Times,* July 11, 1948.

217   a rare genius   Rex Harrison, *Rex* (New York: Morrow, 1975), pp. 101, 103.

219   the only one   André Bazin, reprinted in *Le Cinéma de la cruauté* (Paris: Flammarion, 1975), p. 52 (trans. DS).

220   The most   PS to John Hertz, Jr., Aug. 10, 1948.

220   Preston was like   Maxine Merlino to DS, July 15, 1989.

221   Betty Grable couldn't   Cesar Romero to DS, Oct. 2, 1988.

221   low man   Doug Warner, *Betty Grable: The Reluctant Movie Queen* (New York: St. Martin's, 1974), pp. 118, 117.

222   He was efficiency   Marie Windsor to DS, Sept. 27, 1988.

225   His companion   Hedda Hopper, Aug. 7, 1949.

225   Frances and I   Harrison Carroll, *Los Angeles Times,* Mar. 22, 1949.

226   I managed   Alida L. Carey, "Then and Now," *New York Times Magazine,* Dec. 2, 1956, p. 94.

228   He watched   Richard J. Goggin, Jr., to DS, Dec. 7, 1988.

CHAPTER FIFTEEN

230 He described   Sandy Sturges to DS, Sept. 5, 1988.

232 Some of the people   Marvin Chesebro to DS, Sept. 22, 1988.

232 I stayed   M. Zolotow, *New York Times,* Mar. 26, 1951.

236 elegant but autocratic   Dolores Gray to DS, Aug. 27, 1988.

237 It was   Katharine Hepburn to DS, April 17, 1989.

239 Esthetically   Phyllis Feldkamp to DS, Dec. 21, 1988.

240 I find working   in Gordon Gow (uncredited), "Conversation with Preston Sturges," *Sight and Sound,* vol. 25, no. 4 (Spring 1956): 183.

241 He's the smoothest   Alida L. Carey, "Then and Now," p. 96.

242 one of the two men   Gaby Sylvia, in Alida Carey, "This Cockeyed Caravan," *North American Review* (Winter 1988), p. 62.

243 after Sandy's father   PS to Grace Barrett, Sept. 3, 1956.

243 Marriage   PS to Steve Brooks, Feb. 4, 1957.

244 his eyes   Andrew Sarris, *Interviews with Film Directors* (New York: Bobbs-Merrill, 1967), pp. 442–443.

245 in case of   PS to Grace Barrett, Aug. 8, 1957.

245 I was paid   Bernard Hiatt to DS, Mar. 1989.

CHAPTER SIXTEEN

250 The best thing   PS to Grace Barrett, Oct. 16, 1958.

251 my favorite   PS, diary, Dec. 23, 1958.

251 But [with Sturges   Peter Turgeon to DS, Dec. 16, 1988.

252 He was certainly   Robert Lescher to DS, Jan. 11, 1989.

253 gave us   Nel King, "Preston Sturges," in *Sight and Sound* 28 (Autumn 1959): 185.

CHAPTER SEVENTEEN

257 He got better   PS, on a piece of Savoy Hotel stationery, London, 1954.

257 too little   reprinted in *Newsletter* (Writers Guild of America west), May 1975, p. 15.

259 I am the   PS to John Hertz, Jr., July 18, 1950.

259 I have had flops   PS to Howard Hawks, Sept. 29, 1956.

Plays

THE GUINEA PIG

Producer: PS. *Director:* Walter Greenough. *Sets:* William Bradley Studio. Opened at the President Theater, New York on January 7, 1929 for 64 performances. *Sam Small:* Alexander Carr. *Catherine Howard:* Mary Carroll. *Wilton Smith:* John Ferguson.

STRICTLY DISHONORABLE

Producer: Brock Pemberton. *Directors:* Pemberton and Antoinette Perry. *Sets:* Raymond Sovey. *Costumes:* Margaret Pemberton. Opened at the Avon Theater, New York on September 18, 1929 for 563 performances.
Giovanni: John Altieri. *Mario:* Marius Rogati. *Tomaso Antiovi:* William Ricciardi. *Judge Dempsey:* Carl Anthony. *Henry Greene:* Louis Jean Heydt. *Isabelle Parry:* Muriel Kirkland. *Gus, Count Di Ruvo:* Tullio Carminati. *Mulligan:* Edward J. McNamara.

RECAPTURE

Producer: A. H. Woods. *Director:* Don Mullally. *Sets:* P. Dodd Ackerman. Opened at the Eltinge Theater, New York on January 29, 1930 for 23 performances.
Henry Martin: Melvyn Douglas. *Patricia:* Ann Andrews. *Mrs. Romney:* Cecilia Loftus. *Gwen:* Glenda Farrell. Also with Hugh Sinclair, Gustave Rolland, Joseph Roeder, Meyer Berenson, Stuart Casey, Louza Riane.

THE WELL OF ROMANCE

Producer: G. W. McGregor. *Director:* J. Harry Benrimo. *Sets:* Gates and Morange. *Book and lyrics:* PS. *Music:* H. Maurice Jacquet. *Costumes:* Eaves, Schneider and

PLAYS

Blythe. Opened at the Craig Theater, New York on November 7, 1930 for 8 performances.
Princess: Norma Terris. *Poet:* Howard March. Also with Laine Blaire, Tommy Monroe, Lina Abarbanell, Elsa Paul, Mildred Newman, Louise Joyce, Joseph Roeder.

CHILD OF MANHATTAN

Producer: Peggy Fears. *Director:* Howard Lindsay. *Sets:* Jonel Jorgulesco. Opened at the Fulton Theater, New York on March 1, 1932 for 87 performances.
Sophie: Helen Strickland. *Eggleston:* Joseph Roeder. *Vanderkill:* Reginald Owen. *Madeleine:* Dorothy Hall. Also with Ralph Sanford, Charles Cromer, Judy Abbot, Mitzi Miller, John Altieri, Douglas Dumbrille.

A CUP OF COFFEE

Written in 1931, first New York production by the SoHo Rep in 1988. *Director:* Larry Carpenter. *Sets:* Mark Wendland. *Costumes:* Martha Hally. *Lighting:* Stuart Duke. *Sound:* Philip Campanella. Opened at Greenwich House, New York, on March 25, 1988 for 16 performances.
Julius Snaith: Willie Carpenter. *Lomax Whortleberry:* Robin Chadwick. *J. Bloodgood Baxter:* Nesbitt Blaisdell. *Oliver Baxter:* Richard L. Browne. *Tulip Jones:* Ellen Mareneck. *Ephraim Baxter:* Gwyllum Evans. *James MacDonald:* Michael Heintzman. *Postman, sign painter and Mr. Rasmussen:* Tom Bloom. *Youth:* George A. Tyger.

PS's play *Unfaithfully Yours,* written in 1932, remains unproduced as of 1989.

In 1951, PS contributed the book for the musical *Make a Wish;* it was largely supplanted by Abe Burrows's subsequent revisions.

In 1953, PS contributed revisions to the book for the musical *Carnival in Flanders* by George Oppenheimer and Herbert Fields.

270

Filmography

In these credits, data have been derived whenever possible directly from the release prints. Films based on Sturges's plays but with whose production he was not actively associated are not included, nor are productions for which he received no onscreen credit. The date following each title is that of the year of release, which is not necessarily that in which the film was actually produced. The following abbreviations apply:

AD: art director(s)/production designer(s)
AP: associate producer(s)
b/o: based on
D: director
DP: director of photography
Ed: editor(s)
M: musical composer
P: producer(s)
S: set designer(s)
Sc: screenwriter(s)
W: wardrobe and costumes

THE BIG POND (1930)

P: Monta Bell. *D:* Hobart Henley. *Sc:* Robert Presnell, Garrett Fort and PS, b/o the play by George Middleton and A. E. Thomas. *DP:* George Folsey. Dialogue staged by Bertram Harrison. *Ed:* Emma Hill. *Musical arranger:* John W. Green. Songs by Al Lewis, Al Sherman, Lew Brown, B. G. De Sylva, Ray Henderson, Irving Kahal, Pierre Norman, Sammy Fain.
Pierre: Maurice Chevalier. *Barbara:* Claudette Colbert. *Ronnie:* Frank Lyon. *Mr.*

271

Billings: George Barbier. *Mrs. Billings:* Marion Ballou. *Pat:* Nat Pendleton. *Toinette:* Andrée Corday. *Jennie:* Elaine Koch.

FAST AND LOOSE (1930)

D: Fred Newmeyer. *Sc:* Jack Kirkland, b/o the play *The Best People,* by David Gray and Avery Hopwood. Dialogue by PS. *DP:* William Steiner.
Marion: Miriam Hopkins. *Henry:* Charles Starrett. *Alice:* Carole Lombard. *Bertie:* Henry Wadsworth. *Bronson:* Frank Morgan. *Carrie:* Winifred Harris. *George:* Herbert Yost. *Lord Rockingham:* David Hutcheson. *Millie:* Ilka Chase. *Judge Sommers:* Herschel Mayall.

THE POWER AND THE GLORY (1933)

P: Jesse L. Lasky. *D:* William K. Howard. *Sc:* PS. *DP:* James Wong Howe. *Ed:* Paul Weatherwax. *AD:* Max Parker. *M:* Louis De Francesco, J. S. Zamencik and Peter Brunelli. *W:* Rita Kaufman.
Tom: Spencer Tracy. *Sally:* Colleen Moore. *Henry:* Ralph Morgan. *Eve:* Helen Vinson. *Tom, Jr.:* Clifford Jones. *Mr. Borden:* Henry Kolker. *Mulligan:* J. Farrell MacDonald. *Edward:* Robert Warwick.

THIRTY DAY PRINCESS (1934)

P: B. P. Schulberg. *D:* Marion Gering. *Sc:* PS and Frank Partos, b/o the novel by Clarence Budington Kelland. *DP:* Leon Shamroy. *Ed:* June Loring. *AD:* Hans Dreier.
Nancy Lane/Princess Catterina: Sylvia Sidney. *Porter:* Cary Grant. *Richard:* Edward Arnold. *King Anatol:* Henry Stephenson. *Count Nicholaus:* Vince Barnett. *Baron Passeria:* Edgar Norton. *Dan:* Ray Walker.

WE LIVE AGAIN (1934)

P: Samuel Goldwyn. *D:* Rouben Mamoulian. *Sc:* Maxwell Anderson, Leonard Praskins and PS, b/o Leo Tolstoy's novel *Resurrection. AD:* Richard Day and Sergei Soudeikin. *M:* Alfred Newman. *DP:* Gregg Toland. *W:* Omar Kiam. *Ed:* Otho Levering.
Katusha: Anna Sten. *Prince Dmitri:* Frederic March. *Missy:* Jane Baxter. *Prince Kortchagin:* C. Aubrey Smith. *Aunt Marie:* Ethel Griffies. *Aunt Sophia:* Gwendolyn Logan. *Simonson:* Sam Jaffe.

THE GOOD FAIRY (1935)

P: Henry Henigson. *D:* William Wyler. *Sc:* PS, b/o the play by Ferenc Molnàr. *DP:* Norbert Brodine. *Ed:* Daniel Mandell. *AD:* Charles D. Hall. *W:* Vera West.

Luisa: Margaret Sullavan. *Dr. Max Sporum:* Herbert Marshall. *Konrad:* Frank Morgan. *Detleff:* Reginald Owen. *Schlapkohl:* Alan Hale. *Dr. Schultz:* Beulah Bondi. *Dr. Motz:* Eric Blore. *Joe:* Cesar Romero. *Barber:* Luis Alberni. *Headwaiter:* Torben Meyer. *Doorman:* Al Bridge. *Movie man:* Frank Moran.

DIAMOND JIM (1935)

P: Edmund Grainger. *D:* A. Edward Sutherland. *Sc:* PS, b/o the book by Parker Morell. *DP:* George Robinson. *Ed:* Daniel Mandell. *AD:* Charles D. Hall. *M:* C. Bakaleinikoff, Franz Waxman, Ferdinand Grofe. *W:* Vera West.
Diamond Jim: Edward Arnold. *Lillian Russell:* Binnie Barnes. *Jane/Emma:* Jean Arthur. *Jerry:* Cesar Romero. *Sampson:* Eric Blore. *Harry:* William Demarest. *Poker player:* Al Bridge.

HOTEL HAYWIRE (1937)

P: Paul Jones. *D:* George Archainbaud. *Sc:* PS. *DP:* Henry Sharp. *M:* Boris Morros. *AD:* Hans Dreier and Robert Odell. *Ed:* Arthur Schmidt.
Dr. Zippe: Leo Carrillo. *Dr. Parkhouse:* Lynne Overman. *Mrs. Parkhouse:* Spring Byington. *Phyllis:* Mary Carlisle. *Bertie:* Benny Baker. *Judge Newhall:* Porter Hall. *O'Shea:* Chester Conklin. *Fuller brush salesman:* Franklin Pangborn.

EASY LIVING (1937)

P: Arthur Hornblow, Jr. *D:* Mitchell Leisen. *Sc:* PS, b/o a story by Vera Caspary. *DP:* Ted Tetzlaff. *M:* Boris Morros. *Ed:* Doane Harrison. *AD:* Hans Dreier. *W:* Travis Banton.
Mary: Jean Arthur. *J. B. Ball:* Edward Arnold. *John, Jr.:* Ray Milland. *Louis:* Luis Alberni. *Mrs. Ball:* Mary Nash. *Van Buren:* Franklin Pangborn. *Wallace:* William Demarest. *Lillian:* Esther Dale. *Butler:* Robert Greig.

PORT OF SEVEN SEAS (1938)

P: Henry Henigson. *D:* James Whale. *Sc:* PS, b/o the play *Fanny,* by Marcel Pagnol. *M:* Franz Waxman. *AD:* Cedric Gibbons. *W:* Dolly Tree. *DP:* Karl Freund. *Ed:* Fredrick Y. Smith.
César: Wallace Beery. *Panisse:* Frank Morgan. *Madelon:* Maureen O'Sullivan. *Marius:* John Beal.

IF I WERE KING (1938)

P/D: Frank Lloyd. *Sc:* PS, b/o the play by Justin Huntly McCarthy. *DP:* Theodore Sparkuhl. *Ed:* Hugh Bennett. *AD:* Hans Dreier. *M:* Boris Morros, Richard Hageman. *W:* Edith Head.

Villon: Ronald Colman. *Catherine:* Frances Dee. *Louis XI:* Basil Rathbone. *Huguette:* Ellen Drew.

NEVER SAY DIE (1939)

P: Paul Jones. *D:* Elliott Nugent. *Sc:* Don Hartman, Frank Butler, PS, b/o the play by William H. Post. *DP:* Leo Tover. *AD:* Hans Dreier, Ernst Fegte. *W:* Edith Head. *Ed:* James Smith. *M:* Boris Morros.
Mickey: Martha Raye. *John:* Bob Hope. *Henry:* Andy Devine. *Prince Smirnov:* Alan Mowbray. *Juno:* Gale Sondergaard. *Papa:* Sig Rumann. *Jeepers:* Ernest Cossart. *Dr. Schmidt:* Monty Wooley.

REMEMBER THE NIGHT (1940)

P/D: Mitchell Leisen. *Sc:* PS. *DP:* Ted Tetzlaff. *Ed:* Doane Harrison. *AD:* Hans Dreier. *M:* Frederick Hollander. *W:* Edith Head.
Lee: Barbara Stanwyck. *John:* Fred MacMurray. *Mrs. Sargent:* Beulah Bondi. *Aunt Emma:* Elizabeth Patterson. *Willie:* Sterling Holloway. *Lee's mother:* Georgia Caine.

THE GREAT MCGINTY (1940)

D/Sc: PS. *P:* Paul Jones. *DP:* William C. Mellor. *AD:* Hans Dreier, Earl Hedrick. *W:* Edith Head. *M:* Frederick Hollander. *Ed:* Hugh Bennett.
Dan McGinty: Brian Donlevy. *Catherine:* Muriel Angelus. *The Boss:* Akim Tamiroff. *Skeeters:* William Demarest. *Tommy:* Louis Jean Heydt. *Madam La-Jolla:* Esther Howard. *Chauffeur:* Frank Moran. *Lookout:* Jimmy Conlin. *Benny:* Dewey Robinson. Also with Byron Foulger, Emory Parnell, Vic Potel, Robert Warwick, Harry Rosenthal, Steffi Duna.
MCA Home Video VHS 80595 and LaserDisc 40595.

CHRISTMAS IN JULY (1940)

D/Sc: PS. *P:* Paul Jones. *DP:* Victor Milner. *AD:* Hans Dreier, Earl Hedrick. *M:* Sigmund Krumgold. *Ed:* Ellsworth Hoagland.
Jimmy MacDonald: Dick Powell. *Betty Casey:* Ellen Drew. *Maxford:* Raymond Walburn. *Baxter:* Ernst Truex. *Bildocker:* William Demarest. *Schindel:* Alexander Carr. *Don Hartman:* Franklin Pangborn. *Harry:* Harry Rosenthal. *Mrs. MacDonald:* Georgia Caine. *Mr. Schmidt:* Torben Meyer. *Hillbeiner:* Al Bridge. *Jenkins:* Byron Foulger. *Zimmerman:* Julius Tannen. Also with Harry Hayden, Vic Potel, Robert Warwick, Jimmy Conlin, Dewey Robinson, Frank Moran, Georges Renavent and PS.
MCA Home Video VHS 80207.

THE LADY EVE (1941)

D/Sc: PS, b/o a story by Monckton Hoffe. *P:* Paul Jones. *DP:* Victor Milner. *AD:* Hans Dreier, Ernst Fegte. *M:* Sigmund Krumgold. *Ed:* Stuart Gilmore. *W:* Edith Head.

Charles Pike: Henry Fonda. *Jean/Eve:* Barbara Stanwyck. *Harrington:* Charles Coburn. *Pike:* Eugene Pallette. *Muggsy:* William Demarest. *Alfred MacGlennon-Keith:* Eric Blore. *Gerald:* Melville Cooper. Also with Robert Greig, Luis Alberni, Frank Moran, Evelyn Beresford, Harry Rosenthal, Julius Tannen, Jimmy Conlin, Al Bridge, Vic Potel, Torben Meyer, Robert Warwick.

MCA Home Video and Laser Videodisc 40353.

SULLIVAN'S TRAVELS (1942)

P/D/Sc: PS. *AP:* Paul Jones. *DP:* John Seitz. *AD:* Hans Dreier, Earl Hedrick. *M:* Leo Shuken, Charles Bradshaw, Sigmund Krumgold. *Ed:* Stuart Gilmore. *W:* Edith Head.

Sullivan: Joel McCrea. *The girl:* Veronica Lake. *LeBrand:* Robert Warwick. *Jones:* William Demarest. *Casalsis:* Franklin Pangborn. *Hadrian:* Porter Hall. Also with Bryon Foulger, Robert Greig, Eric Blore, Torben Meyer, Al Bridge, Esther Howard, Almira Sessions, Frank Moran, Georges Renavent, Vic Potel, Jimmy Conlin, Roscoe Ates, Dewey Robinson, Julius Tannen, Emory Parnell, Chester Conklin, Harry Rosenthal, J. Farrell MacDonald, PS.

MCA Home Video VHS 08551.

THE PALM BEACH STORY (1942)

P/D/Sc: PS. *AP:* Paul Jones. *DP:* Victor Milner. *AD:* Hans Dreier, Ernst Fegte. *M:* Victor Young. *Ed:* Stuart Gilmore. *W:* Irene.

Gerry Jeffers: Claudette Colbert. *Tom Jeffers:* Joel McCrea. *Princess:* Mary Astor. *Hackensacker:* Rudy Vallee. *Toto:* Sig Arno. Also with Robert Warwick, Torben Meyer, Jimmy Conlin, Vic Potel, Franklin Pangborn, Al Bridge, Frank Moran, Harry Rosenthal, Esther Howard, William Demarest, Robert Greig, Roscoe Ates, Dewey Robinson, Chester Conklin, Julius Tannen, Byron Foulger, J. Farrell MacDonald.

MCA Home Video and Laser Videodisc 40380.

THE MIRACLE OF MORGAN'S CREEK (1944)

P/D/Sc: PS. *DP:* John F. Seitz. *M:* Leo Shuken, Charles Bradshaw, Sigmund Krumgold. *AD:* Hans Dreier, Ernst Fegte. *Ed:* Stuart Gilmore. *W:* Edith Head.

Norval Jones: Eddie Bracken. *Trudy Kockenlocker:* Betty Hutton. *Emmy:* Diana Lynn. *Kockenlocker:* William Demarest. Also with Porter Hall, Emory Parnell, Al

Bridge, Julius Tannen, Vic Potel, Brian Donlevy, Akim Tamiroff, Almira Sessions, Esther Howard, J. Farrell MacDonald, Frank Moran, Georgia Caine, Torben Meyer, Jimmy Conlin, Harry Rosenthal, Chester Conklin, Byron Foulger.
Paramount Home Video 4312.

HAIL THE CONQUERING HERO (1944)

P/D/Sc: PS. *DP:* John F. Seitz. *Ed:* Stuart Gilmore. *AD:* Hans Dreier. *M:* Sigmund Krumgold, Werner Heymann. Song "Home to the Arms of Mother" by PS.
Truesmith: Eddie Bracken. *Libby:* Ella Raines. *Sergeant:* William Demarest. *Mayor Noble:* Raymond Walburn. *Mrs. Truesmith:* Georgia Caine. Also with Al Bridge, Esther Howard, Elizabeth Patterson, Jimmy Conlin, Franklin Pangborn, Vic Potel, Torben Meyer, Chester Conklin, Robert Warwick, Dewey Robinson.

THE GREAT MOMENT (1944)

P/D/Sc: PS, b/o book by René Fülöp-Miller. *DP:* Victor Milner. *M:* Victor Young. *AD:* Hans Dreier, Ernst Fegte. *Ed:* Stuart Gilmore. *W:* Edith Head.
Morton: Joel McCrea. *Elizabeth Morton:* Betty Field. *Warren:* Harry Carey. *Eben Frost:* William Demarest. *Wells:* Louis Jean Heydt. *Jackson:* Julius Tannen. Also with Porter Hall, Franklin Pangborn, Harry Hayden, Torben Meyer, Vic Potel, J. Farrell MacDonald, Robert Greig, Harry Rosenthal, Frank Moran, Dewey Robinson, Al Bridge, Georgia Caine, Roscoe Ates, Emory Parnell, Chester Conklin, Esther Howard, Byron Foulger, Jimmy Conlin, Sig Arno.

THE SIN OF HAROLD DIDDLEBOCK (1947)

P/D/Sc: PS. *DP:* Robert Pittack. *M:* Werner R. Heymann. *AD:* Robert Usher. *Ed:* Thomas Neff.
Diddlebock: Harold Lloyd. *Miss Otis:* Frances Ramsden. *Wormy:* Jimmy Conlin. *Waggleberry:* Raymond Walburn. *Bartender:* Edgar Kennedy. Also with Arline Judge, Franklin Pangborn, Rudy Vallee, Lionel Stander, Torben Meyer, Margaret Hamilton, Al Bridge, Frank Moran, Robert Greig, Vic Potel, Georgia Caine.
Hal Roach Video V029.

UNFAITHFULLY YOURS (1948)

P/D/Sc: PS. *DP:* Victor Milner. *MD:* Alfred Newman, b/o music from Rossini, Wagner, Tchaikovsky. *AD:* Lyle Wheeler, Joseph C. Wright. *Ed:* Robert Fritch. *W:* Charles LeMaire, Bonnie Cashin.

Sir Alfred de Carter: Rex Harrison. *Daphne:* Linda Darnell. *Barbara:* Barbara Lawrence. *August:* Rudy Vallee. *Anthony:* Kurt Kreuger. Also with Lionel Stander, Edgar Kennedy, Al Bridge, Julius Tannen, Torben Meyer, Robert Greig, Georgia Caine, J. Farrell MacDonald, Frank Moran.
CBS Fox Video VHS 1249.

THE BEAUTIFUL BLONDE FROM BASHFUL BEND (1949)

P/D/Sc: PS, b/o a story by Earl Felton. *DP:* Harry Jackson. *AD:* Lyle Wheeler, George W. Davis. *Ed:* Robert Fritch. *W:* Charles LeMaire, Rene Hubert. *M:* Cyril Mockridge.
Freddie: Betty Grable. *Blackie:* Cesar Romero. *Hingelman:* Rudy Vallee. *Conchita:* Olga San Juan. Also with Sterling Holloway, Hugh Herbert, Porter Hall, Margaret Hamilton, Emory Parnell, Al Bridge, J. Farrell MacDonald, Georgia Caine, Esther Howard, Chester Conklin, Torbin Meyer, Dewey Robinson, Marie Windsor.
Key Video VHS 1727.

LES CARNETS DU MAJOR THOMPSON/THE FRENCH THEY ARE A FUNNY RACE (1957)

D/Sc: PS, b/o essays by Pierre Daninos. *P:* Alain Poire, Paul Wagner. *DP:* Maurice Barry, Christian Matras, Jean Lallier. *Ed:* Raymond Lanny. *AD:* Serge Pimenoff. *M:* Georges Van Parys. *W:* Suzanne Revillard.
Thompson: Jack Buchanan. *Martine:* Martine Carol. *Taupin:* Noël-Noël. *Miss Ffyth:* Totti Truman Taylor. *Ursula:* Catherine Boyl.

Preston Sturges also appeared (and spoke) briefly in two films — as himself in Paramount's *Star Spangled Rhythm* (1942), and in the role of "Serge Vitry" in *Paris Holiday* (1958), starring Bob Hope.

Lyrics

Many of these songs exist only in fragmentary or inchoate form. Where the date of composition and/or name of the composer is known, that information is included in parentheses. The manuscripts and texts are in the private collection of Sandy Sturges; her permission to include this list is gratefully acknowledged. Except where noted, the songs written remain unpublished.

A Fool in Love (1932)
After the Rain (1929)
Again (1936: Ted Snyder)
All the Time
Ambling Along
Ashes of Love
Asia Minor Blues
At Nighttime
The Bell in the Bay (1942: melody also by PS; marked "for Harry Rosenthal," written for and included in *The Miracle of Morgan's Creek*)
Blue Wedding (1928)
Day by Day
The Donkey and the Moon
Down Where the Sun Shines (1927)
Dream of Dreams
Echoes
Even the Skies Are Crying (1928)
Flat Foot Blues
For You Alone (1935: Ted Snyder, arranged by Franz Waxman)
Get on Your Bicycle (1936, with added variations: *Where the Deuce Were You This Evening, Bruce* [1947])

LYRICS

The Ginsbergs Are Coming

The Green-Eyed Waltz (1927)

Happy Days (1932)

Here's Hopin' (1927)

Home to the Arms of Mother (1943: music and lyrics by PS, written for and included in the film *Hail the Conquering Hero;* published by Famous Music Corp.)

I Couldn't Say It Before

In My Cradle of Dreams (1929: Ted Snyder)

Italian Night (1927: alternate titles: *Italian Miss, A Night in Italy*)

Jazz Baby (1928)

Just Because You Smiled (1928)

Just a Pretty Little Miss

Kansas City Belle

Like a Thief in the Night (1928)

Love (melody only: by PS?)

Love Song (1944: in French)

Maybe You'll Be My Baby (1928: arranged by Sam Grossman)

Morning After Blues

My Love

Oh Minnie (1928: Sam Grossman)

Only Meant for You (1934)

No No No (1927)

Now That You've Gone (1928: music by Elmo Russ)

One Night (1930)

One Starry Night (1928)

Out on a Limb

Paris in the Evening (1935: Ted Snyder; for the film *The Gay Deception*)

Rambling Along (1927)

Roses Bring Sadness to Me (1927)

Samarkand Blues (1927)

Sandy Shores

Secret Rendezvous (1936: music by Ralph Irwin, French lyrics by Pierre Fernay, as *Une Longue Nuit;* for the film *One Rainy Afternoon*)

She's My Gal (1927)

Sleepy Summer Days (1942)

Smilin' Your Troubles Away

The Sun's Gonna Shine By and By (1927)

Sweet Honey Chile (1927)

Then I'll Marry You (1927)

Waiting

Wedding of the Painted Moll

Who Do (1945)

The Whole Town Knows I'm in Love with You
Winky (1912?)
Words Fail Me (1936: Ted Snyder)
You Will Be My Only You (1935: Ted Snyder)

FOR THE OPERETTA *THE WELL OF ROMANCE* (1929):

At Twilight
Be Oh So Careful, Ann (orig. 1927)
Dream of Dreams
For You and For Me
I'll Never Complain
Melancholy Lady
Rhapsody
Well of Romance

FOR THE UNPRODUCED FILM *LOOK, MA, I'M DANCIN'* (1952):

That's How They Done It in the Good Old Days
From the Very First Moment

Bibliography

Curtis, James. *Between Flops*. New York: Harcourt Brace Jovanovich, 1982.

Dickos, Andrew. *Intrepid Laughter: Preston Sturges and the Movies*. Metuchen: Scarecrow, 1985.

Harvey, James. *Romantic Comedy*. New York: Knopf, 1987.

Henderson, Brian, ed. *Five Screenplays by Preston Sturges*. Berkeley: University of California Press, 1985. Contains the screenplays for *The Great McGinty, Christmas in July, The Lady Eve, Sullivan's Travels* and *Hail the Conquering Hero*.

Ursini, James. *The Fabulous Life and Times of Preston Sturges, An American Dreamer*. New York: Curtis Books, 1973.

In addition to those essays and articles cited in the Notes above, a list of major articles on PS to 1984 may be found in:

Cywinski, Ray. *Preston Sturges: A guide to references and resources*. Boston: G. K. Hall, 1984.

Index

INDEX

INDEX

INDEX

290

INDEX